MERSEY TUGS

THROUGH TIME

Ian Collard

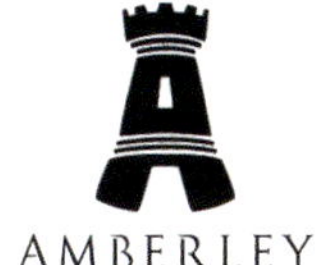

First published 2016

Amberley Publishing
The Hill, Stroud
Gloucestershire, GL5 4EP

www.amberley-books.com

ISBN 978 1 4456 5410 2 (print)
ISBN 978 1 4456 5411 9 (ebook)

British Library Cataloguing in Publication Data.
A catalogue record for this book is available from the British Library.

Typeset in 9.5pt on 12pt Celeste.
Typesetting by Amberley Publishing.
Printed in the UK.

Introduction

As ships increased in size, and became larger and more powerful, smaller vessels were required to assist them to their berths. These ships were used to navigate the larger vessels into narrow waterways, around shallow water and into tight docking areas. A tug is described as a boat that moves vessels by pushing or towing them. They are highly manoeuvrable and have propulsion systems that have been developed to increase their power and safety.

The early tugs were fitted with paddle wheels but these were soon replaced by propeller-driven vessels. They are very powerful for their size and are strongly built. Some are also ocean-going and others serve as salvage vessels, offshore support, and ice-breaking and fire-fighting vessels. However, the majority of vessels described in this book are harbour tugs that assist in berthing and un-berthing vessels in the dock system and the River Mersey. Towing is a vital part of the work in any major port as ships would not be able to use the facilities provided without the tugs assistance in manoeuvring to and from the berths.

In the seventeenth century, the Port of Liverpool increased its trade with the British colonies. London merchants preferred to ship goods from the United States to Liverpool and transport them by land to the south of England. In this period Liverpool shipowners carried goods to Africa, slaves to the southern ports of America and sugar, rum and tobacco back to Britain. During Queen Anne's reign a new dock was planned, which was to be the first commercial wet dock in England. Thomas Steer was given the responsibility to survey the ground and provide plans for its construction, which included lock gates to retain water levels. The dock was opened in 1715 but was not completed until 1720. However, it soon proved insufficient in dealing with the increased trade that was developing in the port. South Dock, later Salthouse Dock, was opened in 1753 and Georges Dock was completed in 1771. Lighthouses were built and dues levied on all vessels were brought under the control of dock trustees appointed by the town council.

It has been claimed that the *Charlotte Dundas* was the first tug as she towed two loaded barges along the Forth & Clyde Canal in 1802. The use of steam-powered tugs was recognised by shipowners when their vessels were delayed because of high winds or other weather, or tidal related issues. The paddle steamers were driven by low-pressure boilers that supplied steam to the side lever engines, and in the second half of the century tugs were built with two engines side by side. This enabled the paddles to be controlled independently, and gave the vessel a great deal of manoeuvrability. The *Francis B Ogden* was the first screw tug and she was followed by the deep-sea vessel *Archimedes.* Compound engines gave greater power and better fuel consumption and enabled the tug owners to increase their profits.

Between 1800 and 1831 the number of ships and cargo transhipped through the port increased dramatically:

1800	4,746 ships	450,000 tons
1810	6,729 ships	734,391 tons
1819	7,849 ships	867,318 tons
1831	12,537 ships	1,592,436 tons

Occasionally, passenger ferries were taken out of service on the Mersey and placed on towing duties, much to the annoyance of intending commuters. In 1816 the steamer *Princess Charlotte* towed the *Harlequin* out of the Mersey, and the *Hero* was also used for towing duties. The 1823-built *Druid* is reputed to have been the first purpose-built tug on the river and the *Eagle* was also used for this purpose at times. The Liverpool Steam Tug Company purchased the *Eleanor, Ormerod, Druid* and *Hero. Queen* and *Victoria* were built at Birkenhead in 1837. Both new tugs developed 100 hp and the *President* was introduced in 1839, with *Albert* introduced in the following year. The new tugs also undertook seagoing duties and *Victoria* completed a tow from Shannon to Liverpool in 1843. *Eleanor* rescued passengers and crew from the *General Gascoyne* in 1837 and *Victoria* took part in a rescue in January 1839, helping to save the lives of 104 passengers and crew from three vessels that were wrecked during a storm. The Liverpool Steam Tug Company purchased its own lifeboat in 1839 and operated excursion trips by its tugs when they were not occupied on towing duties. By 1848 the company owned nine tugs, and William Willoughby & Son operated six vessels.

The Mersey Towing Company became the Mersey Tug Company in 1850, and it later became the New Mersey Tug Company. The Hercules Steam Tug Company, owned by Henry Cruise and William Downham, and the Independence Steam Tug Company were also operating by 1852. The master mariner William Jolliffe and passenger steamer owner Thomas Jolliffe also introduced the *Lion* in 1852.

Commercial traffic through Liverpool and Birkenhead Docks increased dramatically during the American War of Independence and Kings, Queens, Princes and Coburg Docks were built. A new customs house was completed in 1839 and Brunswick Dock was opened in 1832 for the timber trade. Waterloo, Clarence and Victoria Docks were built for the coastal trade and the famous Albert Dock and warehouses were opened by Prince Albert in 1846. The following year the Birkenhead Docks Company was formed and Egerton and Morpeth Docks were opened. Over the following years the expansion of the dock system continued, but merchants became dissatisfied as they felt that the dues paid to the corporation were being spent on the town of Liverpool, and not the harbour or the facilities in the docks.

A Royal Commission was appointed in 1853 to investigate the complaints and it recommended that a new body be formed to take over the running and operation of the docks. A Bill was introduced in 1857 and after a long and expensive struggle it was passed by both Houses of Parliament. The Bill created the Mersey Docks & Harbour Board, which was responsible for all the port accommodation and control was given to twenty-eight dock trustees. The first work it undertook was to build Canning Dock for the timber trade and to construct Herculaneum Graving Docks.

In 1857 the St George's Steam Tug Company was formed by H. J. Ward, a ship's chandler. The United Steam Tug Company began operating the same year and the Mersey Steam Tug Company began in 1857 with the new *Great Conquest. Resolute* was also introduced that year as the largest and most powerful tug in the United Kingdom. John Prendiville became manager of the Mersey Steam Tug Company, which was later renamed the Mersey Original Steam Tug Company. John Watkins introduced the *John Bull* in 1853, but the company only survived for six years and closed down at the end of the decade.

The *Defiance* of 1841 was claimed to be the first iron tug and was followed by the *Liver* in 1848. The Liverpool Steam Tug Company increased their fleet by introducing eleven iron tugs between 1851 and 1857. *Iron King, Lioness* and *Toward Castle* were also iron vessels. The *Blazer,* owned by the Liverpool Steam Tug Company, was 383 tons, and the *Victoria* 152 tons. The larger tugs were usually fitted with engines that generated higher boiler pressures and, consequently, were more powerful. The Gamecock Steam Towing Company and W. H. J. Alexander began operating tugs on the Thames around 1880 and the Jolliffe tugs took on the family name. The *Thomas Jolliffe* was introduced in 1879 and the *William Jolliffe* followed six years later. The Liver Steam Tug Company, the Caledonian Steam Tug Company and the Star Steam Tug Company all operated on the River Mersey at this time.

It was in this period that Liverpool shipowners took the lead in the list of British merchant fleets. Alfred Holt, Booth, Harrison, Cunard, Houlder Brothers and Lamport & Holt all invested in ships and increased the size of their fleets to satisfy the demands of international trade. There were also large fleets of coastal vessels trading to Ireland, Scotland and the Isle of Man. Cotton, cattle, grain, tobacco, woollen and linen goods and metals, timber and machinery were the main items passing through the port. In 1876 Georges Stage, used by the Mersey ferries, was joined together with Princes Stage and expanded.

In 1873 a further Act of Parliament was passed to enable the board to spend £4 million to construct Langton, Alexandra and Hornby Docks, which created improved facilities for the larger vessels using the port. A further £3 million was spent on deep water berths at Langton and Canada Docks, and a new graving dock was later built at Canada Dock. For the year ending 1 July 1874 the number of ships entering the Port of Liverpool was 19,186, with a total tonnage of 6,710,093 tons. The gross revenue derived from the ships was £380,588; the amount from goods was £562,910, and from other sources £233,731, including rents of property and revenue from dock traffic, dock line of railway, weighing materials and dock warehouses. The total gross revenue amounted to £1,177,230 and the surplus (after setting aside £80,000 for taxes) was £173,994.

An Act of Parliament in 1906 allowed the Mersey Docks & Harbour Board to construct Gladstone and Gladstone Graving Dock, which was opened by King George V on 11 July 1913. The whole project was completed in 1927 and at that time the system contained the biggest and deepest docks in the world. Morpeth and Alfred Docks had been built at Birkenhead and the Great Float was completed in 1866. New entrances were built at Alfred Dock and were opened by His Royal Highness the Duke of Edinburgh on 21 June 1866.

William Becket Hill formed the Liverpool Screw Towing & Lighterage Company in 1877. He came from Lancaster and was educated in Somerset, becoming a clerk at Pilkington & Wilson. Five years later he gained employment at the Montreal Steamship Company (Allan Line) as the freight manager and became a partner in 1883. He founded the Hill Line, which operated vessels on the London–New York route, and was appointed Liverpool agent for the City Line. He was involved in the establishment of the Shipping Federation and became its first vice chairman. William Becket Hill was a firm believer in screw-driven vessels and introduced the *Bantam Cock* and *Stormcock.*

The *Stormcock* operated as a tender to the Allan liners and on 22 January 1880 she conveyed HRH Princess Louise, who was sailing on the *Sarmation* to join her husband, the Marquis of Lorne, Governor General of Canada. The princess was seen off by her brothers, the Prince of Wales, later King Edward VII, and the Duke of Edinburgh. The royal party were taken to the *Sarmation,* which was at anchor off Egremont, and *Stormcock* followed the liner out of the river to Waterloo, where the brothers were taken off and transferred to the Admiralty yacht *Lively. Stormcock* was chartered by the government, who sent her to Egypt in 1882, where she carried troops along the Suez Canal and was later purchased by the Admiralty from her owners.

Gamecock was launched in September 1879 by Thomas Brassey & Company at Birkenhead. In 1889 she towed the *Yarrowdale* from St Vincent to Dunkirk. The tow covered a distance of 2,560 miles and took fourteen days to complete. The next two vessels named *Stormcock* were also sold to the Admiralty. *Stormcock* of 1883 became HMS *Traveller* in 1885. She was present at the Diamond Jubilee Naval Review at Spithead in 1897 and saw service in the Queenstown Command, and also in the Mediterranean during the First World War. The third *Stormcock* was launched by Laird Brothers at Birkenhead on 28 September 1885. In November that year she towed the sailing vessel *Ardencaple* from Fernando Noronha to Greenock, a distance of 4,000 miles, in thirty days, with a short stop at St Vincent and Las Palmas to take on coal. She was purchased by the Admiralty in 1896 and was renamed HMS *Alligator. Blackcock* was equipped with triple-expansion machinery and entered service in 1886. Her machinery was the first to be installed in a tug and on trials she achieved a speed of 13 knots. *Blackcock* left Liverpool on 19 March 1888 for St Helena to tow the *Norham Castle* back to the United Kingdom. The tow commenced on 25 April, arriving at London on 28 May after a distance of 4,500 miles.

Skirmisher was built as a tender to the ocean liners and was used to escort the royal yacht *Victoria and Albert* at the opening of the Manchester Ship Canal in 1894. Prior to the opening of the canal, the Liverpool Screw Towing & Lighterage Company acquired a number of flats, barges and steam barges, The 51-ton barge *Cicely* had been built at Winsford in 1844, *Pride* dated from 1869, *Mary* entered service in 1873, *Liberator* in 1874, *Ballet Girl* in 1876, *Bar One* and *Straight Tip* in 1877 and the steam barges *Wirral, Lord Clive* and *Pride o' th' Weaver. Moorcock* had originally been built in 1866 as the sailing trawler *Herring* and was converted to steam in 1879. She was purchased in 1892 and saw service with the company until she was sold to J. L. Gordon of Liverpool in 1898. *Little England* was purchased in 1895 and renamed

Sedgecock. Prairiecock operated from 1896 to 1936, when she was broken up at New Ferry, and *Heathcock* from 1897 to 1910. The fourth *Stormcock* was purchased in 1898 and was fitted with compound engines, developing 600 hp. She was also requisitioned by the Admiralty during the First World War and became HMS *Storm Bird.*

One of the most significant tugs owned by the Liverpool Screw Towing and Lighterage Company was the *East Cock,* which was launched at Birkenhead on 8 December 1908. She was similar to the *North Cock* and *South Cock,* which had both entered service in 1903, and achieved 11.61 knots on her trials. In 1957 she assisted in the salvage of the *Olympic Rock,* which was stranded in the Mersey and survived in service for another three years, when she was broken up on Bromborough beach.

George Bell Cowl, a lawyer, opened his tug business 1882 and was operating with five second-hand vessels by 1887 when his company was taken over by the Alexandra Towing Company. They established their headquarters in Cowl's offices at Langton Dock and the Alexandra Towing Company began with a capital of £25,000 in £5 ordinary shares. George Bell Cowl was invited onto the board of directors and was given 400 shares in the company. The Mack family held the most significant number of shares, and the *Alexandra* was purchased in 1888. *Alexandra* took its name from the new company, but also from one of Liverpool's docks and this started the fashion of naming their vessels after Liverpool Docks. However, when they later expanded to other ports this system was adhered to with local names. The company was well managed and was able to keep revenue up and costs down, but in one month in 1889 three tugs were involved in five accidents and a reserve fund was set up. Tug masters and engineers then received a half-yearly bonus as an incentive if their vessel had not been involved in any incidents.

The Master Mariners William and Thomas Jolliffe had founded their towing company in 1854 with their first paddle tug, the *Lioness.* She was followed in 1859 and 1860 by the *Lion* and *Emperor* and their vessels were also involved in the excursion trade to North Wales in the summer months. *Great Emperor* and *Great Western* were introduced in 1864 and were followed by the screw tug *Thomas Jolliffe* in 1879. *William Jolliffe* followed six years later and was sold to Canadian Pacific Steamships in 1914, renamed *Nitinat* and used for barge towing and salvage duties. In 1924 she was purchased by the Pacific Salvage Company, becoming Salvage Chief, and was wrecked on Merry Island on 7 February the following year. The two-funnelled *Jane Jolliffe* entered service in 1888 and *Sarah Jolliffe* two years later. The *Andrew Jolliffe* was built at South Shields in 1894, *Vivian Jolliffe* in 1897 and *Hannah Jolliffe* in 1900. In 1908 the business of William and Thomas Jolliffe was acquired by the Alexandra Towing Company and the *Andrew Jolliffe* was renamed *Wapping.*

Russell Rea set up his business as a coal merchant in Liverpool in 1872, and went into partnership with his brother James Rea in 1879. They established the Rea Towing Company two years later and entered into the bunkering trade with the *Cumbria,* which was later renamed *Hallgarth. Holmgarth* followed in 1899, *Aysgarth* in 1900 and *Fallgarth* and *Edengarth* in 1902 and 1903 respectively. *Aysgarth* was the first of their tugs to be registered in Liverpool and gave good service to the company until she was sold to James Dredging, Towage & Transport Company Limited in 1932. The Rea Transport Company was formed in 1902 to service the coaling activity in the Mersey, delivering the fuel by barge to vessels anchored at the Sloyne. *Fellgarth* and *Edengarth* entered service and spent most of their careers towing Rea's barges on the Mersey and the Manchester Ship Canal. In 1919 both tugs were transferred to Rea Limited, and then to the Rapid Coaling Syndicate in 1947. They were broken up by William Cubbin Limited at Birkenhead and Routledge Brothers, Garston in 1960.

The coal elevators Canada, Sandon, Salisbury and Nelson were taken over in 1913/14 from the Liverpool Barge & Coaling Company and the company provided tugs to tow them around the river and docks. The powerful tugs *Yewgarth* and *Cairngarth* were built in 1913 to handle the large coal elevators. *Yewgarth* was transferred to Rea Limited in 1920 and to Rea Towing Company Limited in 1924. She was broken up at Garston in 1959. *Cairngarth* was similarly transferred within the company and was requisitioned by the Admiralty in 1939 to operate at Devonport, being returned to her owners the following year. She arrived at Barrow on 14 September 1960 and was broken up.

Working life and conditions on the Mersey tugs at the beginning of the twentieth century was described by J. H. Cropper of Wallasey,

> I joined the firm's tug Wallasey as a fireman on 5 June 1905. Life was very hard in those Days and if we were ashore for two nights each week we considered ourselves fortunate. Each member of the crew had also to take a turn watching the tug in the docks during the liberty hours. It was seven days a week duty with no stipulated hours and fixed wages. These were the days when radio was in its infancy and our information on the movements of ships came from the Coastguard Stations, and the daily morning and evening newspapers. Tugs had to be constantly on the alert, sometimes for days before the expected vessel actually arrived. Never the less crews were happy; the spirit was like that of a family and men would stay in one tug for years. For my own part I spent seventeen years in the Victoria and twelve in the Formby.

Overgarth and *Nethergarth* entered service in 1907, *Stanegarth* was introduced in 1910 and *Ullsgarth* in 1912. *Danegarth* and *Graygarth* were built in 1915 for work at Bristol and Southampton respectively. However, *Graygarth* later worked on the Mersey for many years from 1920, and was originally registered at Southampton until 1953, when this was changed to Liverpool. In August 1961 she completed her service with the company and was beached at Garston, where she was broken up. *Graygarth* was similar to *Cairnsgarth* and *Yewgarth.* In 1922 the Rea Towing Company was formed and *Carlsgarth, Dongarth, Langarth, Minegarth, Yorkgarth* and *Poolgarth* were delivered to Rea's by Smith's Dock Company Limited for service on the Mersey. Their names were adapted from the names of collieries in the Yorkshire, Nottinghamshire and Derbyshire coalfields. The tugs were seen assisting vessels of the Blue Funnel Line, Federal Line, New Zealand Shipping Company and other major shipping lines operating on the Mersey. They were occasionally sent to Barrow to help during the launch of vessels at the shipyard. *Minegarth* also held a passenger certificate to enable her to transport groups of dock workers to vessels loading explosives in the Crosby Channel.

During the First World War the *Sarah Jolliffe, Hannah Jolliffe* and *T A Jolliffe* were requisitioned by the Admiralty, as was *Herald, Flying Kestrel* and *Flying Breeze.* These were later followed by *Herculaneum, Harrington, Wallasey, Alexandra* and *Hornby*. *Wapping* saw service in the Mediterranean and was later in the Persian Gulf, and for most of the war around a third of the fleet were away from the Mersey. Between 1919 and 1923 the Alexandra Towing Company managed the tugs *Dandy, Jaunty, St Catherine, St Erth, St Faith, St Giles, St Omar* and *Spry* for the Ministry of Transport. The concrete dumb barges *A C W 10* and *A C W 11* were owned by the company and the barges *Cretealp* and *Cretefield* were also managed by the Alexandra Towing Company.

In 1916 James H. Lamey established a towing company. James, and his brother and partner William, had been pilots on the Manchester Ship Canal and purchased the paddler *Hero* under the name of the Hero Tug Company, managed by Marwood & Company. The Lamey family came from Appledore, Devon, where they had been owners of coastal sailing vessels, some of which carried clay to Runcorn, where it was loaded into barges and sent to the potteries by canal. Lamey also owned the schooner *Irish Minstrel* and the auxiliary schooner *Puseyjones No 2*. The *Hero* was built in Bristol in 1896 and was purchased by The London Grain Elevator Company in 1898. She was sold to John Ryan of Birkenhead in 1906 and acquired by Lamey in 1916. The name of the business was changed to J. H. Lamey & Company in 1920.

Resolute was in service for Lamey's from 1919 until the following year, when she became a total loss off Hoylake. *Iris* was purchased in 1920 and she survived with the company for seven years, when she was broken up at New Ferry. The *Hull* followed in 1928 when she was purchased from the London & North Eastern Railway Company and sold to the South Caernarvonshire Yacht Company in 1939. *Dorunda* came into the fleet in 1929, followed by *Florida* in 1933 and the *Troon* the following year. *Troon* assisted the tow of some sections of the Mulberry Harbour from Deganwy in North Wales, where they had been constructed, to the beaches of Normandy in 1944. The *B. C. Lamey* entered service in 1938 and *Energy* was bought from the Workington Harbour Board. The motor launches *Margo* and *Montila* were acquired to assist in the movement of invasion barges in the dock systems at Liverpool and Birkenhead.

The West Coast Towing & Salvage Company was set up in 1917, taking over the Star Tug Company, the Steam Tug Expert Company and the Sunshine Tug Company. However, they only survived until 1924. In 1919, when the Cunard Steamship Company moved some of its operations to Southampton, the Alexandra Towing Company also established a base at that port. It was at this time that investment in R. & J. H. Rea was encouraged to enable the company to invest in new ships and infrastructure following losses during the First World War. Rea Limited was formed with Alfred Holt & Company as a major investor. A takeover offer was received from William Cory & Son Limited and the Rea Transport Company was purchased by them, which included interests outside the River Mersey. 50 per cent of Rea Limited was acquired by William Cory and the Rea Transport Company Limited was restyled as R. & J. H. Rea Limited in 1919.

The Rea Towing Company purchased three tugs from the Manchester Ship Canal Company in 1927. MSC *Ellesmere Port* became *Ellesgarth*, MSC *Salford* was renamed *Salgarth* and MSC *Runcorn* became *Rungarth*. Their duties involved towing dumb sand hopper barges to the deposit buoy in Liverpool Bay and assisting ships in and out of the Manchester Ship Canal. They had replaced the Bridgewater side-lever tugs *Earl of Ellesmere, Brackley, Dagmar* and *St*

Winifred, which had been built between 1859 and 1870 and were broken up in 1926/27. The three tugs survived until they were broken up at Barrow; *Salgarth* in 1955, *Rungarth* in 1956 and *Ellesgarth* the following year.

The Alexandra Towing Company sold the *Coburg, Alfred, Huskisson, Wapping, Nelson, Hornby, Ryde, Albert* and *Toxteth* in the mid-1930s, and eight new tugs were ordered to replace them. These were the *Coburg, Huskisson, Nelson, Salthouse, Hornby, Wapping, Alfred* and *Crosby.* Cock tugs also introduced the new *Grebe Cock* in 1935, *Storm Cock* in 1936 and *Black Cock* in 1939.

During the Second World War many tugs were damaged by enemy action. *Crosby* was hit by an incendiary bomb, *Nelson* caught fire, *Wellington* and *Coburg* were badly damaged, *Alexandra* was set on fire, *Collingwood* was damaged by a bomb, *Hornby* was sunk and *Canning* and *Brunswick* also needed repairs following enemy action. Rea's *Poolgarth* sank and all her crew were lost when she hit a mine off Canada Dock on 22 December 1940. The tugs *Greetings, Musca, Vespa, Earner, Empire Ben, Empire Darby, Empire Joan, Empire Sara, Empire Walter, T I D No. 1* and *T I D No. 16* were managed by the Alexandra Towing Company for the Ministry of Transport between 1939 and 1945.

At the end of war J. H. Lamey purchased the *Assistant* from the Mersey Docks & Harbour Board and she was renamed *J. H. Lamey* following the fitting of a mainmast, the provision of a top bridge and the installation of VHF radio-telephone equipment. She was the first Mersey tug to have this communication facility fitted. It is reported that when the *Baltic Queen* sank in a collision in the Mersey in February 1948, the incident was witnessed by W. H. Lamey from his home at New Ferry. He immediately made a call to the *J. H. Lamey,* which was soon on her way to rescue some of the survivors. The *J. H. Lamey* was broken up at Garston in 1962.

Partington was purchased from the Manchester Ship Canal Company in 1946 and was renamed *William Lamey.* She was followed by her sistership *Eastham,* which became the *Edith Lamey. Athlete,* acquired in 1947, retained her original name and was broken up at Preston in 1955. *West Creek* and *Darent* were purchased in 1949, becoming *Margaret Lamey* and *Alfred Lamey* respectively. *Cruiser* was renamed *B. C. Lamey* in 1951 and *Thunderer* was purchased and renamed *Anita Lamey. Wrestler* was acquired from Steel & Bennie Limited in 1953, and was renamed *Irene Lamey.* The following year *Momentum* joined the fleet from the Ridley Steam Tug Company Limited of Newcastle, and became *Marie Lamey.* She was fitted with a Kort nozzle rudder by Grayson Rollo & Clover Docks Limited at Birkenhead, and this was the first installation of its type to be fitted to an existing tug.

The tanker *World Jury* stranded in the Eastham Channel in February 1956 and was refloated by the *Irene Lamey, Anita Lamey, Edith Lamey, J H Lamey* and *Margaret Lamey.* In 1958 the *Marie Lamey, Anita Lamey* and *Irene Lamey* towed the landing craft LCT *4025, 4049* and *4098* from Bangor, North Wales to Liverpool. On arrival they left Liverpool for Canada in tow of the United Towing Company's *Merchantman, Masterman and Tradesman* on 3 April. They had been purchased by the Canadian government, and arrived at Quebec three weeks later. *John Lamey* was introduced in 1957 as the first oil-engined tug in regular Mersey ship-towing service. *Sparkler* also entered service as *Alfred Lamey* the same year, and the second *Edith Lamey* was introduced together with the *James Lamey* two years later.

The *William Lamey* was launched on 25 March 1959 from the Gateshead yard of T. Mitchison & Company Limited. She was propelled by two Lister Blackstone oil engines geared to one shaft and developing 1088 bhp. *William Lamey* was equipped with radar, VHF radio-telephone and the twin uptakes in place of a funnel gave the master a completely unobstructed view of the towing operation. She was followed by the *J. H. Lamey* in 1963 and *B. C. Lamey* in 1966.

In 1951 the institutional shareholders of the Liverpool Screw Towing & Lighterage Company formed North West Tugs, with Cammell Laird as the main shareholder. The new company was managed by the Liverpool Screw Towing & Lighterage Company, and *Fighting Cock* and *Game Cock V* were launched by Cammell Laird & Company Limited at Birkenhead in 1953. The firm became the Liverpool Screw Towing Company in 1956 when their barges were sold. The *Heath Cock* entered service in 1958 and was the first to be powered by oil engines. Her sister *West Cock* was followed by *Pea Cock, Flying Cock* and *Weather Cock,* which was the first tug working in Britain to be fitted with a two-speed gearbox.

In the early 1950s the Rea Towing Company placed orders for the construction of six new tugs for service on the River Mersey. The first of these was the *Aysgarth,* which was launched at Aberdeen on 20 August 1951, followed by *Applegarth, Bangarth, Grassgarth, Rosegarth* and *Throstlegarth,* which was launched in 1954. These, together with the Alexandra Towing Company's war replacement vessels, would be the last steam tugs to be built for the Mersey. Coal was becoming expansive and oil was cheap and was more acceptable because it was pollution free. *Aysgarth* towed the second of the lock caissons of the Queen Elizabeth II Oil Dock from Barrow to the Mersey in August 1953. The third caisson was towed from Barrow to Eastham by the *Bangarth* and *Grassgarth* in November that year.

Applegarth sank in Canning Dock on 19 August 1954 following an overhaul in Canning Dry Dock. She was raised three days later but sank in the Mersey on 13 January 1960 while assisting the Perthshire off Birkenhead. Her master and crew of six were lost and she was raised on 28 January 1960, returning to service six months later. *Bangarth* and *Grassgarth* assisted the tanker *Velletia* to her berth at the Queen Elizabeth II Oil Dock at Eastham at the official opening of the dock. The two tugs also assisted the oil-tanker *Olympic Rock* on 22 January 1957 when it had stranded off Egremont. *Bangarth* also rescued the crew of the *Lurcher,* which was sinking after a collision with the *Stamatios G Embiricos* in the river on 21 January 1961. Just after the crew were taken off the *Lurcher* she sank. *Rosegarth* towed the *Rungarth* to Barrow to be broken up in March 1956 and the Isle of Man steamer *Victoria* to Barrow for scrapping in January 1957. All six tugs were converted to oil burning between 1956 and 1959. The *Incegarth* was built by Isaac Pimblott & Company Limited of Northwich in 1958, followed by the larger *Elmgarth* and *Pinegarth* in 1960 and 1961.

The oil-burning tug *Hazelgarth* was launched at Appledore on 18 July 1958 and delivered to the Rea Towing Company in May 1959, followed by *Willowgarth, Cedergarth* and *Maplegarth* in 1962 and *Beechgarth* in 1964. *Hazelgarth* and *Willowgarth* were employed at the inauguration of the Tranmere Oil Terminal on 8 June 1960, assisting the Shell tanker *Zenatia* to the North Jetty. *Hazelgarth* and *Willowgarth* were also employed at Barrow for the launch of the Orient liner *Oriana,* and *Hazelgarth* assisted at the launch of HMS *Dreadnought,* Britain's first nuclear-powered submarine, in 1960. Two more powerful vessels, *Hollygarth* and *Brackengarth,* were introduced in 1969 to provide towing services to Shell's very large oil tankers at the Tranmere Oil Terminal. In 1960 Rea's acquired the lighterage and barge business of William Bate & Company Limited and their tugs *Redcroft* and *Firefly*. *Redcroft* was immediately sold to Routledge Brothers and was broken up at Garston.

The diesel-powered *North Isle* and *North Loch* were delivered to the Alexandra Towing Company in 1958/59, and three Furness Withy's Johnstone Warren Line tugs were purchased. The Britannia Steam Towing Company was taken over by Alexandra in 1962. The company owned a fleet of three tugs and had been established for over eighty years. For several years it had been operating a joint service with the Alexandra Towing Company, which had seven tugs based at Swansea and three at Port Talbot. The Alexandra Towing Company also acquired one third of the shares in J. H. Lamey that year, as well as North West Tugs and the Liverpool Screw Towing Company with their fleet of tugs in 1967. The company then acquired the remaining two thirds interest in J. H. Lamey the following year. In 1970 their tugs were renamed as follows:

Fighting Cock	*Sloyne*
Game Cock V	*Wellington*
Heath Cock	*Collingwood*
West Cock	*Morpeth*
Pea Cock	*Canada*
Flying Cock	*Gladstone*
Weather Cock	*Formby*
William Lamey	*Wapping*
J. H. Lamey	*Hornby*
B. C. Lamey	*Salthouse*
Alfred Lamey	*Coburg*
James Lamey	*Huskisson*

Herculaneum was built in 1961 and was followed by a new *Alexandra, Langton, Brocklebank* and *Egerton*. Richard Dunston of Hessle delivered the *Romsey, Brockenhurst* and *Ventnor*. *Trafalgar* and *Nelson* were delivered in 1966 and the three Furness Withy's Johnston Warren tugs were sold to Rea in 1968.

In 1896 the Johnston Line ordered a tug from A. W. Robertson Limited of London to assist with the docking arrangements for its deep-sea vessels in the Mersey. The original tug was named *Amore* and she worked in conjunction with vessels of other companies. In 1916 she was requisitioned by the Admiralty, reboilered and based at Queenstown. The Johnston Line was taken over by Furness, Withy & Company Limited in 1916 and she was joined by the tugs *Beemore* and *Ceemore* in 1929. *Amore* was replaced by *Deemore* the following year. *Beemore* was sold to the Alexandra Towing Company in 1958 and renamed *Mumbles*. Later that year Alexandra's purchased the *Deemore*, which became the *Margam*. *Ceemore* was also purchased in 1959 and was renamed *Murton*. The three vessels were originally employed at Liverpool but were later transferred to work at Swansea. *Murton* was broken up at Briton Ferry in 1964,

Margan at Silloth in 1965 and *Mumbles* at the River Neath. *Rossmore, Foylemore* and *Kilmore* were delivered in 1958 and were painted with the name 'Furness Lines' on their hulls three years later.

The *Wapping* sailed from Swansea in 1973 to undertake towage duties at Gibraltar. The following year the Alexandra Towing Company acquired London Tugs, which became Alexandra Towing Company (London) Limited. The Medway Dry Dock & Engineering Company at Sheerness and the Britannia Marine Towing Equipment also came under its control at this time. Bulk Cargo Handling Services, and the thirty-one barges of the Liverpool Lighterage Company, were acquired by Alexandra in 1971. The following year they also bought the barge fleet owned by Rea Towing Limited and one of their barge tugs. Bulk Cargo Handling Services purchased the seven elevators of the United Grain Elevators in 1973, and ordered three new grain barges. *Alfred* and *Crosby* were delivered in 1971, and *Albert* and *Victoria* the following year. R. & J. H. Rea took over Steel & Rennie of Glasgow and the Newport Screw Towing Company in 1970. R. & J. H. Rea Limited was restyled as Cory Ship Towage Limited in 1970 and the fleet, except that of the Rea Towing Company on the Mersey, was repainted into the new livery.

In 1972 Cory acquired the Grangemouth & Forth Towing Company, the Clyde Shipping Company and W. H. Reynolds of Plymouth, the following year. The *Waterloo, Wellington, Wallasey, Sun London, Sun Essex* and *Sun Kent* were delivered. A share of ITM Offshore Limited was acquired in 1973, and the Alexandra Marine Transportation Company was formed to oversee the operation of Alexandra's offshore services. The grain business of Bulk Cargo Handling Services in Liverpool was closed in 1985 and staff made redundant. *Indomitable* and *Formidable* were delivered in 1978/79, *Canada* in 1980, *Collingwood* in 1981, and *Sun Thames* and *Ganges* in 1982.

Following their sale to Greek owners in 1981, *Heath Cock, Pea Cock* and *Weather Cock* left the Mersey as *Vernicos Barbara IV, Vernicos Georgis* and *Vernicos Alexia* respectively. *Vernicos Georgis* (ex-*Pea Cock*) was responsible for towing the other two vessels and off St David's Head she developed engine problems. While these were being resolved, a tow line fouled her propeller. The three tugs were driven ashore on 18 October 1981, near Solva in St Brides Bay, and were wrecked.

Sun Anglia was delivered in 1984 and *Bramley Moore* the following year. *Redoubtable* was purchased in 1982 and *Implacable* and *Invincible* the following year. In 1983 Rea's took over C. J. King of Avonmouth. Alexandra Marine Transportation Limited was an offshore division of the Alexandra Towing Company and was structured as a marketing company for anchor-handling tugs, supply vessels and flat-top pontoon barges.

The Alexandra Towing Company with operations in Liverpool, London, Felixstowe, Southampton, Swansea and Gibraltar was taken over by the Australian Howard Smith Group in 1992, when a bid of £52 million was accepted. However, it was not until the spring of 1994 that the Alexandra livery finally disappeared from the entire fleet of fifty-three vessels, and the rectangular Howard Smith logo appeared on the superstructure. The following year Howard Smith Towage & Salvage announced an order for six new tugs, two for Felixstowe, one to Southampton and one for use by the Medway Towage operation at Sheerness. Options would be taken on two further vessels.

In May 2001, the towage operations of Howard Smith was acquired by Adsteam Marine Limited, becoming Adsteam Towage Limited, based at Huskisson Dock, Liverpool, with its head office in Hull. In 2007 the Adsteam board accepted an offer from Svitzer Wijsmuller to take over the company and the group was renamed Svitzer. The Competition Commission agreed to the acquisition subject to the sale of Adsteam's harbour towage operations at Liverpool. Adsteam entered into negotiations with interested parties and on 13 March 2007 the Competition Commission approved Smit Lloyd as a suitable purchaser of Adsteam's Liverpool business, and the sale was completed later that month. On 14 January 2000, Cory Towage Limited was sold to Wijsmuller for £81.8 million, becoming part of the Svitzer Marine Group in 2006. In 2010 Boskalis acquired Smit International N V for £1.35 million, with a pledge to retain the Smit name and its operations.

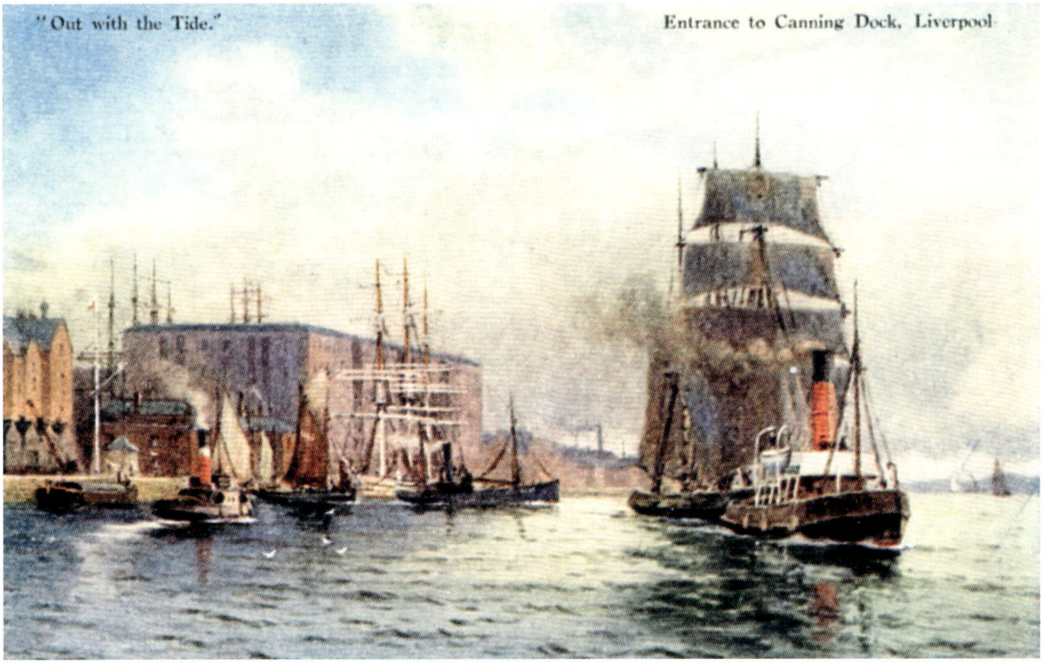

"Out with the Tide."

Entrance to Canning Dock, Liverpool

The River Mersey off Canning Dock.

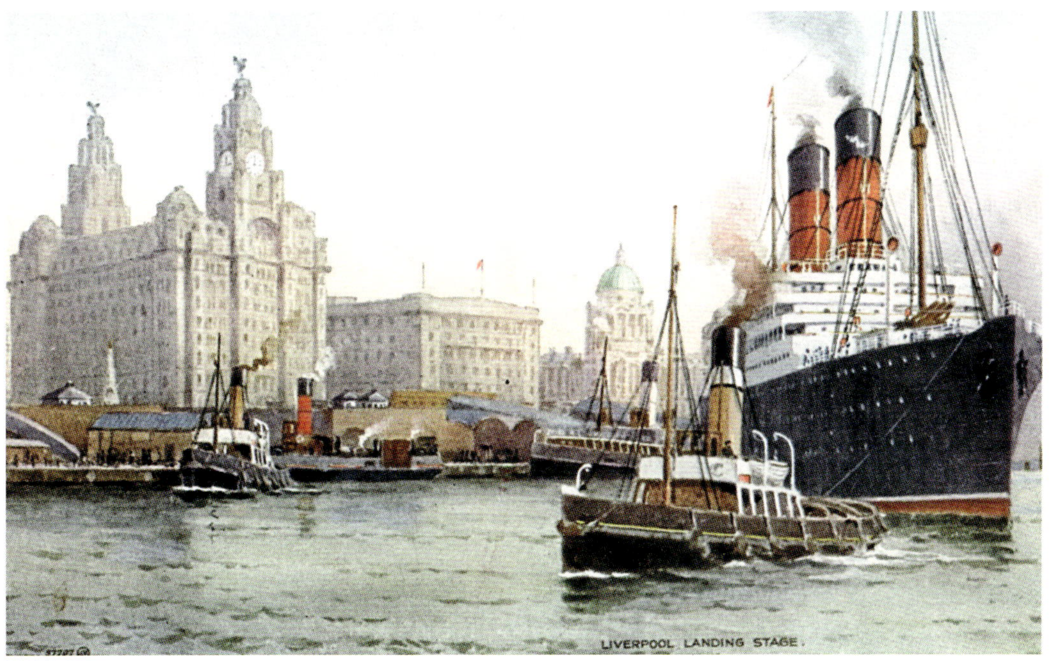

An Alexandra tug assists a Cunard liner off the landing stage at Liverpool.

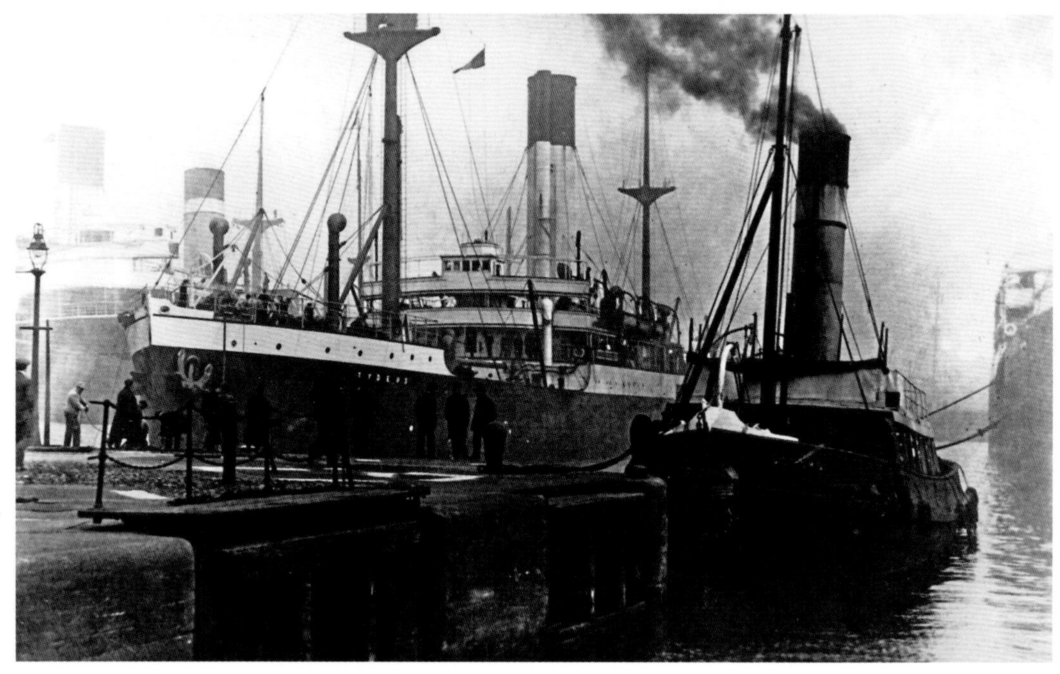

Coburg (1934/201 grt) in Alfred Dock, Birkenhead ahead of the Blue Funnel cargo vessel *Tydeus* (1901/7,441 grt).

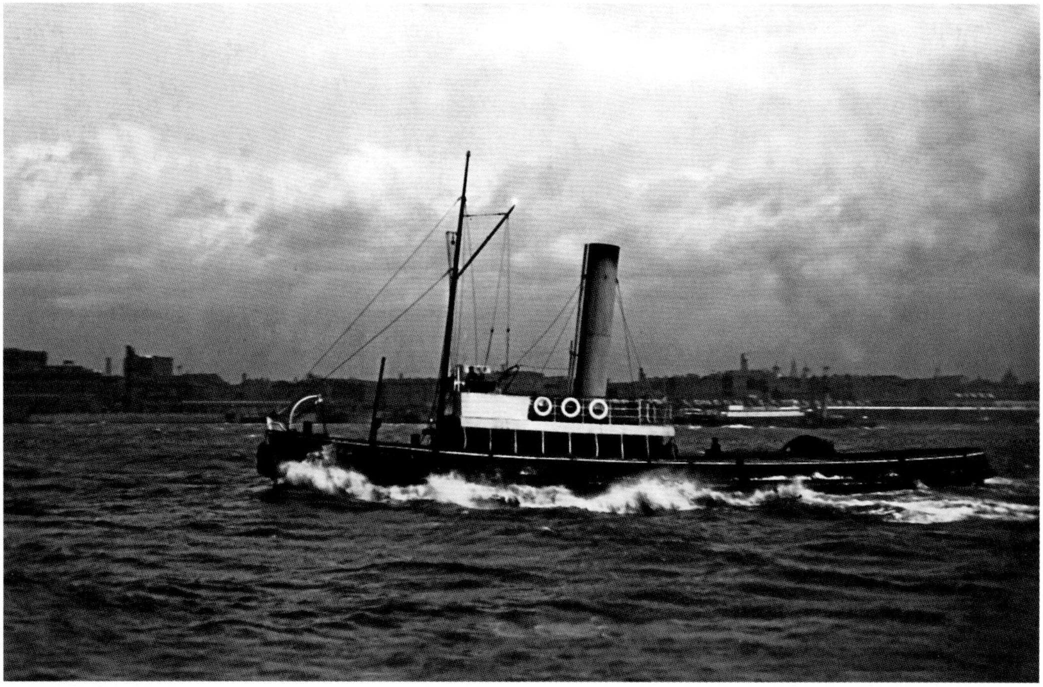

East Cock (1909/139 grt/650 hp/steam) of the Liverpool Screw Towing & Lighterage Company. She was broken up at Bromborough in 1960.

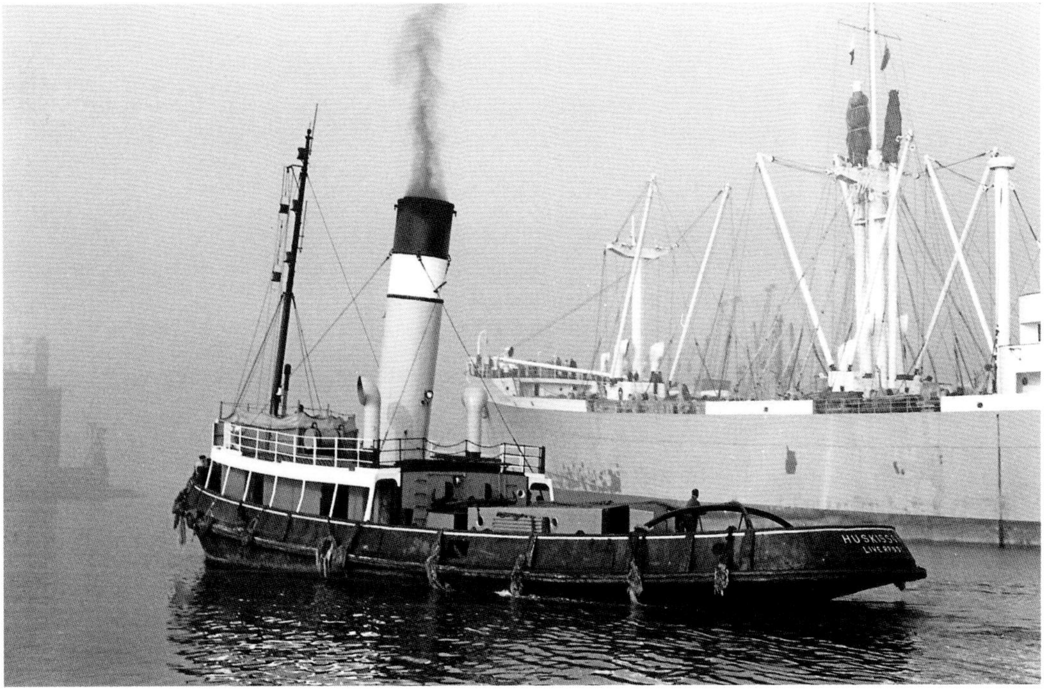

Huskisson (1934/201 grt) assists a Safmarine vessel in the West Float, Birkenhead. *Huskisson* was broken up in 1965.

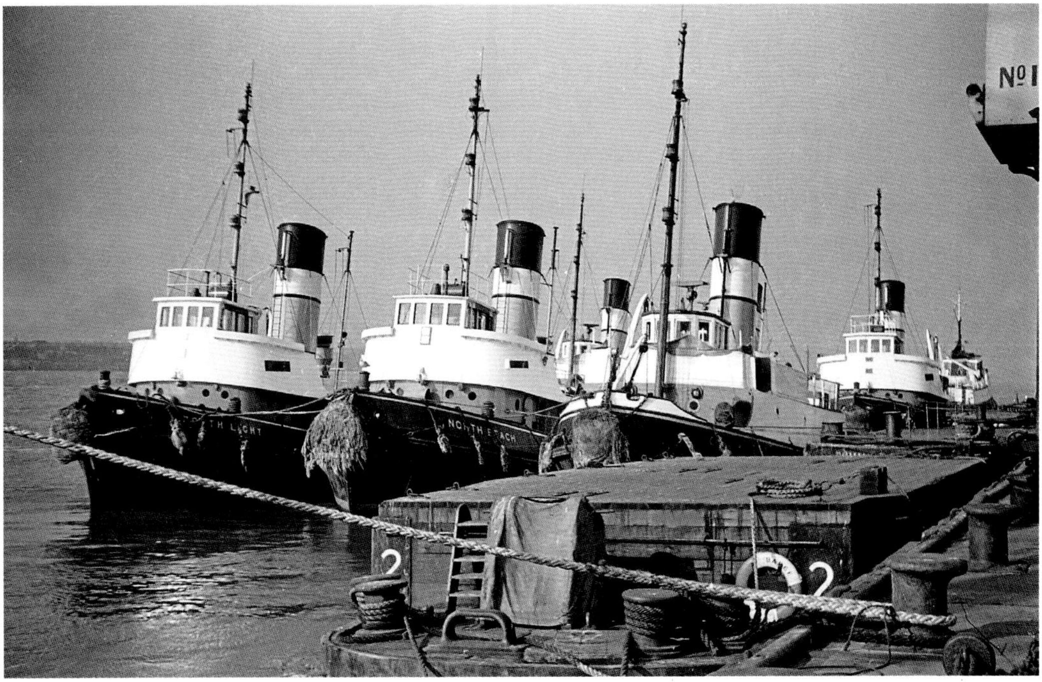

Alexandra and Rea tugs berthed at Princes Landing Stage in the 1960s.

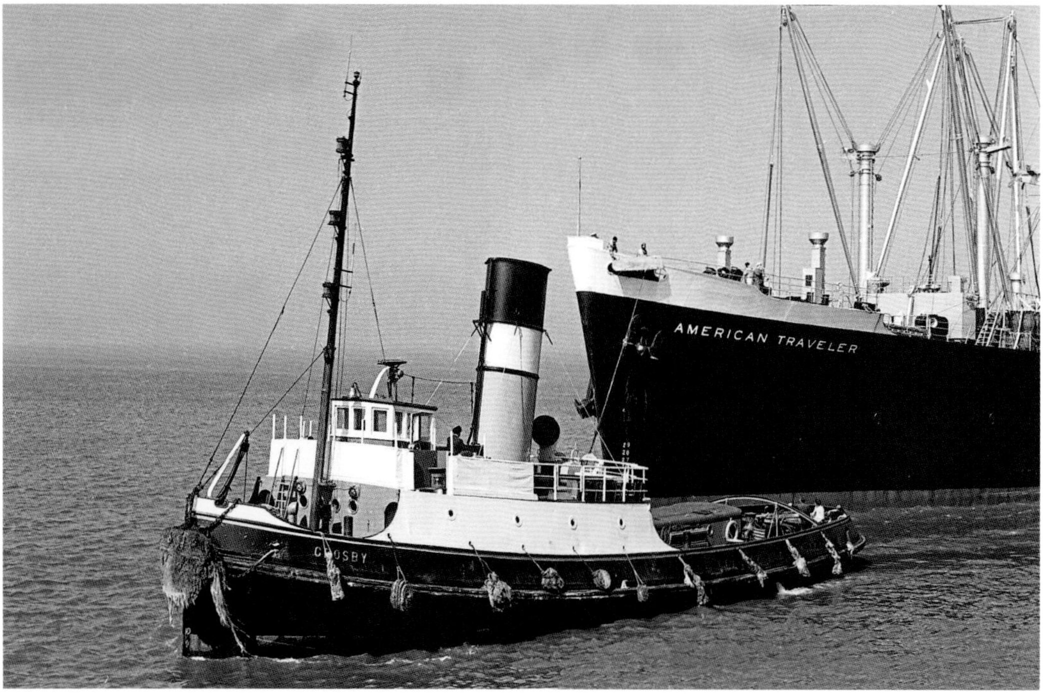

Crosby (1937/215 grt) towing the United States Line vessel *American Traveler* off Gladstone Dock. She was broken up at Dalmuir in 1968.

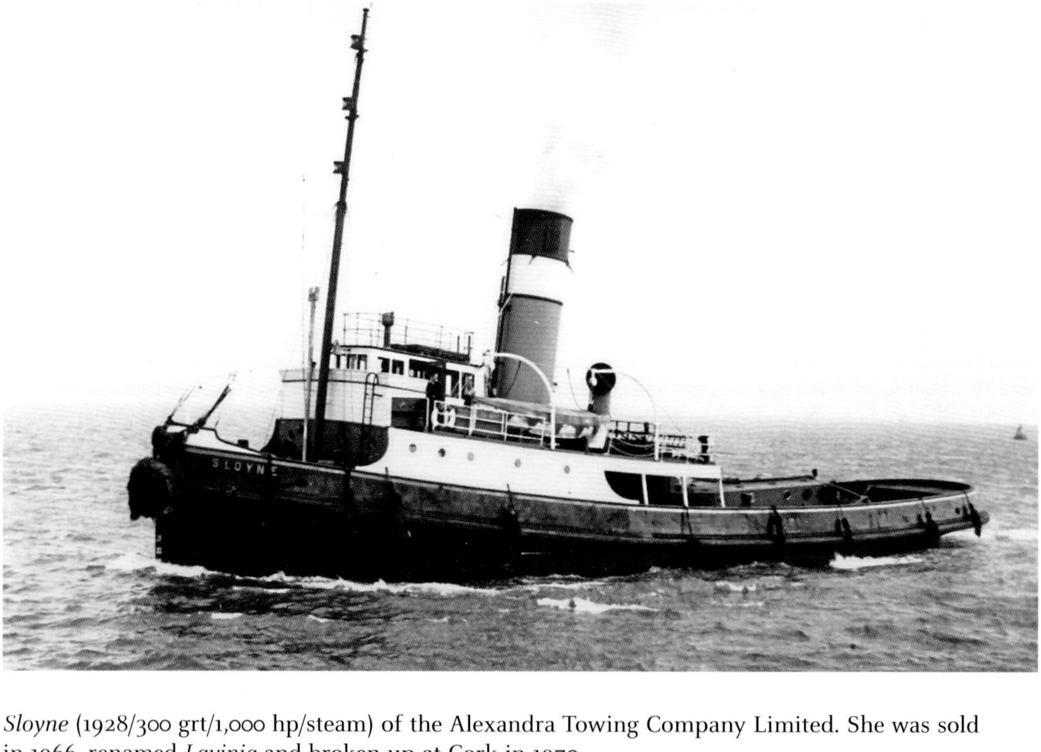

Sloyne (1928/300 grt/1,000 hp/steam) of the Alexandra Towing Company Limited. She was sold in 1966, renamed *Lavinia* and broken up at Cork in 1970.

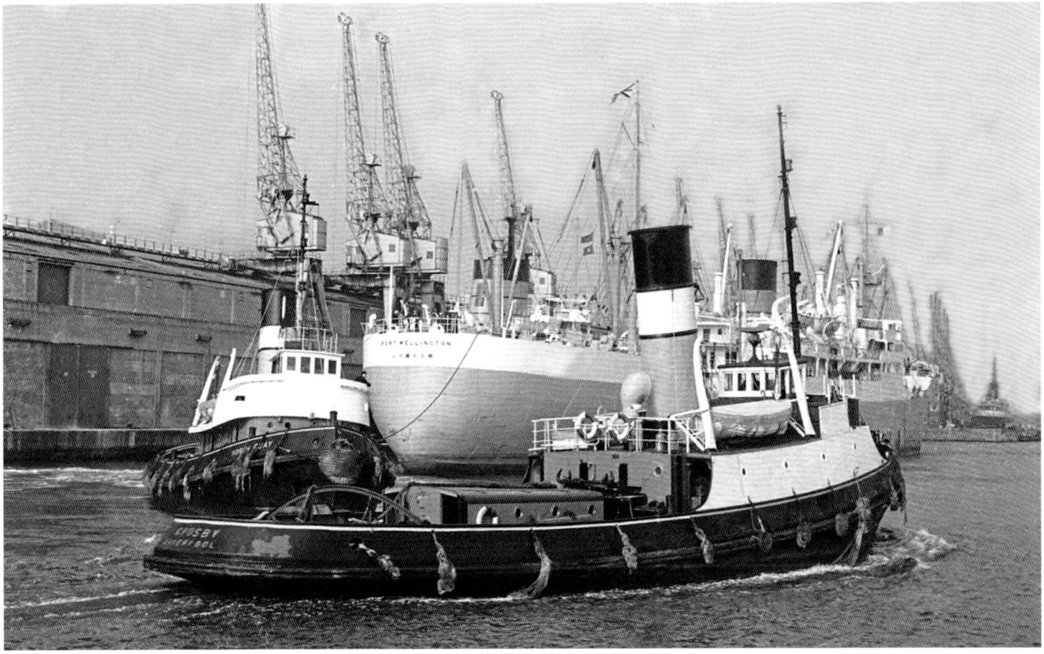

Crosby (1937/215 grt) and *North Quay* (1956/219 grt) in Huskisson Dock, Liverpool. *Crosby* was broken up at Dalmuir in 1968.

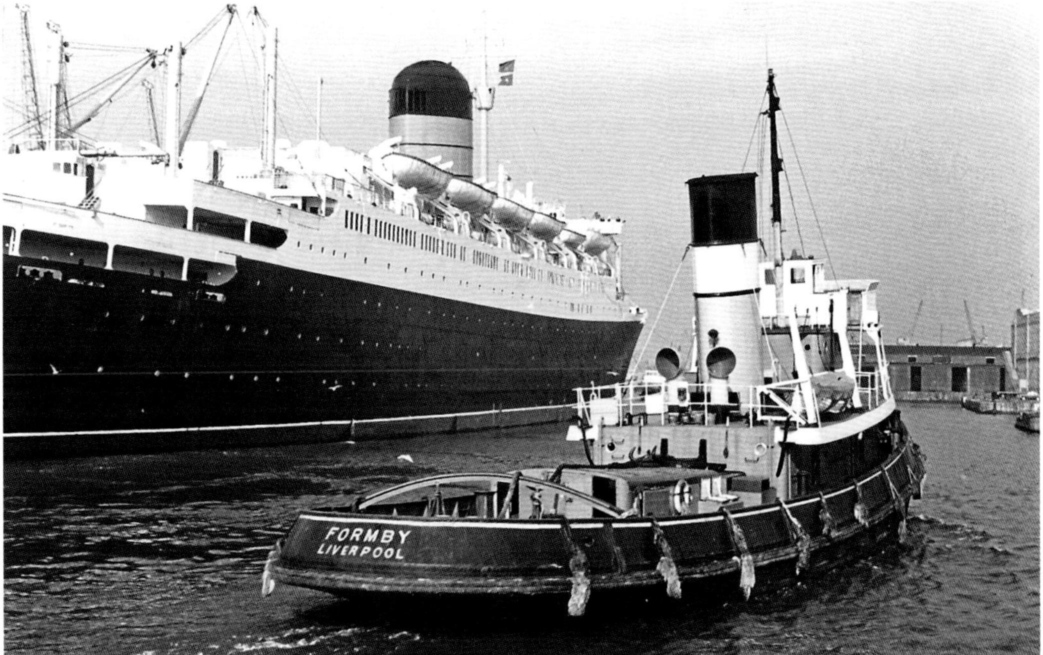

Formby (1951/237 grt) helps manoeuvre the Cunard liner *Sylvania* (1957/22,017 grt) to her berth in Huskisson Dock. *Formby* was sold to Impresa Fratelli Barretta of Italy in 1969 and was renamed *Poderoso*.

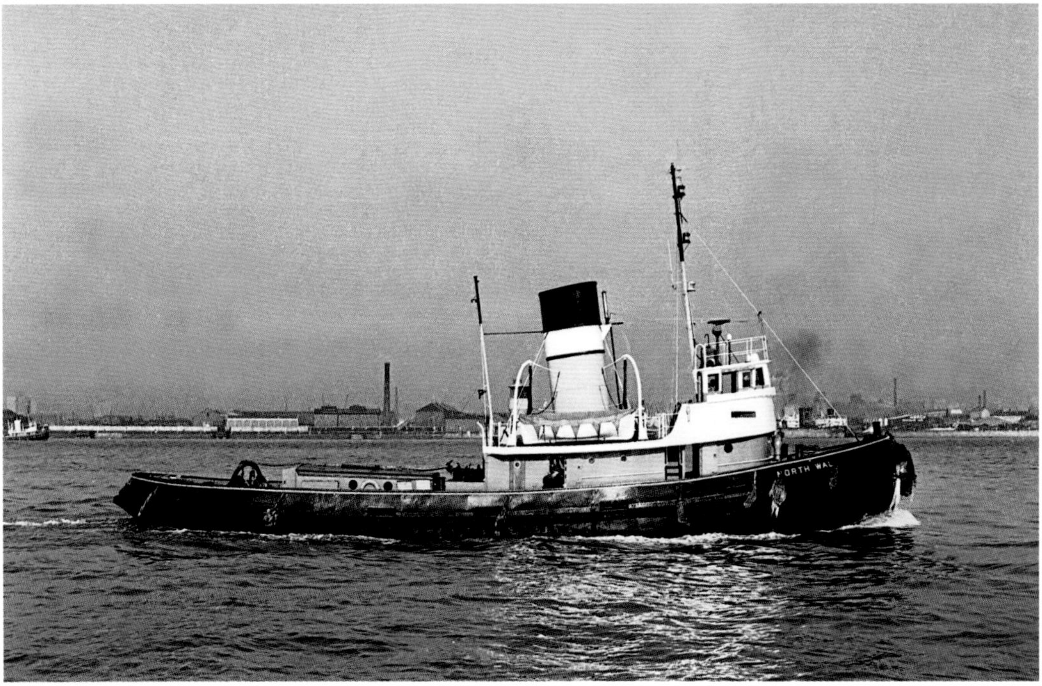

North Wall (1959/219 grt/1,000 hp/steam) of the Alexandra Towing Company Limited. She was purchased by Italian owners at Brindisi in 1973 and renamed *Maestoso*.

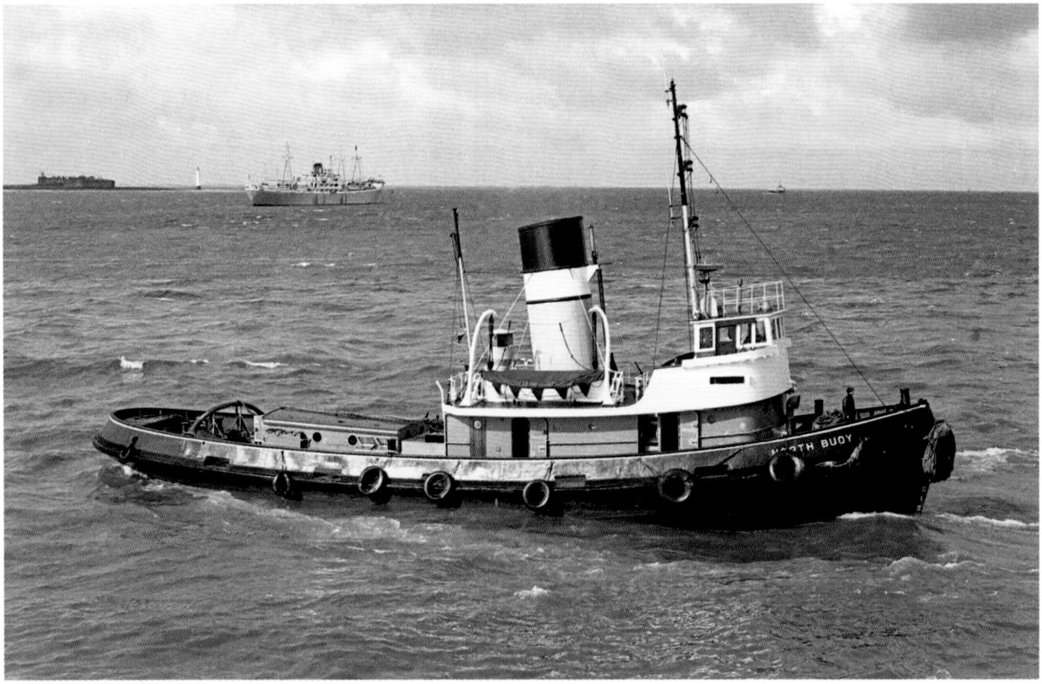

North Buoy (1959/219 grt/1,000 hp/steam) of the Alexandra Towing Company Limited. In 1973 she was sold to Italian operators, renamed *Coraggioso* and broken up at Brindisi in 1988.

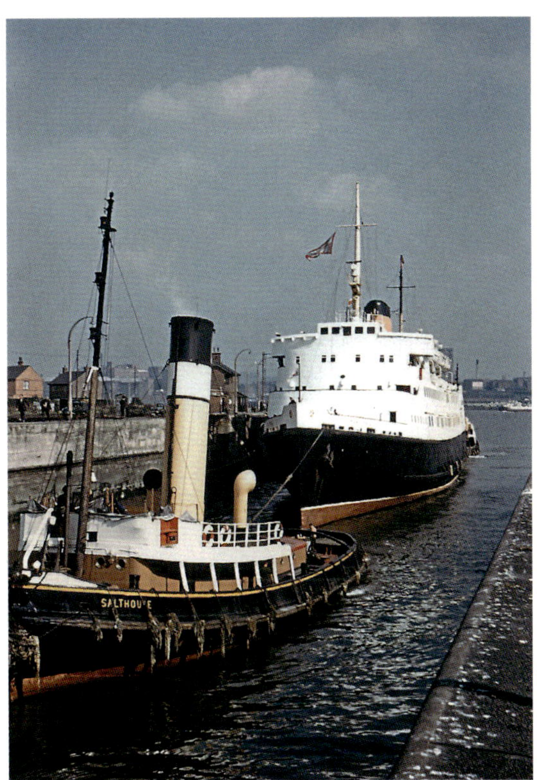

The Alexandra Towing Company tug *Salthouse* (1935/192 grt) ahead of the Manx car ferry *Manx Maid* (1962/2,724 grt) in Alfred lock at Birkenhead. *Salthouse* was broken up at Preston in 1965.

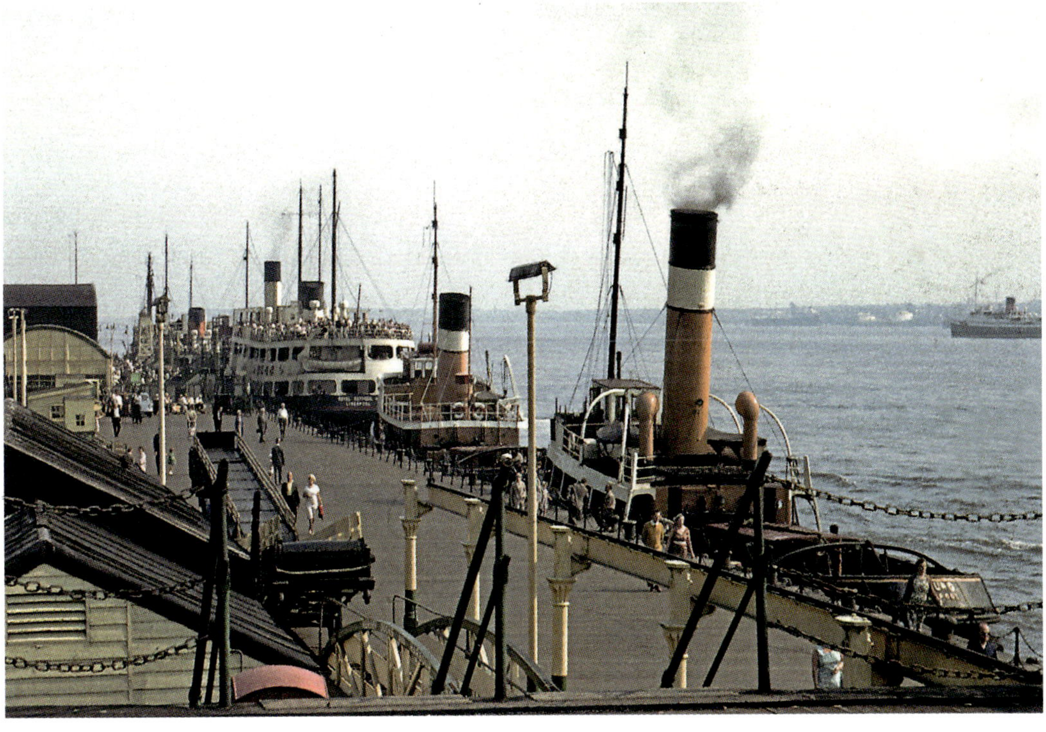

Alexandra tugs await orders at Princes Landing Stage, Liverpool.

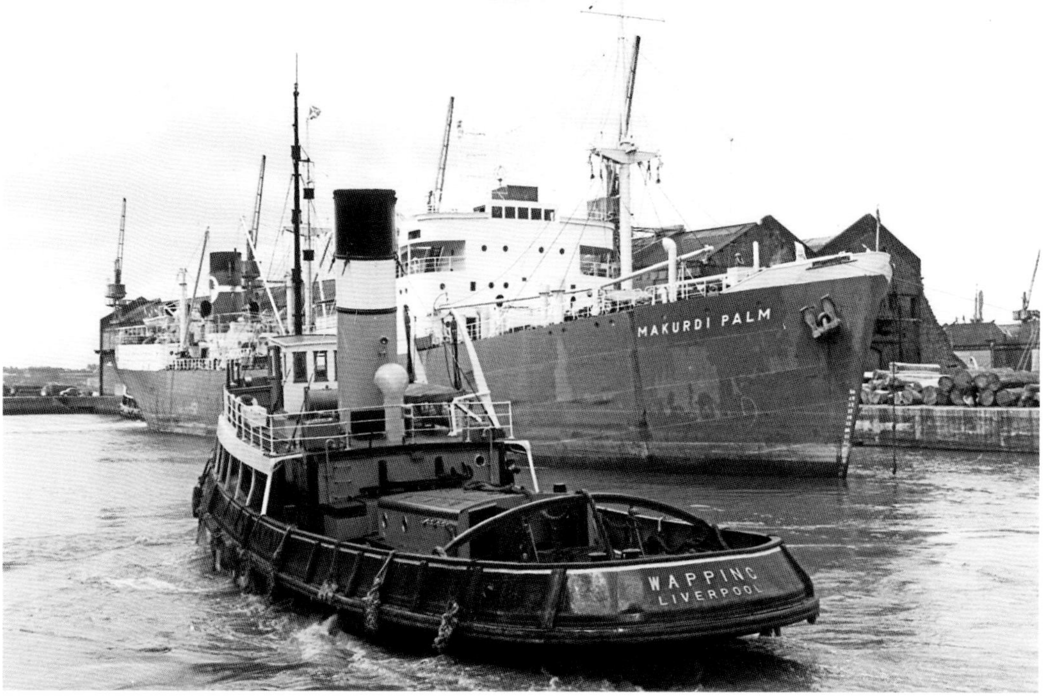

Wapping (1936/201 grt) and the Palm Line vessel *Makurdi Palm* in the North Dock's system at Liverpool. *Wapping* became *Marsh Cock* in 1967 and was broken up at Dalmuir the following year.

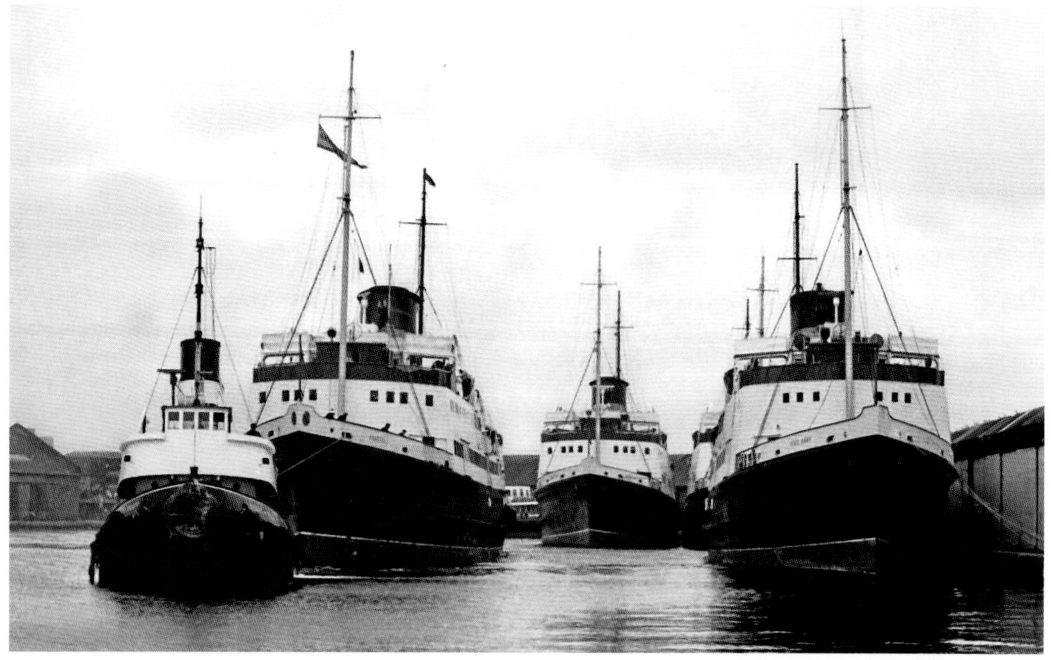

North Buoy (1959/219 grt) assists *Snaefell l* (1948/2,489 grt) berth alongside *King Orry* (1946/2,485 grt)in Morpeth Dock, Birkenhead at the end of the summer season in 1965.

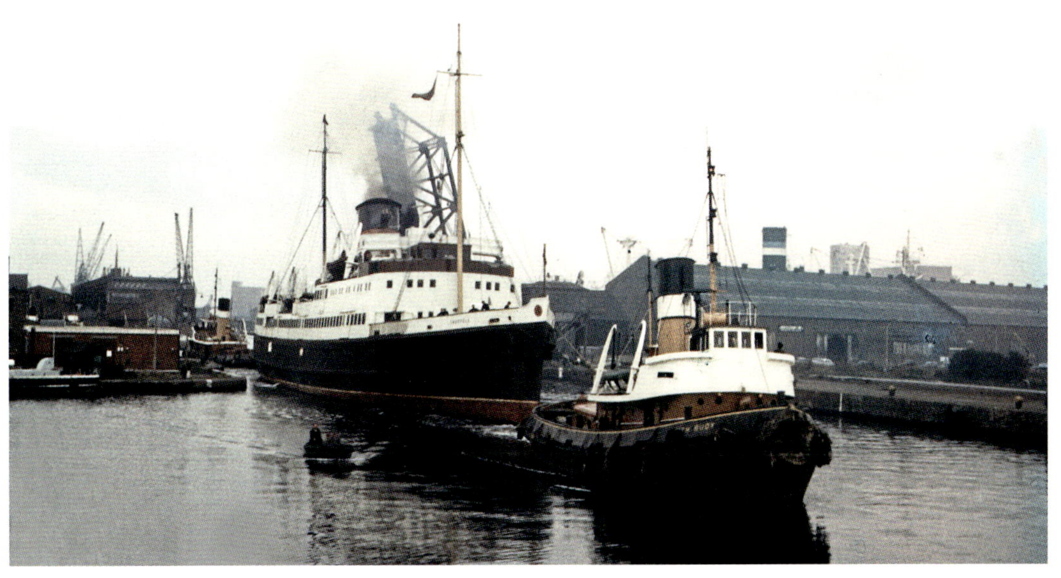

North Buoy and *North Wall* with *Snaefell* in Egerton Dock, Birkenhead.

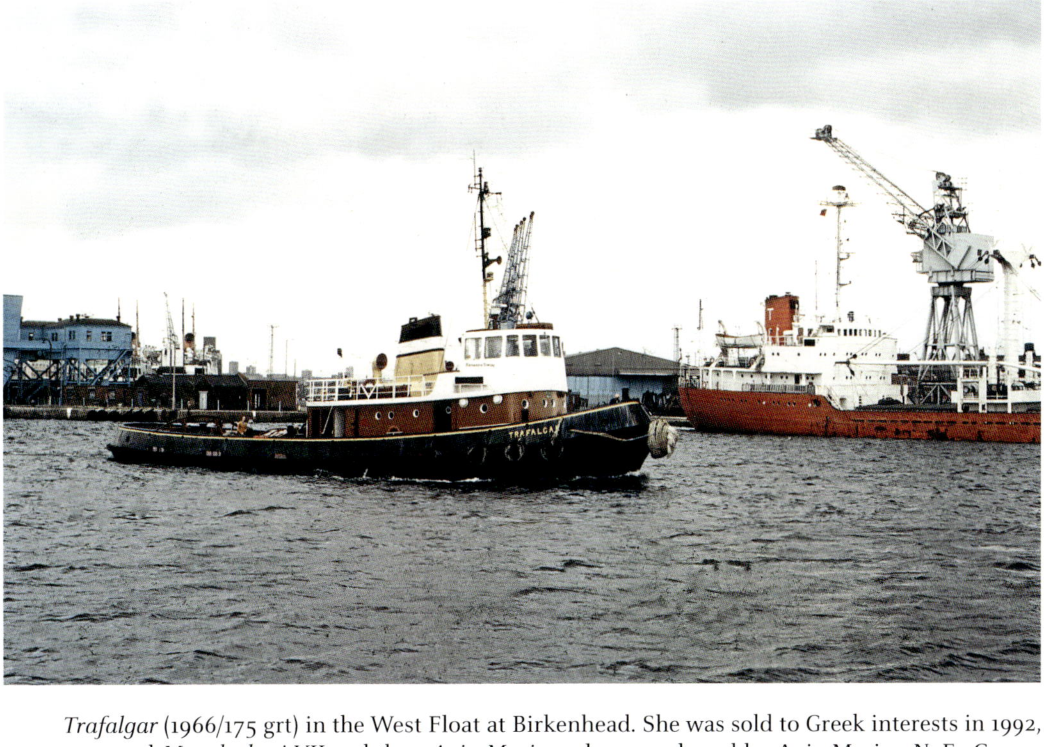

Trafalgar (1966/175 grt) in the West Float at Birkenhead. She was sold to Greek interests in 1992, renamed *Megalochari VII* and then *Agia Marina* when purchased by Agia Marina N. E., Greece in 2000. She was broken up at Aliaga in 2011.

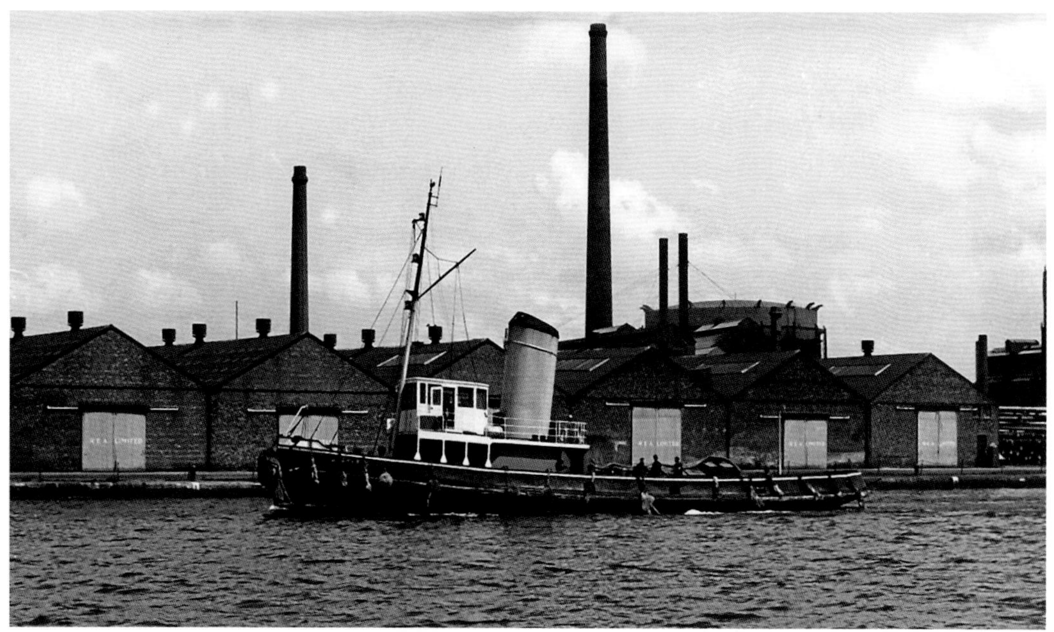

Grebe Cock (1935/169 grt) in the West Float at Birkenhead. She was broken up at Troon in 1967.

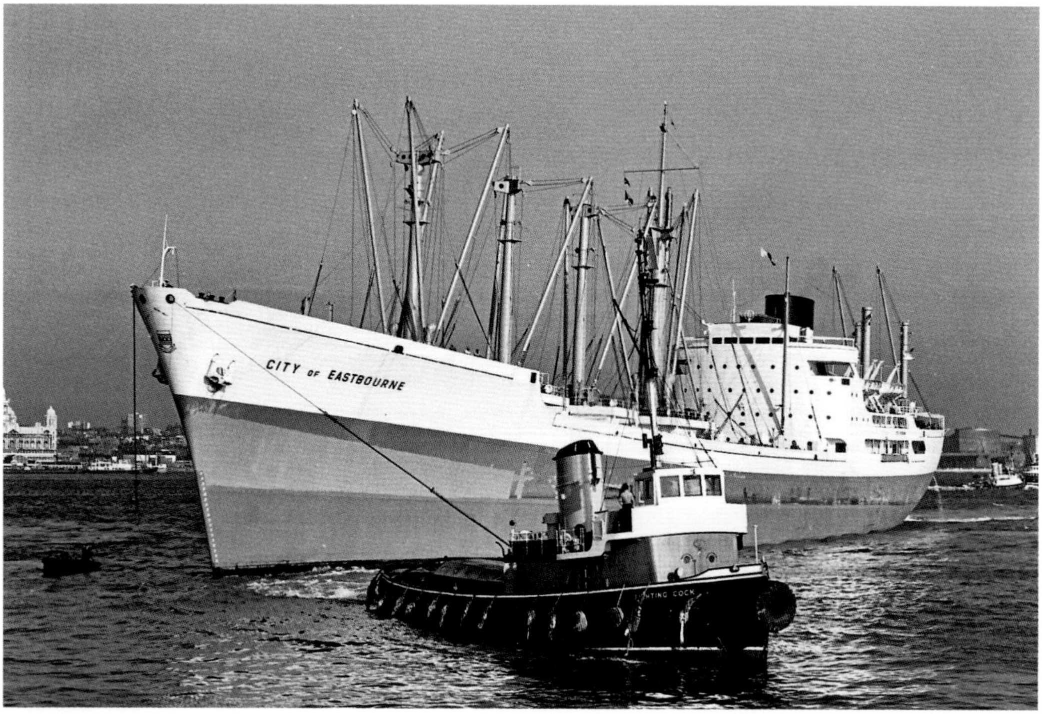

Fighting Cock (1953/218 grt) assists the Ellerman cargo vessel *City of Eastbourne* (1962/10,006 grt) into Alfred Dock, Birkenhead. *Fighting Cock* was converted to oil burning in 1960, when her funnel height was reduced. In 1970 she was renamed *Sloyne* and sold to Vernicos Shipping of Greece the following year, becoming *Vernicos Nicos*. She was broken up in 1988.

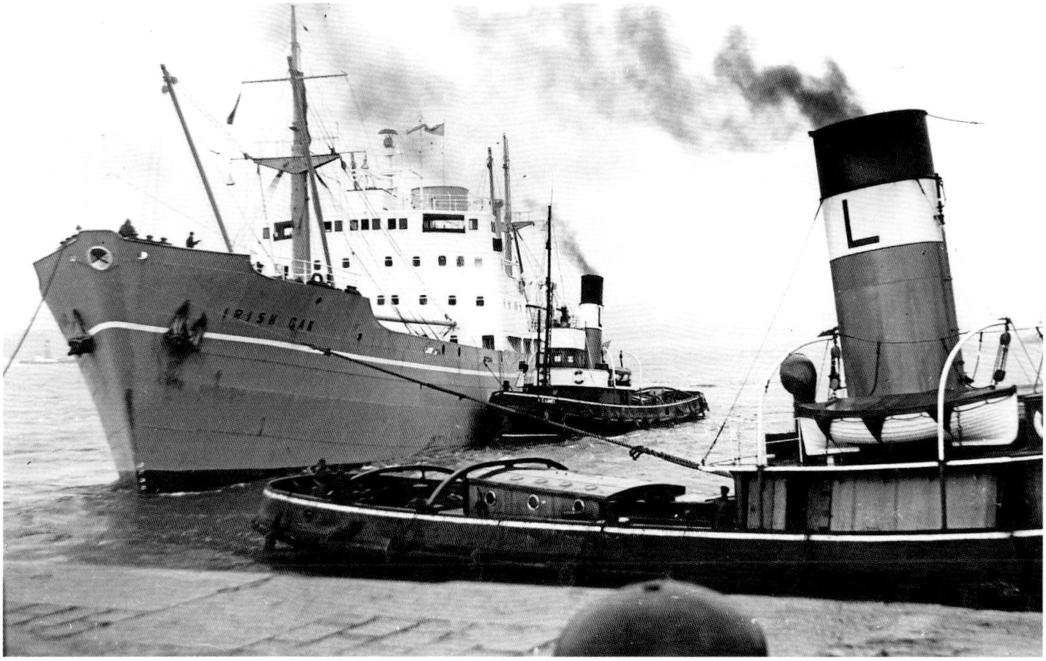

Lamey tugs bring *Irish Oak* (1949/5,077 grt) into Alfred lock at Birkenhead.

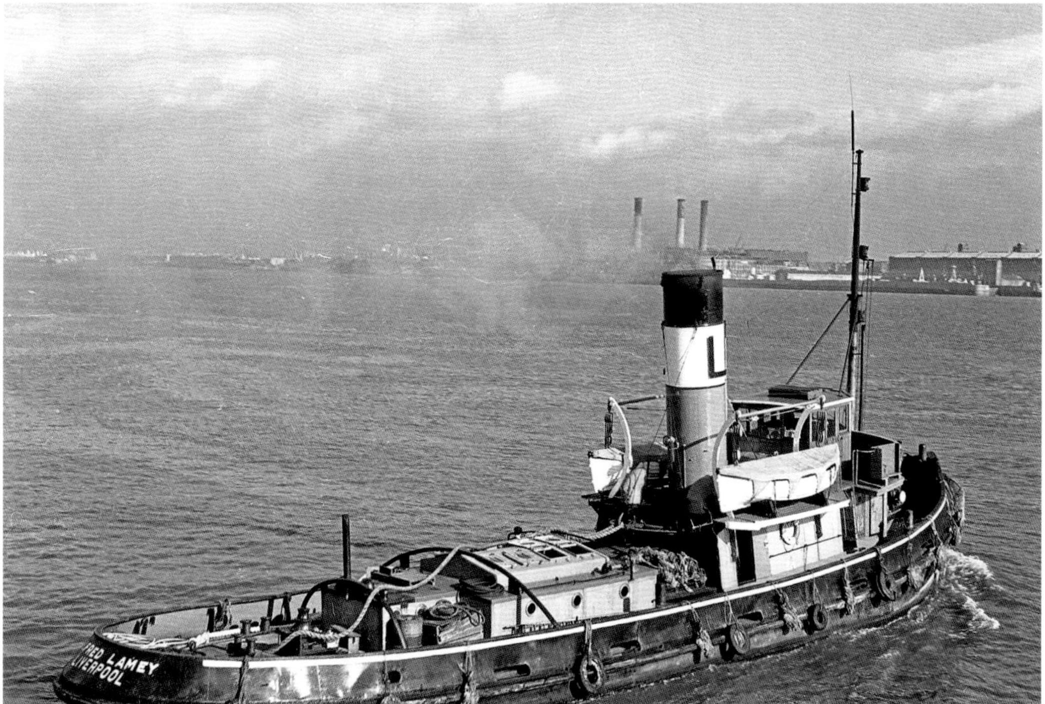

Alfred Lamey (1908/172 grt/750 hp/steam) of J. H. Lamey Limited. She was broken up at Barrow in 1957.

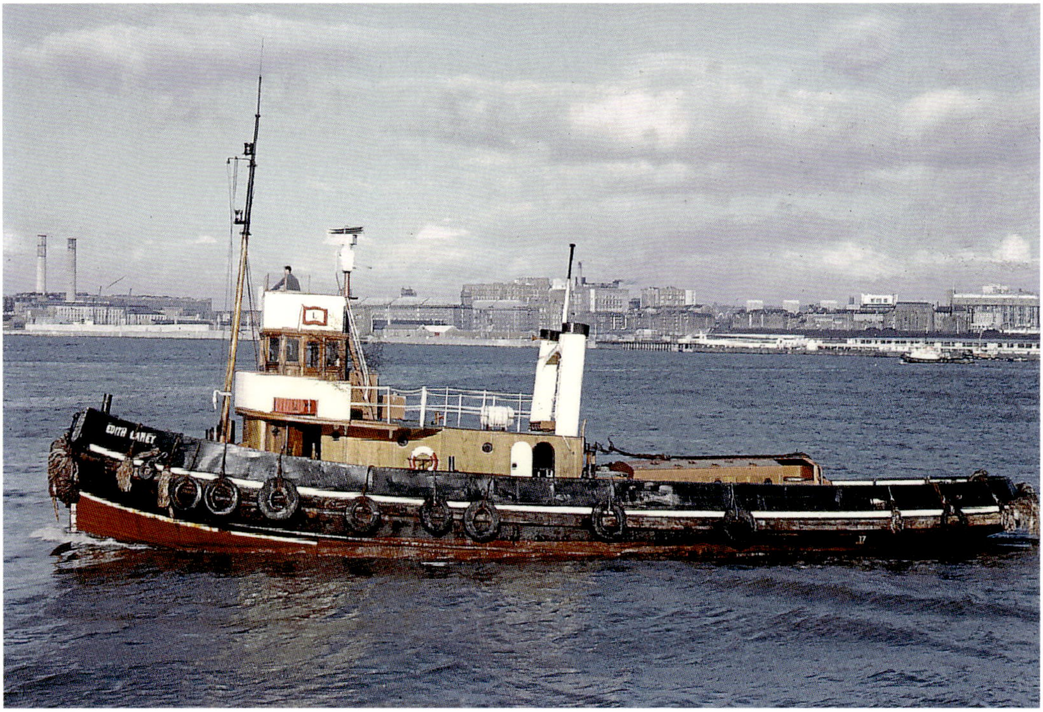

The Lamey tug *Edith Lamey* (1942/147 grt) docking at Birkenhead. She was broken up in 1969.

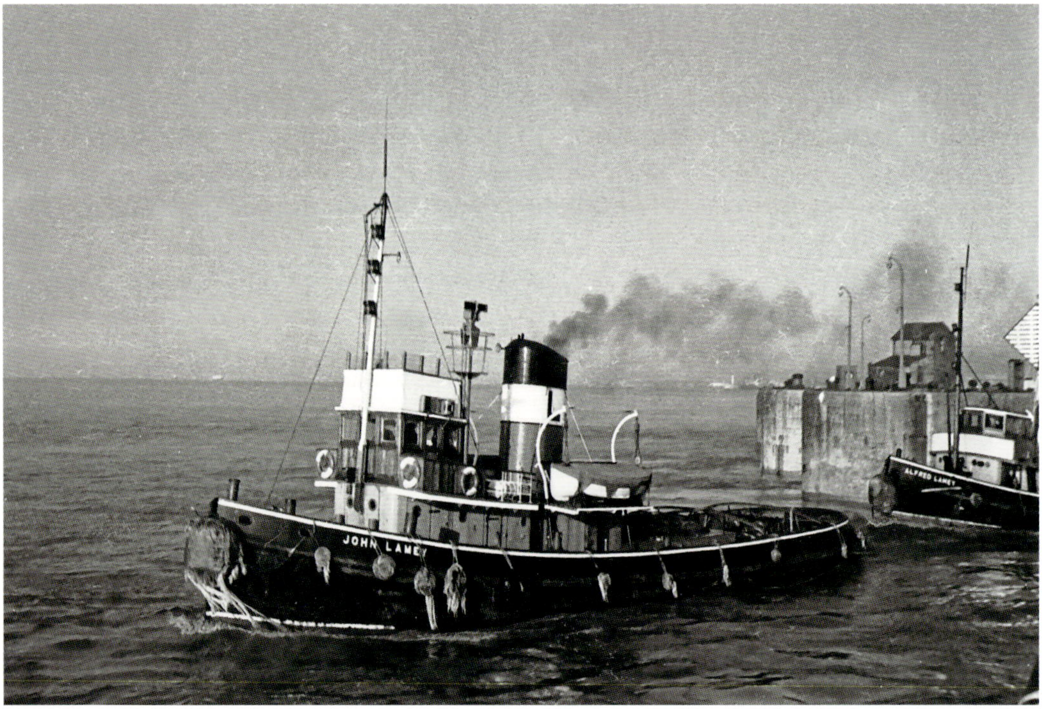

John Lamey (1927/185 grt) and *Alfred Lamey* (1960/141 grt).

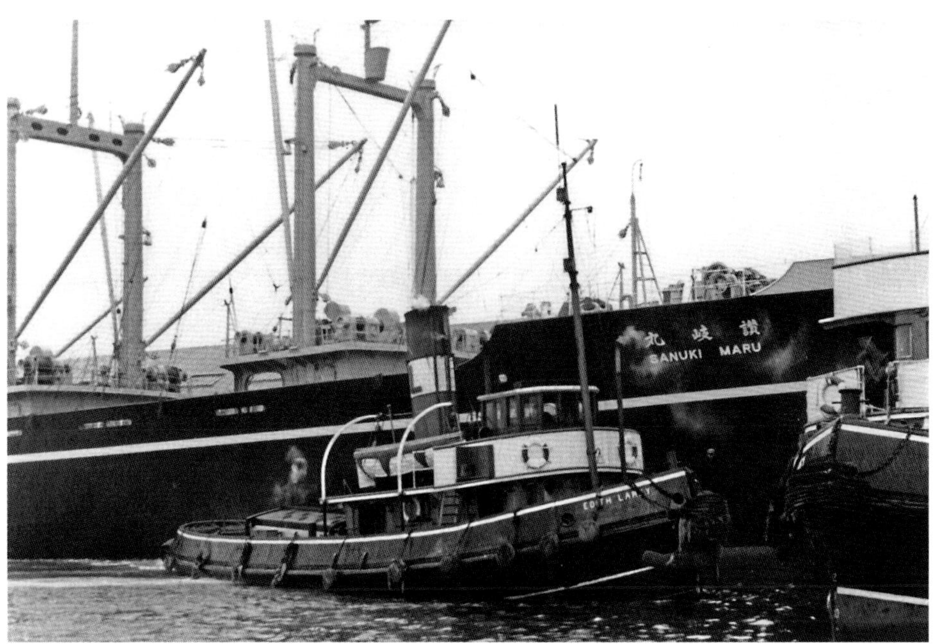

Edith Lamey at the bow of the NYK vessel *Sanuki Maru* (1955/9,308 grt).

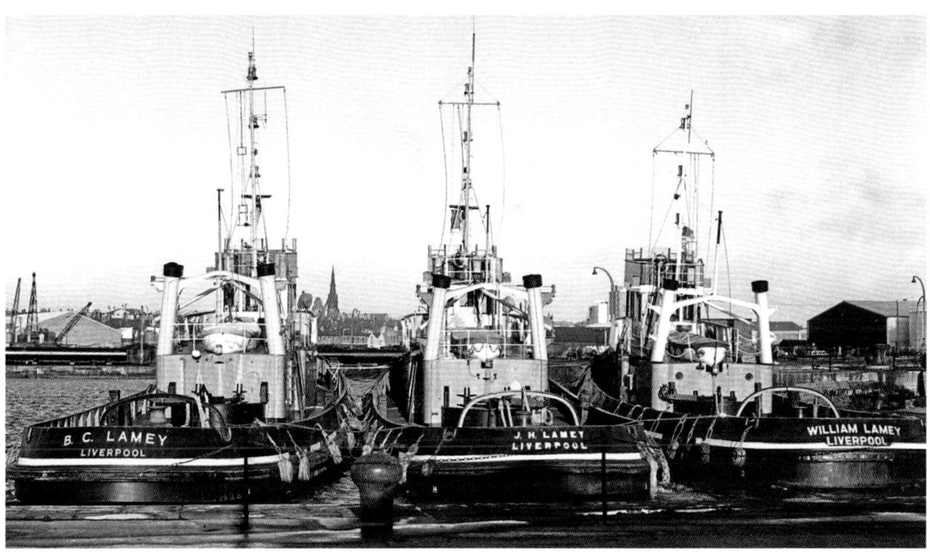

B. C. Lamey (1966/225 grt), *J. H. Lamey* (1964/216 grt) and *William Lamey* (1959/166 grt) berthed in Alfred Dock, Birkenhead. *B. C. Lamey* became *Salthouse* in 1970 and *David F* in 1984 before being sold to Maltese interests, becoming *Zamtug II* in 1987. Shortly after her sale she left Liverpool for Malta in December 1987 in tow of the Mersey Docks & Harbour Company floating crane *Samson*. On 12 December an RAF helicopter was called to rescue the two-man crew of the floating crane, after the tow had parted and she was adrift. The *Samson* grounded near Ram Head and was later declared a total loss. The *J. H. Lamey* was renamed *Hornby* when Lamey's were taken over by the Alexandra Towing Company. She was sold to operate in Northern Ireland in 1984 and her name was changed to *Samuel F. William Lamey*, becoming *Wapping* in 1970, *Theodoros 1* in 1985, *Agios Rafail* in 2002, *Fox 1* the following year and *Andreas L* in 2008.

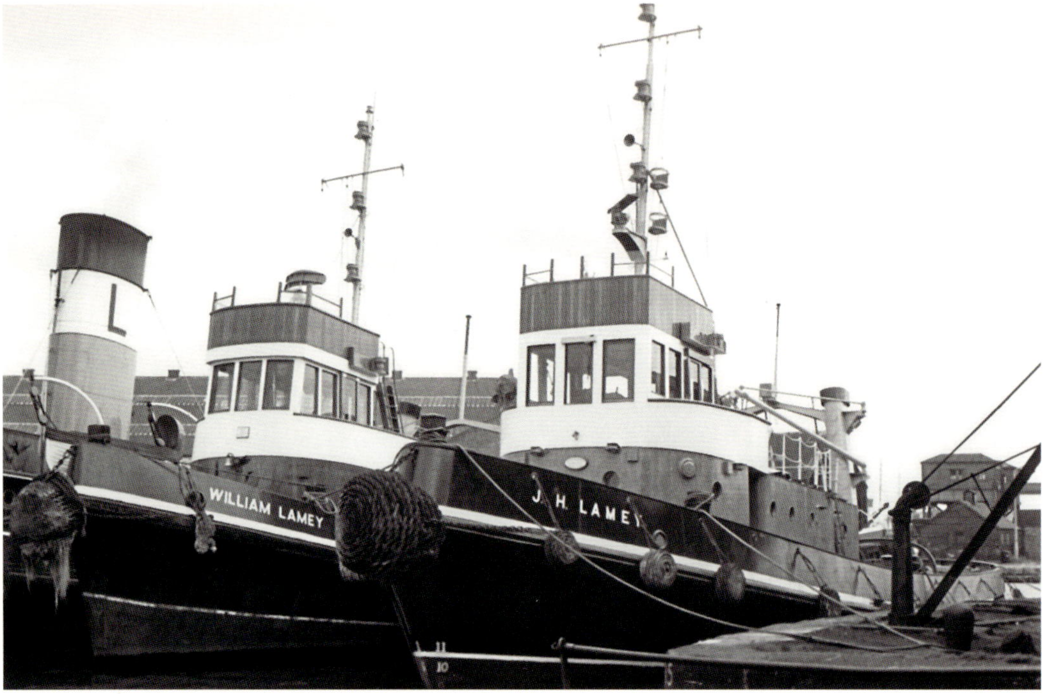

Lamey tugs 'at rest' in the East Float at Birkenhead.

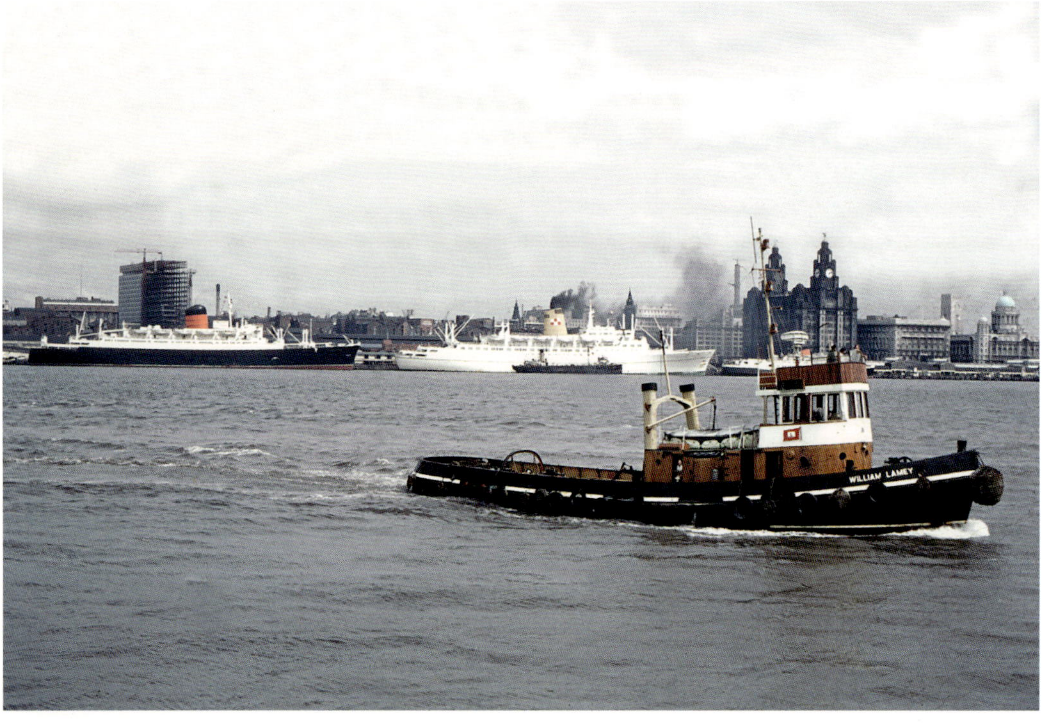

Sylvania (1957/22,017 grt), *Empress of Canada* (1961/25,585 grt) and *William Lamey* (1959/166 grt) in the River Mersey.

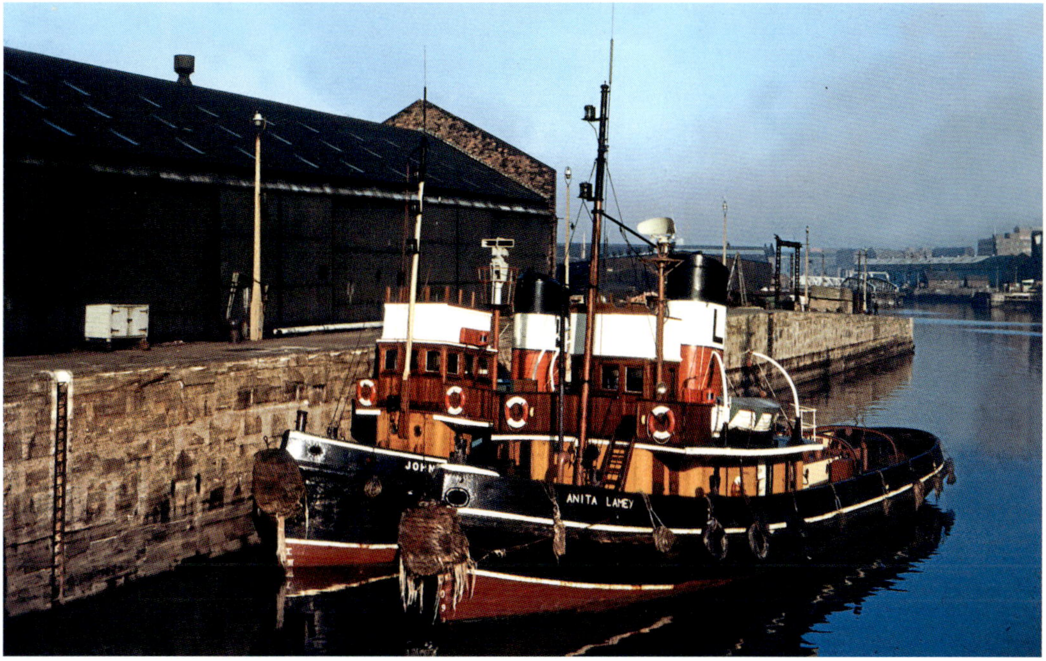

John Lamey (1927/185 grt) and *Anita Lamey* (1920/172 grt) at Brunswick Dock, in the South Dock's system at Liverpool. *John Lamey* was sold in 1967, becoming *Harry Sharman*. In November 1970 she sank off the Isle of Wight while attempting to salvage the oil tanker *Pacific Glory*.

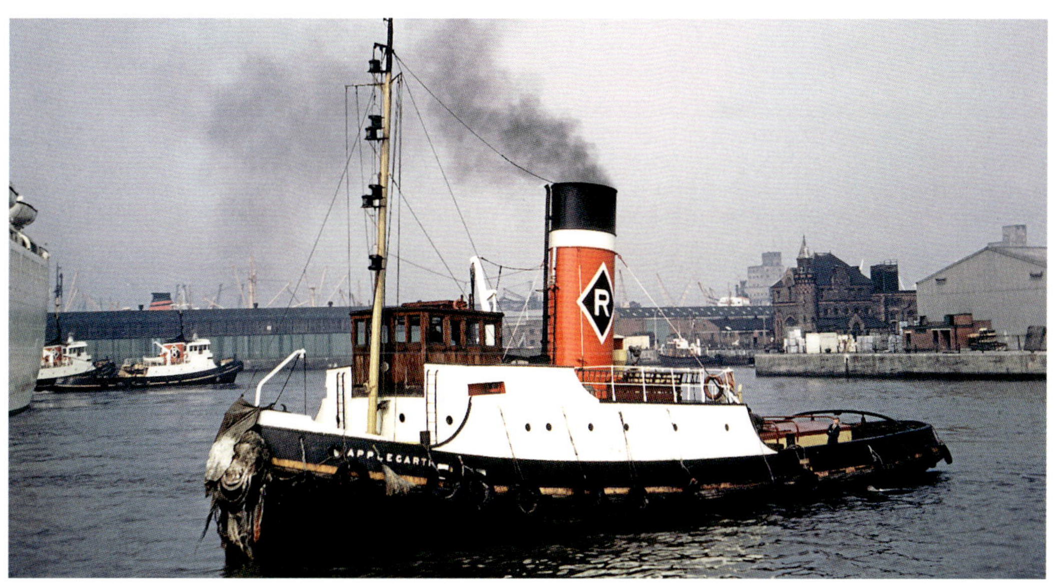

Applegarth (1951/231 grt/1,120 hp/steam) of the Rea Towing Company Limited. On 13 January 1960 she sank as she was working with the cargo vessel *Perthshire* off Woodside Landing Stage. One of the crew of six was rescued by the *Throstlgarth*. She was later raised, refitted and returned to towing duties the following year. In 1971 she was sold to the Holyhead Towing Company and renamed *Afon Cefni*. In 1973 she was purchased by Greek interests, becoming *Achilles*, then *Vernicos Christina* in 1975 and was broken up in Greece in 1980.

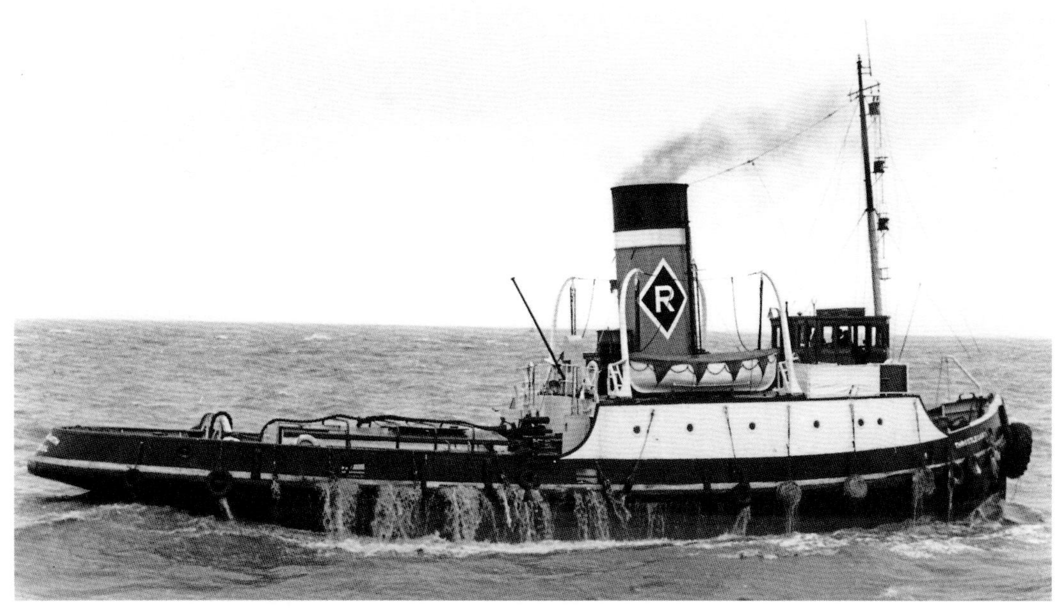

Throstlegarth (1954/231 grt) deals with a heavy swell in the Mersey. She was sold to the West of Scotland Shipbreaking Company, arrived at Troon on 11 November 1972 and broken up.

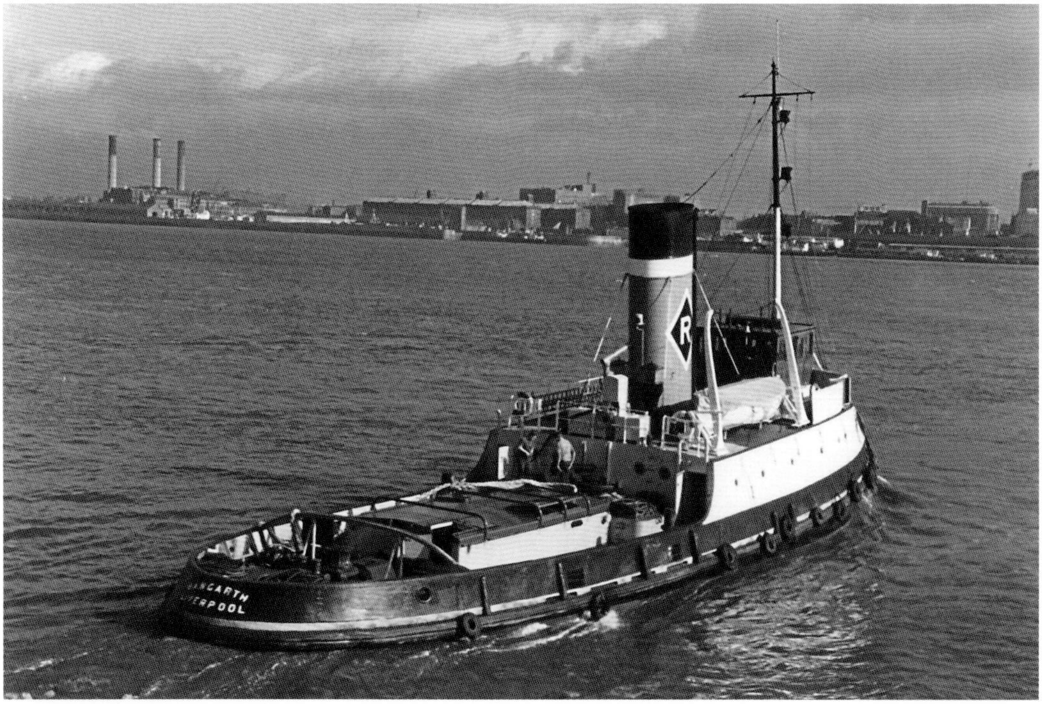

Bangarth (1951/231 grt) sails from Alfred Dock, Birkenhead. On 23 October 1969 she foundered in tow off Srumble Head.

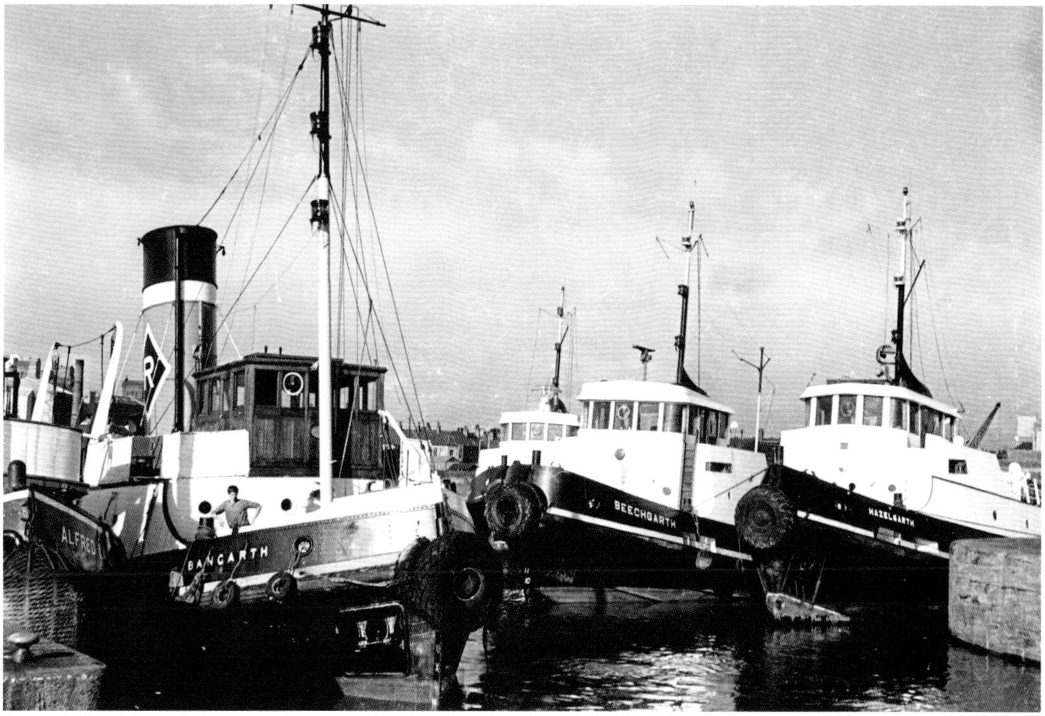

Alfred Lamey, Bangarth, Maplegarth, Beechgarth and Hazelgarth entering south Alfred lock at Birkenhead.

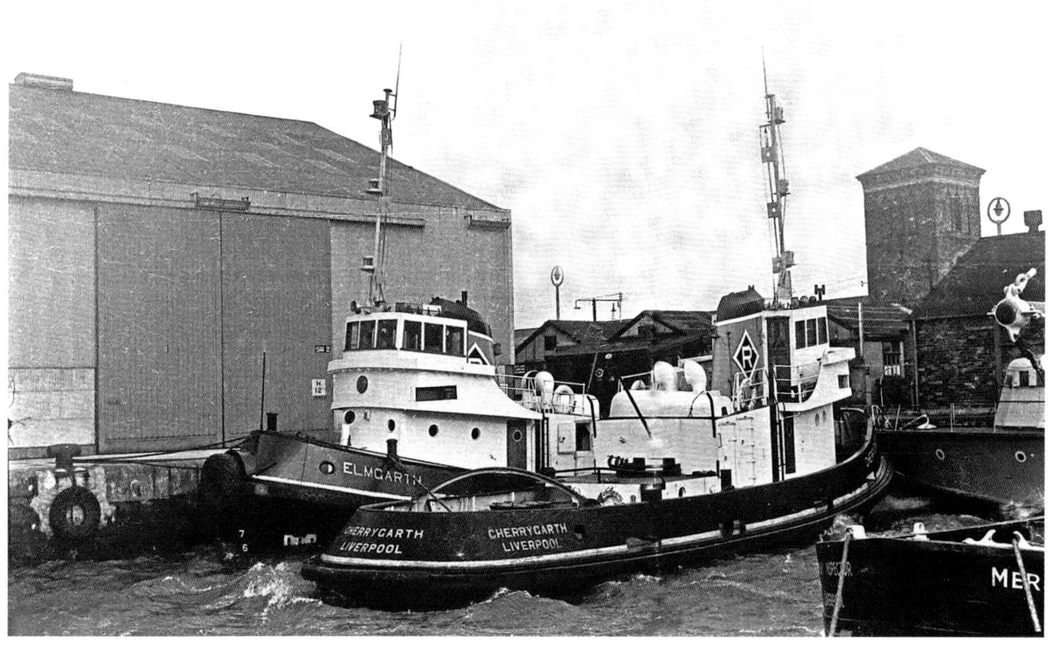

Elmgarth (1960/75 grt) and *Cherrygarth* (1963/62 grt) in Alexandra Dock on a stormy winter's day.

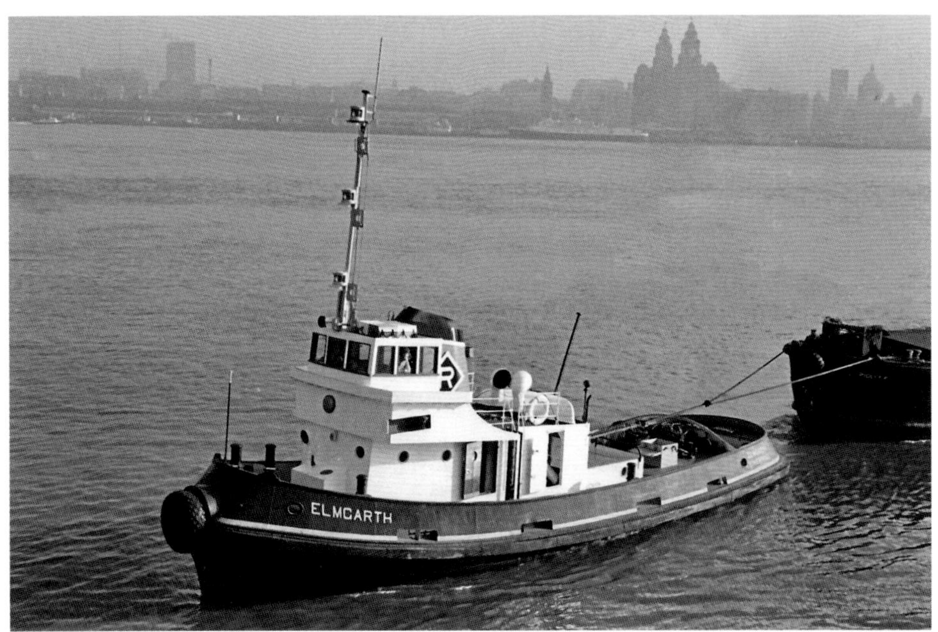

Elmgarth moves a barge from the Manchester Ship Canal to Birkenhead Docks. She was sold to Pevensey Castle Limited in 1972 and renamed *Barkis*. On 16 August 1976 she collided with the *Jupiter* off Lowestoft, capsized and sank.

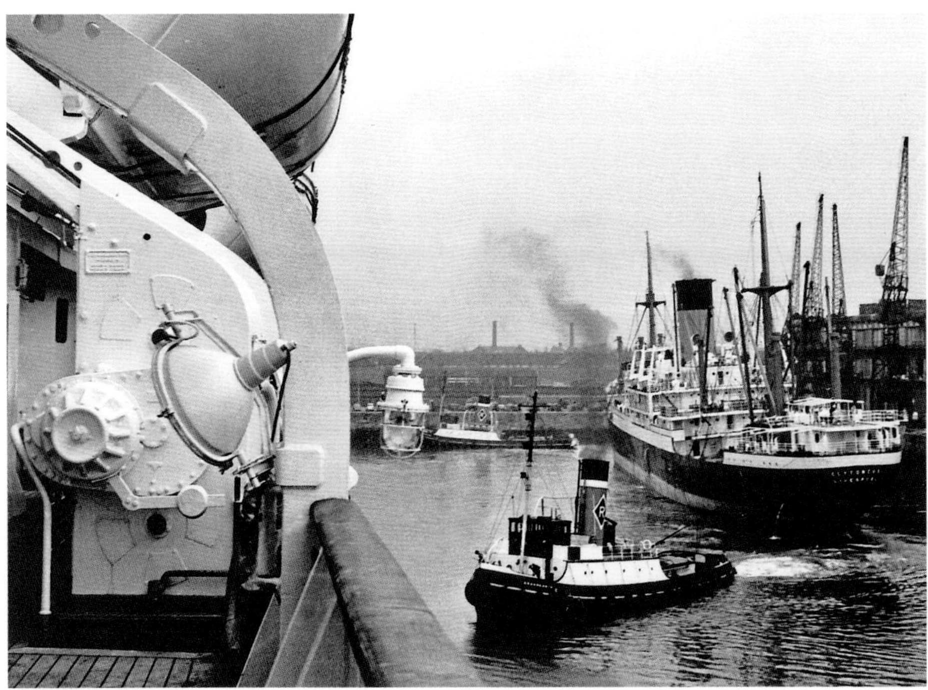

Grassgarth with the Blue Funnel Liner cargo vessel *Clytoneus* at their berth in Gladstone Dock. The photograph was taken from the boat deck of the Canadian Pacific liner *Empress of Canada* (1961/25,585 grt).

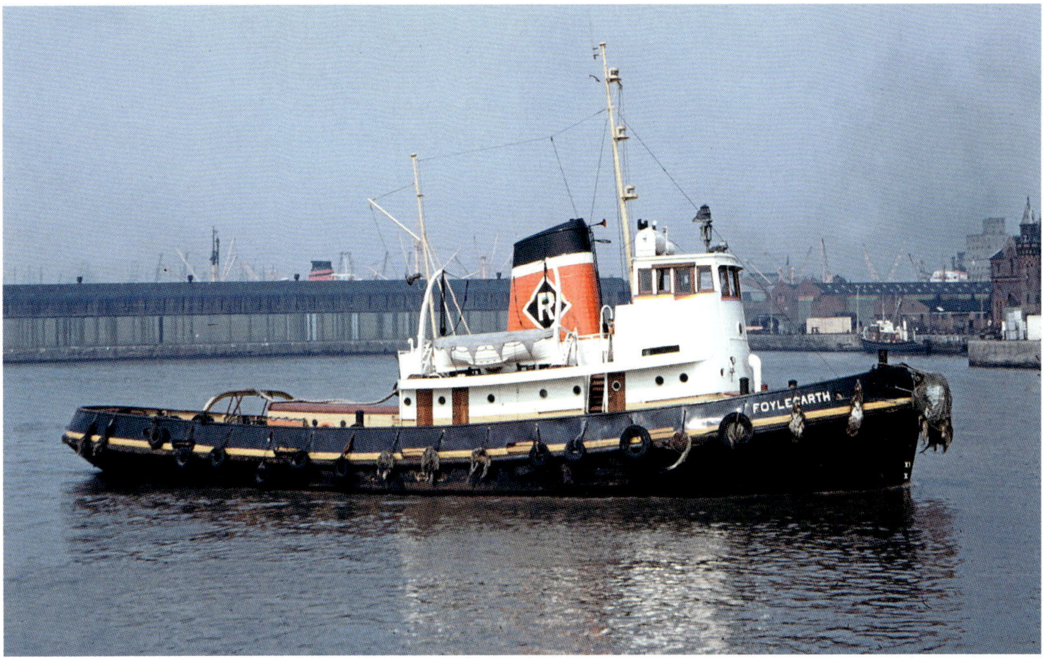

Foylegarth in Langton Dock, Liverpool. She was built by W. J. Yarwood at Northwich in 1958 for Furness Withy's Johnston Warren Lines. *Foylemore, Kilmore* (1958/208 grt) and *Rossmore* (1958/206 grt) were purchased by Rea Towing in 1969 and *Foylemore* became *Foylegarth.* She was sold to H. G. Pounds of Portsmouth in 1983 and renamed *St Budoc,* operating for the Falmouth Towage Company. She became *Frazer Lloyd* in 2003, *St Budoc* again in 2009 and was broken up at New Holland in 2010.

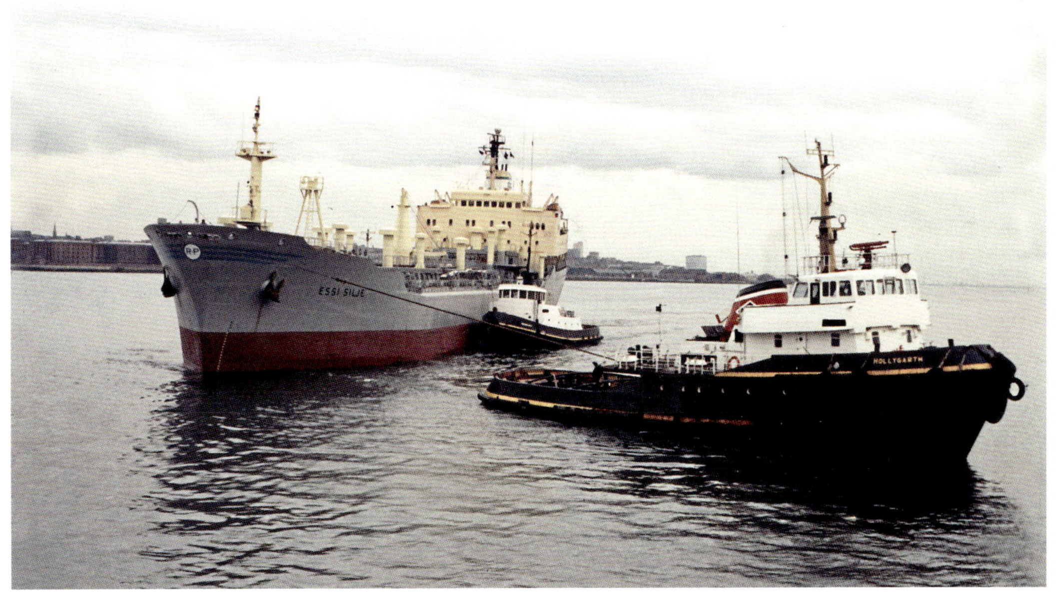

Hollygarth (1969/334 grt) and *Cedergarth* (1962/213 grt) assisting *Essi Silje* off Birkenhead Docks.

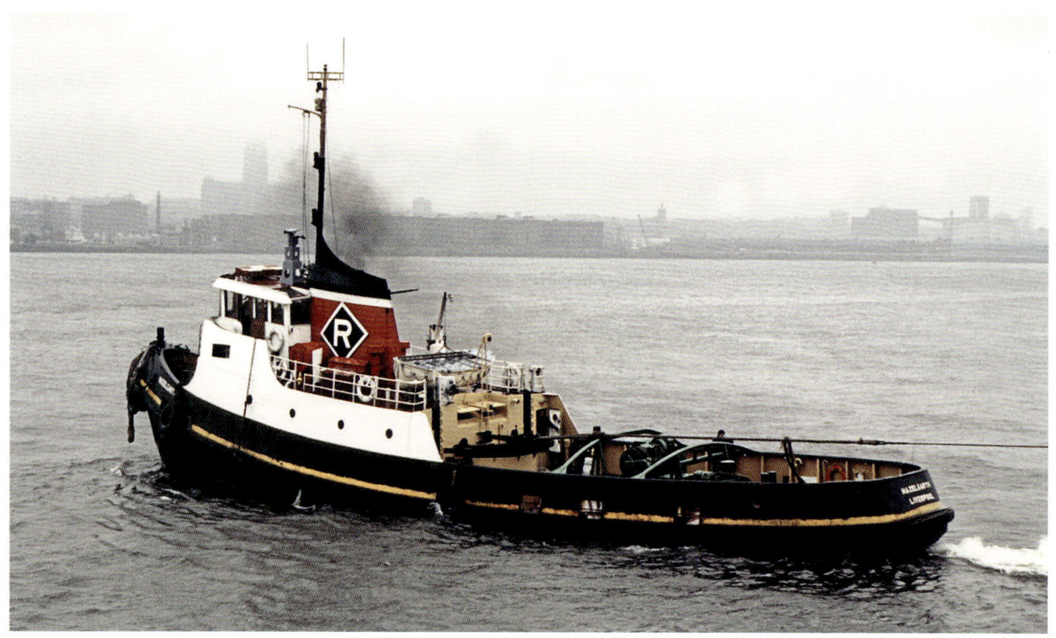

Hazelgarth on towing duties in the river. She became *Mister Cornishman* in 1989, *Shaula* the following year and *Tommy Dev* in 1994.

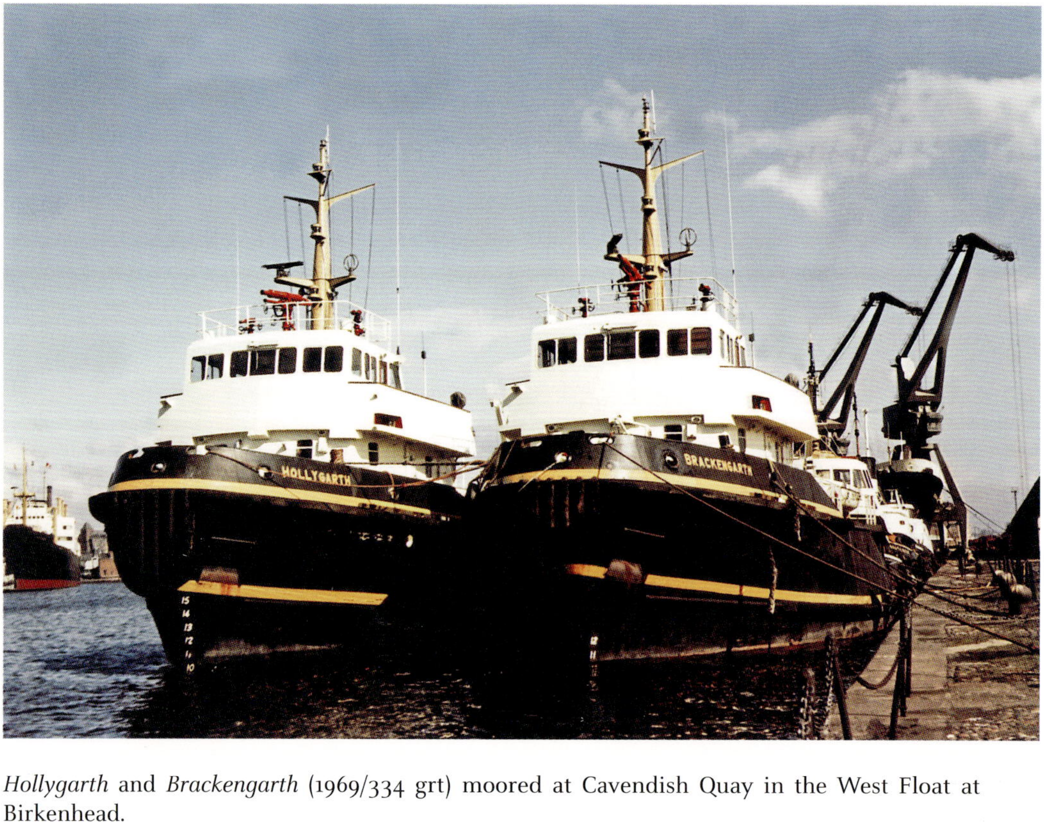

Hollygarth and *Brackengarth* (1969/334 grt) moored at Cavendish Quay in the West Float at Birkenhead.

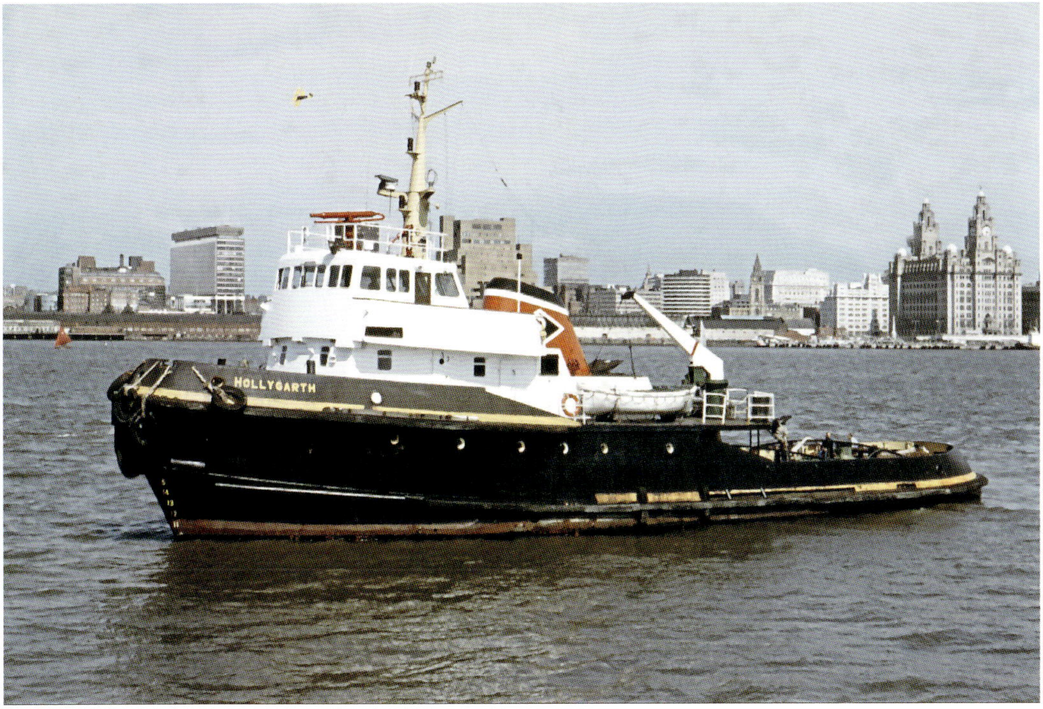

Above and below: Hollygarth off Seacombe Ferry Stage. She became *Towing Wizard* in 1997, *Wizard* in 2003 and *Volshebnik* in 2011. She is seen here (bottom) in the Mersey as *Towing Wizard*.

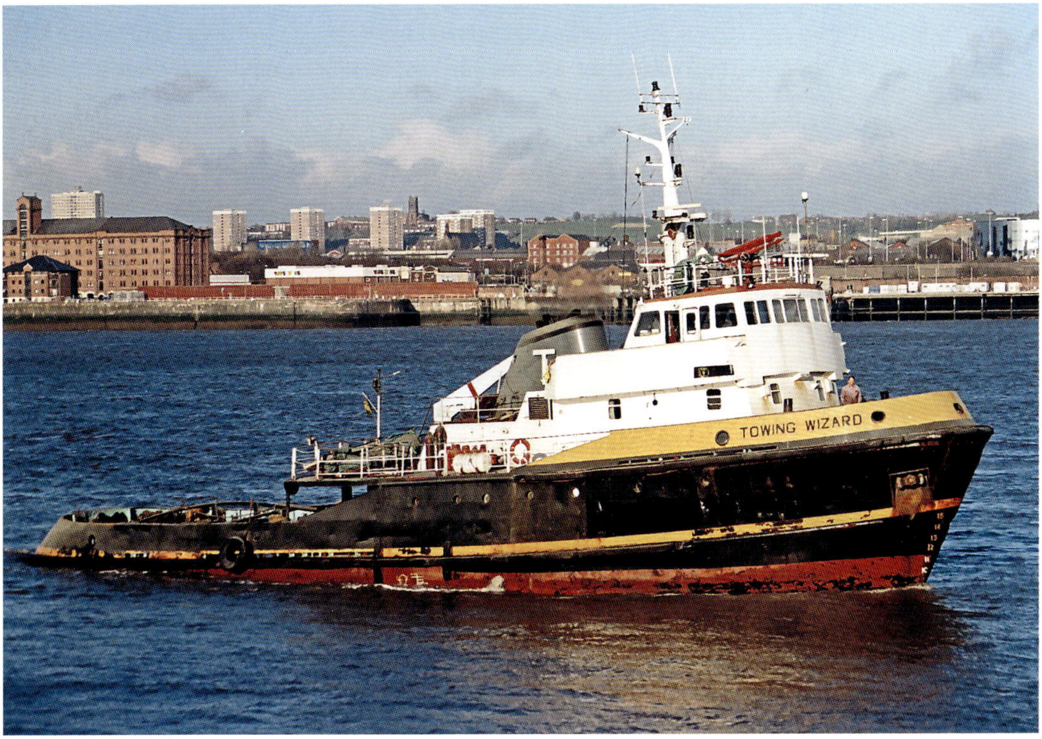

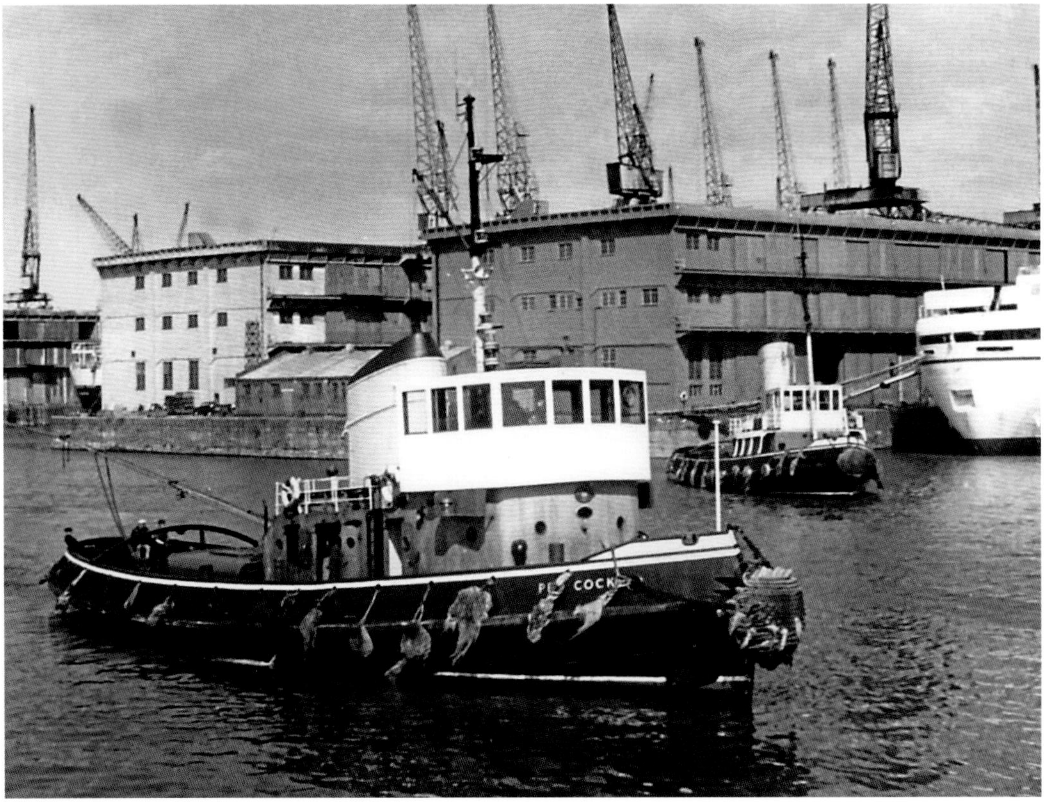
COCK

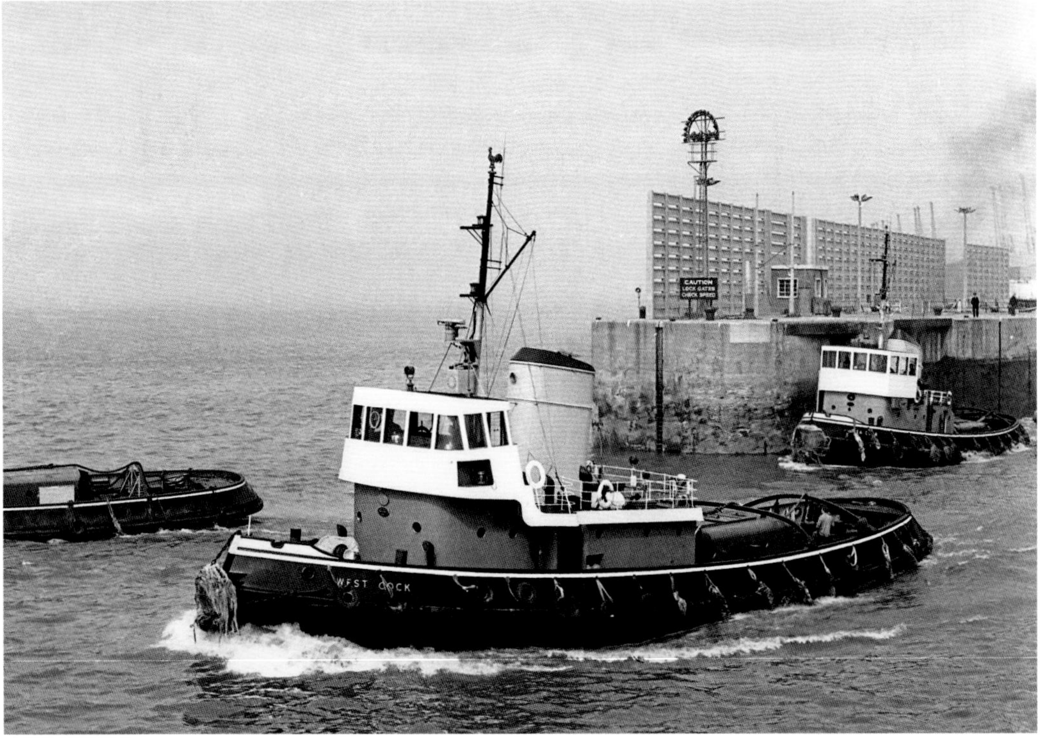
CAUTION
LOCK GATES
CHECK SPEED
WEST COCK

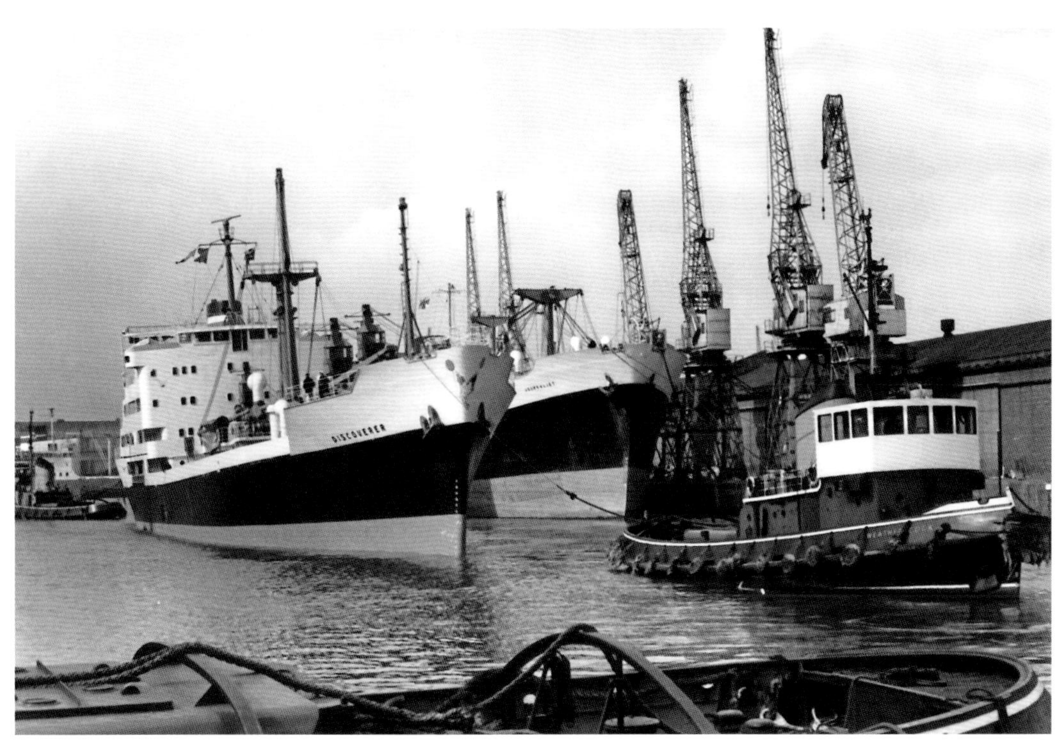

Weather Cock (1960/165 grt) assisting the Harrison cargo vessel *Discoverer* (1964/5,583 grt) to berth ahead of the *Journalist* (1954/8,366 grt) at Canada Dock, Liverpool. She was renamed *Formby* in 1970 and was sold to Vernicos Shipping of Greece in 1981, becoming *Vernicos Alexia.*

Opposite above: *Pea Cock* (1960/165 grt) in Gladstone Dock, Liverpool. She was renamed Canada in 1970 and *Vernicos Georgis* in 1981, when she was sold to Vernicos Shipping.

Opposite below: *West Cock* (1958/193 grt) and *Pea Cock* leaving Langton lock.

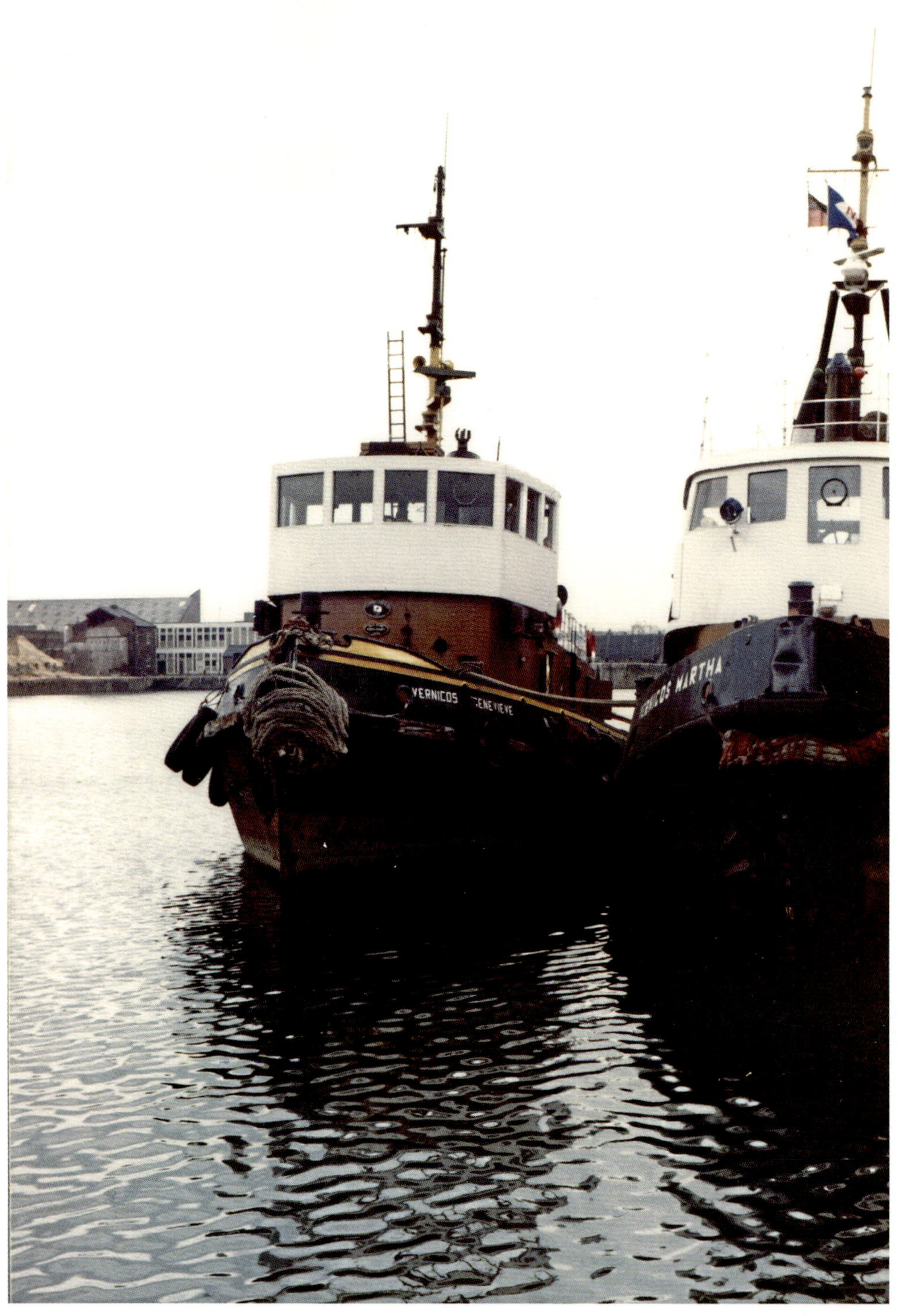

Vernicos Genevieve at Morpeth Dock. She was originally the *Pea Cock* and was briefly named *Vernicos Genevieve* in 1981, following her sale to Greece.

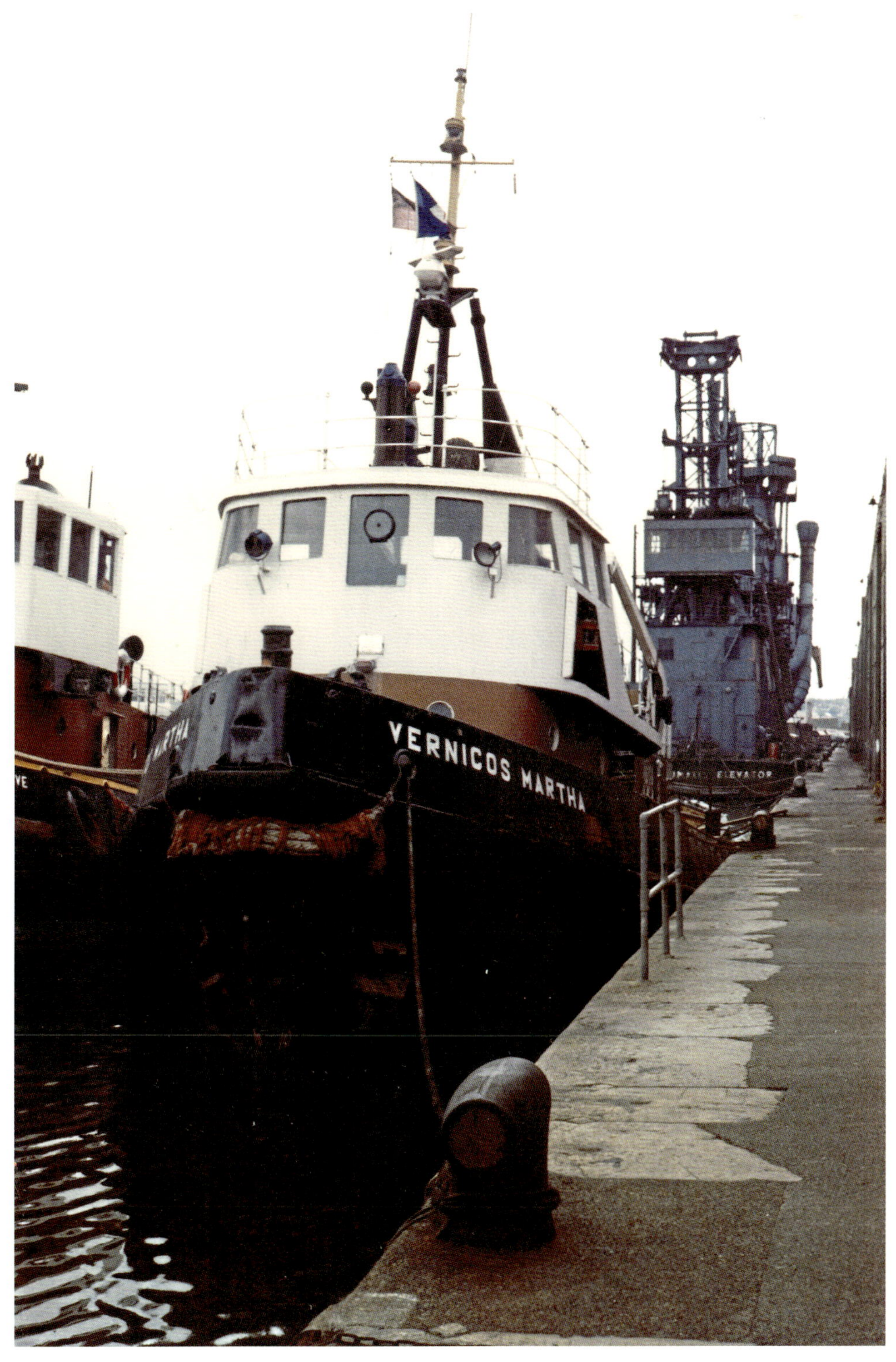

Vernicos Martha (1959/201 grt) was built as Cashel, becoming *Portgarth* in 1974, *Vernicos Martha* in 1981 and *Agios Nikolaos* in 1989.

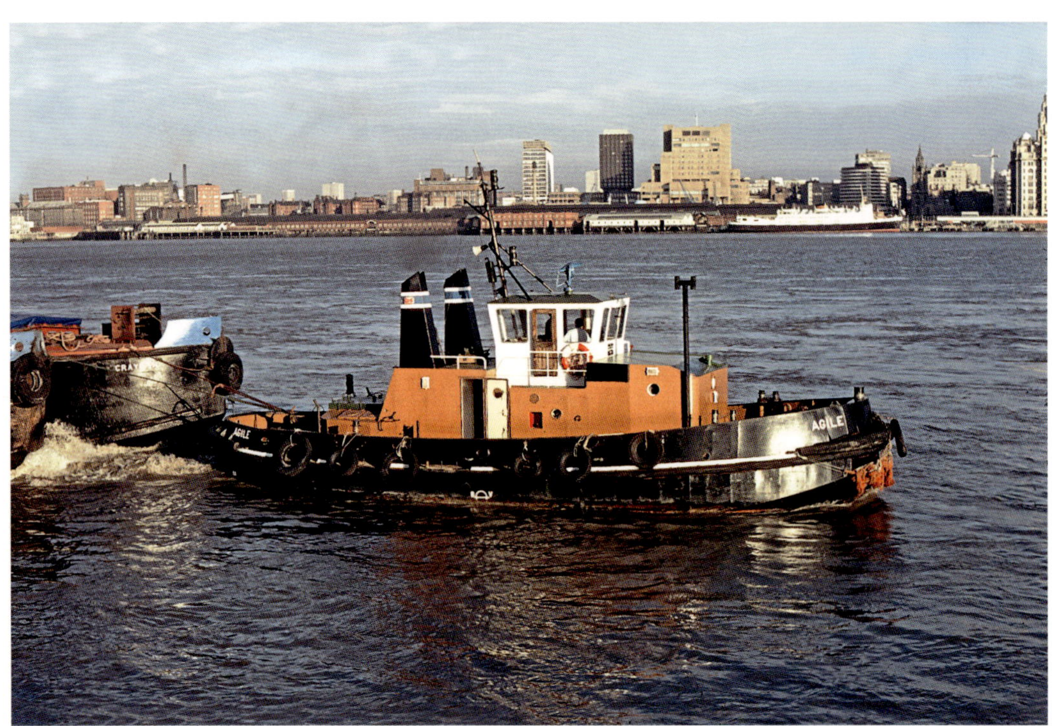

Agile (1971/51 grt) on towing duties in the river. *Agile* and her sister *Adept* were built in 1971 and were purchased from the Port of Dunkirk. *Agile* was originally named *Alerte* and both were employed at Liverpool by Bulk Cargo Handling Services Limited. They were transferred to the Alexandra Towing Company in 1986 and were moved to operate at Gravesend in September 1989. The first section of the tow from Liverpool to Swansea was made by Wallasey, where the two vessels were transferred to the *Victoria*, which took them to the Thames. *Victoria* then sailed to Felixstowe and took up station at that port.

Opposite above: Ardneil (1953/299 grt) was built by Hall Russel & Company at Aberdeen as *Cruiser*. She was re-engined in 1963 and became *Ardneil* in 1969. She was purchased by the Carmet Tug Company in 1984, and sold to Aquatec Diving Services Limited at Takoradi in 1999.

Opposite below: Ceres (1961/43 grt) towing the barge *Artic* into Birkenhead Docks.

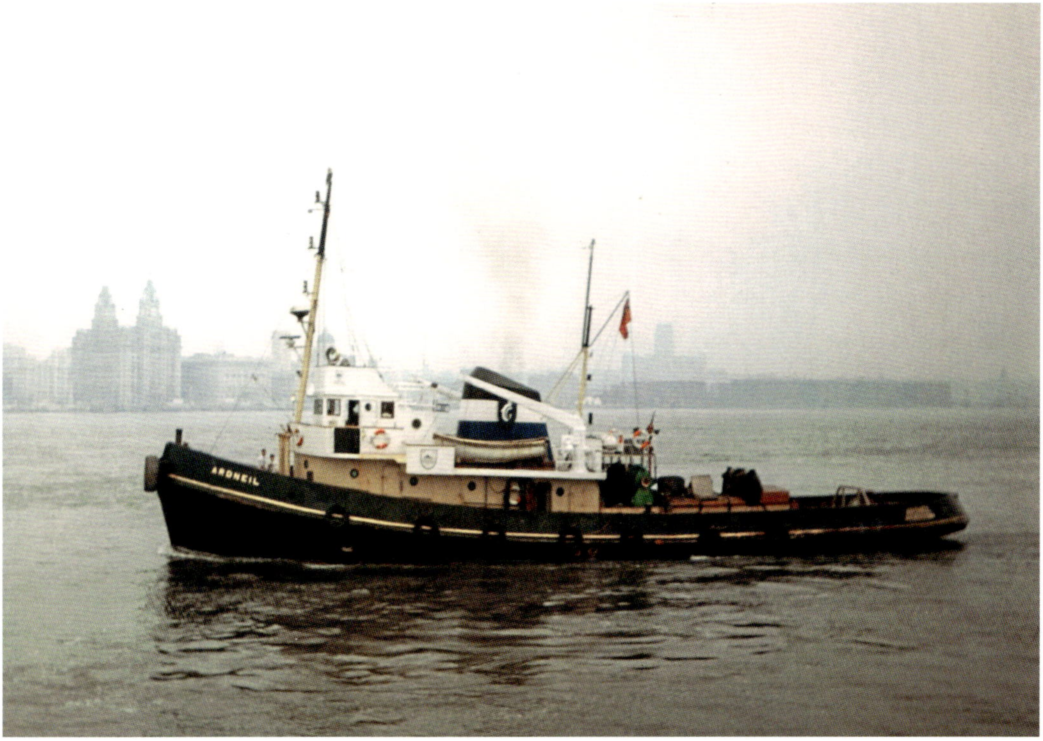

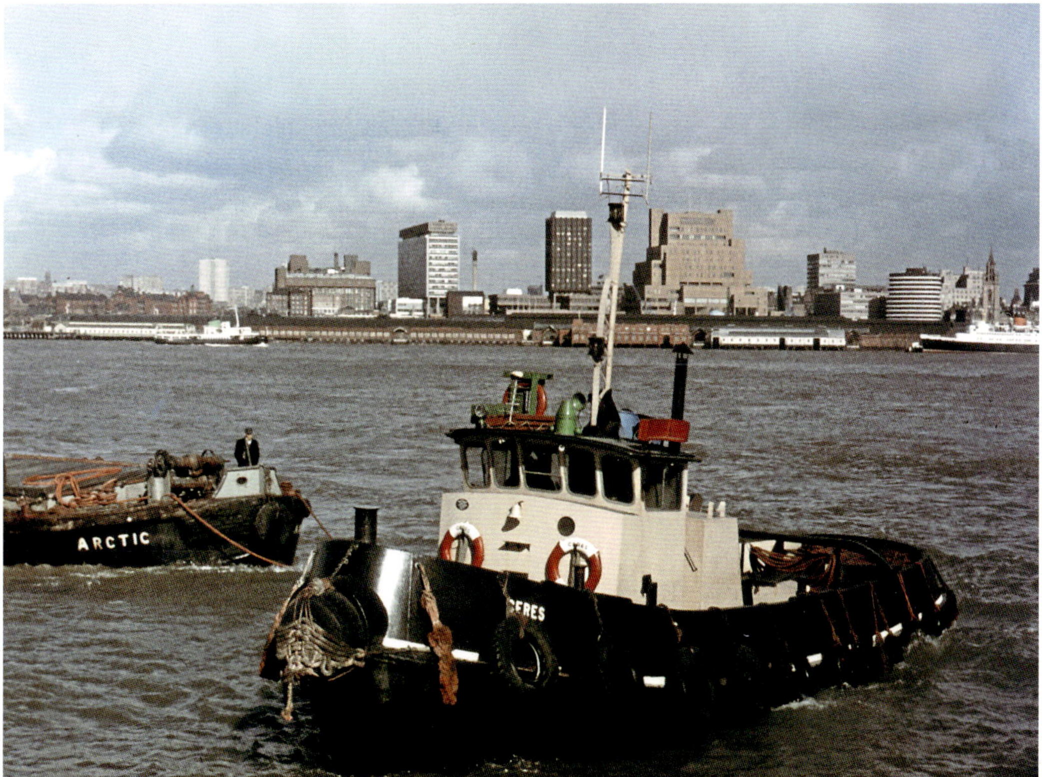

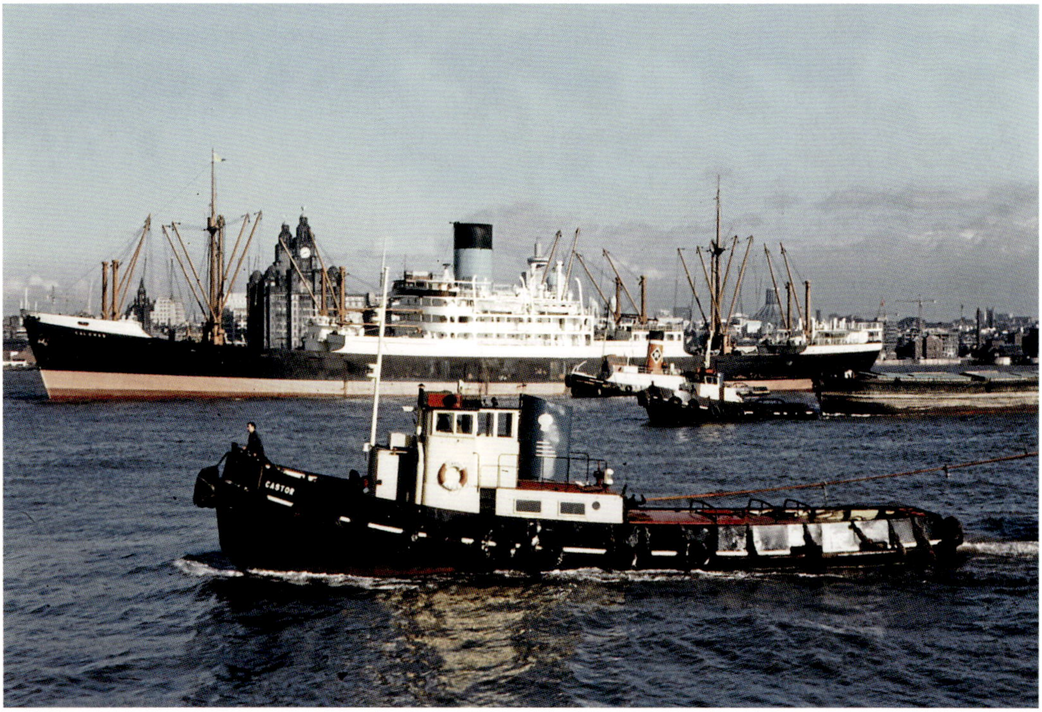

Castor (1944/54 grt).

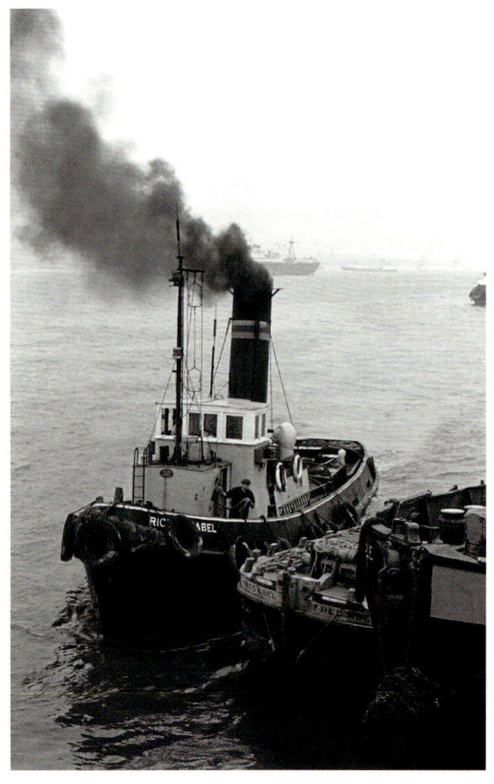

Richard Abel (1944/54 grt/220 hp/steam) of Richard Abel & Sons Limited.

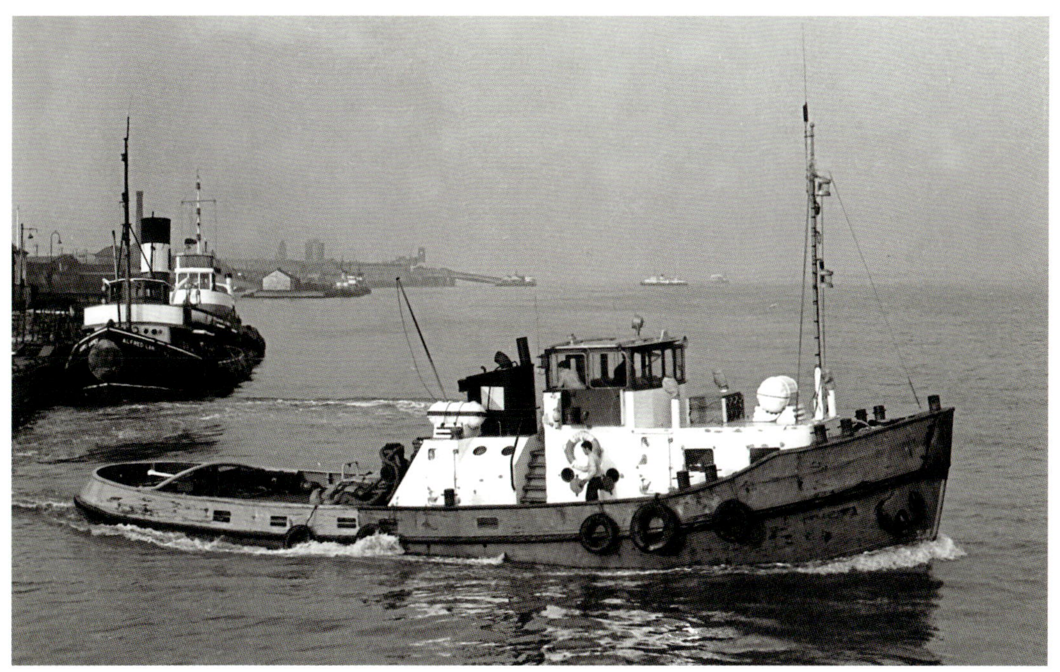

W D 31 off Woodside with *Alfred Lamey* and *William Lamey* berthed at the landing stage awaiting duties.

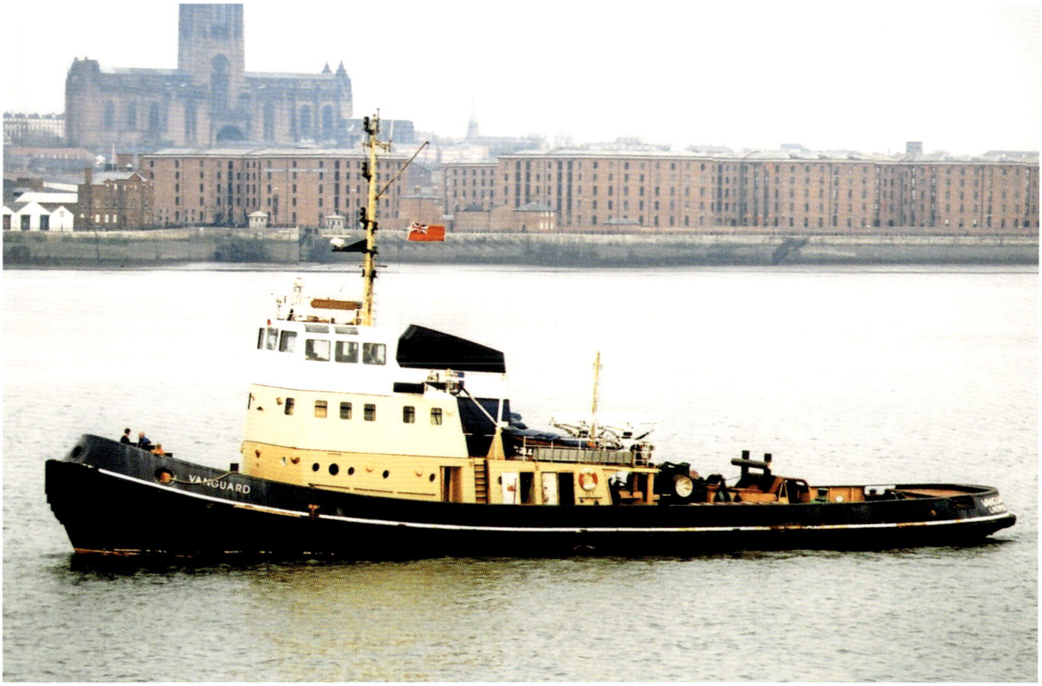

Vanguard (1965/296 grt/1,300 hp/motor) of the Carmet Tug Company Limited. She was built as *Rathgarth*, becoming *Campaigner* in 1977, *Kerry* in 1988 and *Vanguard* in 1991. On 7 September 2004 she was beached and broken up at New Holland in 2010.

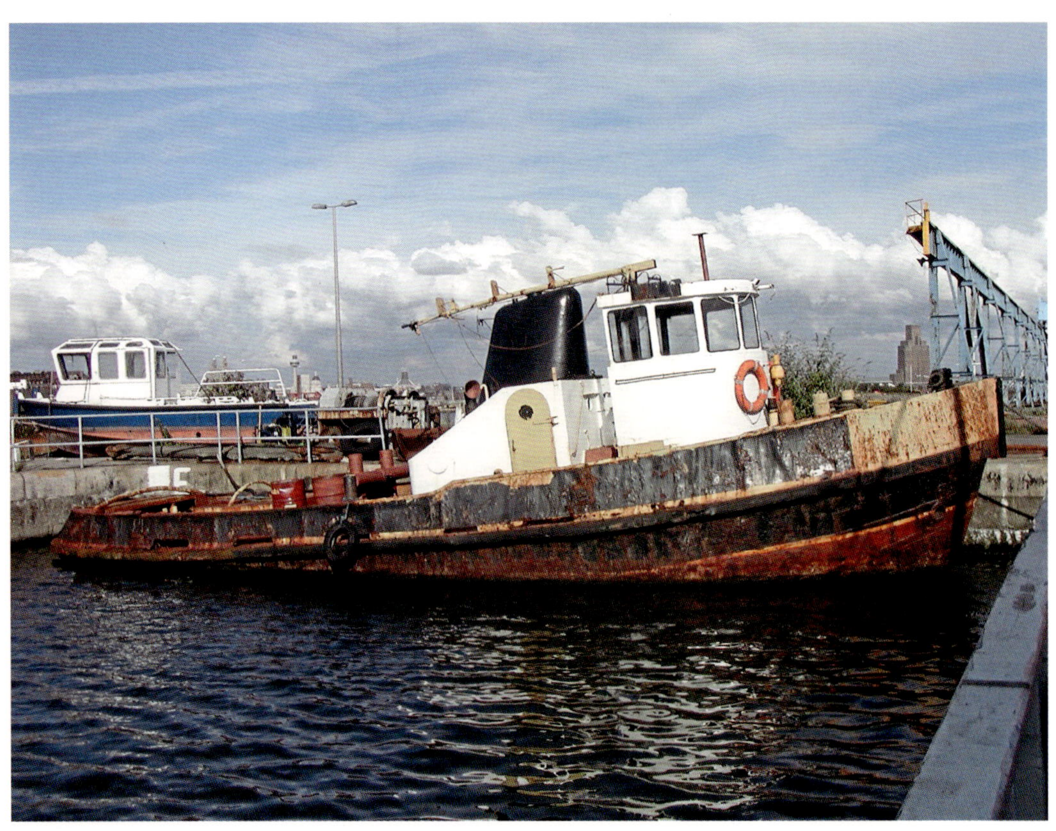

Beaver Gem (1957/34 grt) in Vittoria Dock, Birkenhead.

Opposite: The Dublin tugs *Clontarf* (1963/178 grt) and *Coliemore* (1962/173 grt) in Vittoria Dock. *Clontarf* was built as *Cluain Tarbh*, becoming *Clondarf* in 1992 before being broken up in 2015. *Coliemore* was built as *Applesider*, becoming *Coliemore* in 1972 and was broken up at Cork in 2011.

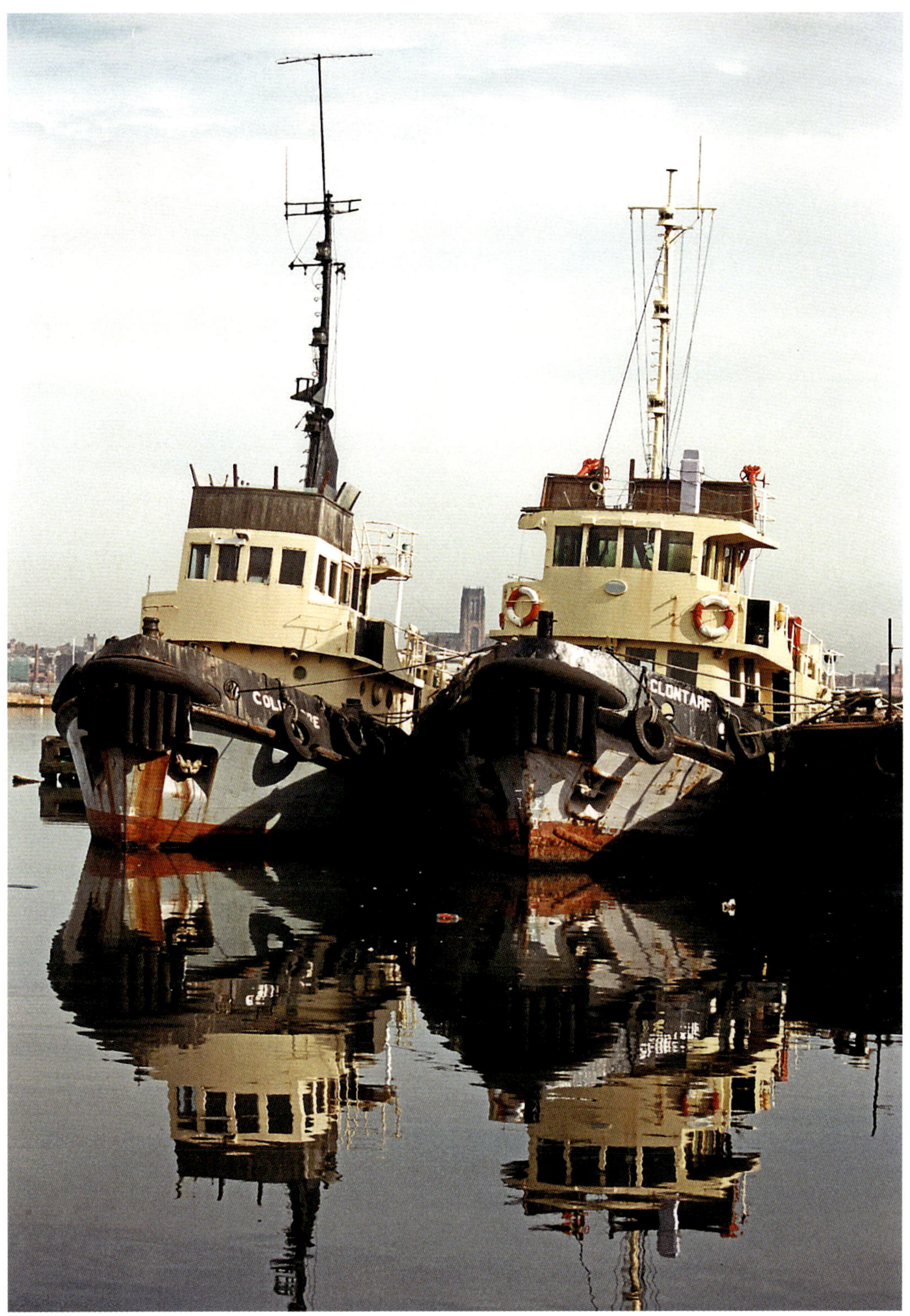
CLONTARF

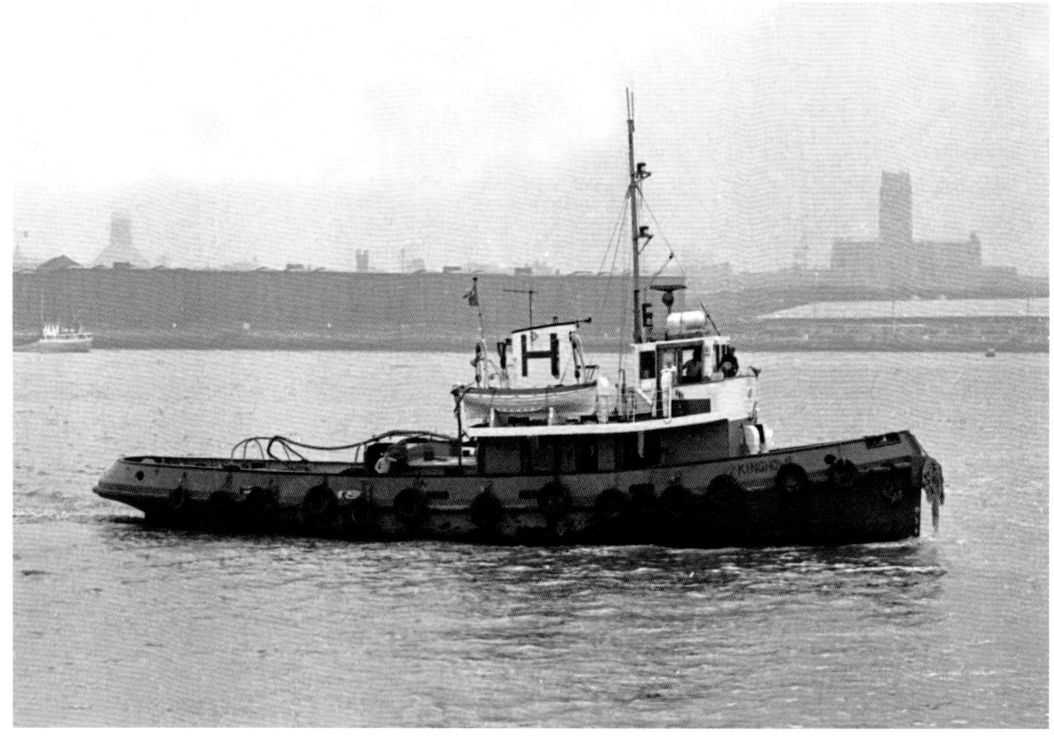

Kinghow. In 1967 John Howard & Company were awarded the contract for the construction of the Royal Seaforth Dock by the Mersey Docks and Harbour Board. The *Charles Hearn* was purchased from the Port of Preston Authority to assist in the work at the new dock. *Charles Hearn* was built in 1959 by Henry Robb Limited at Leith with a gross tonnage of 139, and machinery developing 740 bhp. She went to the rescue of the coaster *Farringay* on her delivery voyage and took her in tow. When the tow line parted she stood by the vessel until a tug arrived from the Mersey to assist. On arrival at Liverpool she was renamed *Kinghow* and was later joined by the *Temhow,* which arrived from Holland as deck cargo on the top barge *Dinhow*. They were followed by the barges *Gibhow, Livhow, Lonhow* and *Seahow,* which were also built in the Netherlands. While at anchor sheltering from a gale in the Menai Straits she heard a distress signal from a vessel in the near vicinity. She set sail and discovered a small fishing boat aground on Puffin Island and assisted the *Beaumaris* lifeboat in the rescue of the crew.

Construction of the Royal Seaforth Dock continued into 1970 when *Kinghow* was surplus to requirements and was laid up. Howard-Marine & Dredging Company Limited was formed in March 1971 and *Kinghow* was employed laying a 3-mile sewer outfall from Meols, on the Wirral, out into Liverpool Bay. She was later used at Amlwch at the site of the Shell Offshore tanker buoy. In 1972, when this work was completed, she moved to the Clyde to work with the Westminster Dredging Company, and then back to the Mersey via a tow to Felixstowe. She was later observed working on the Thames, mooring and unmooring the Howard-Marine barges, and was then laid up at Chatham. At the beginning of the following year she was dry-docked at Great Yarmouth and by May she was again working off Anglesey. *Kinghow* was sold to Greek interests, renamed *Odesseus* and sent to Saudi Arabia to work on a new dock complex at Jeddah.

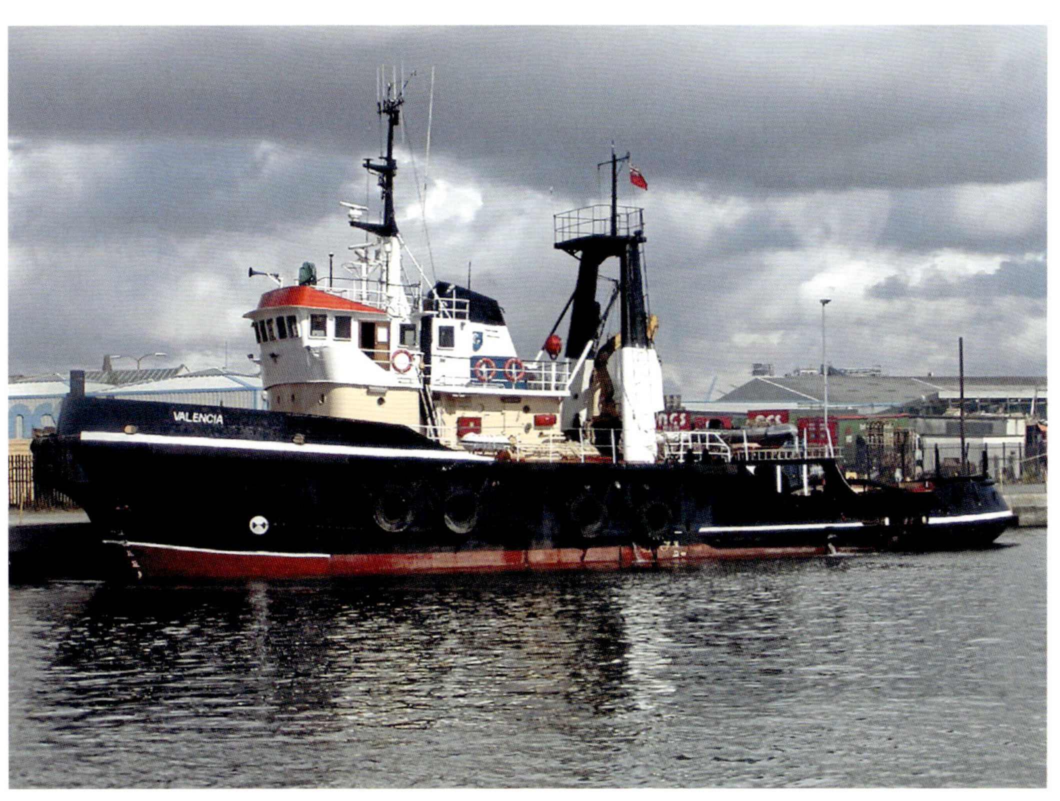

Valencia (1969/338 grt) was built as Aznar Jose Luis, becoming *Boluda Valencia* in 1989, *Valencia* in 1999 and *Valencia Pidesa* in 2004.

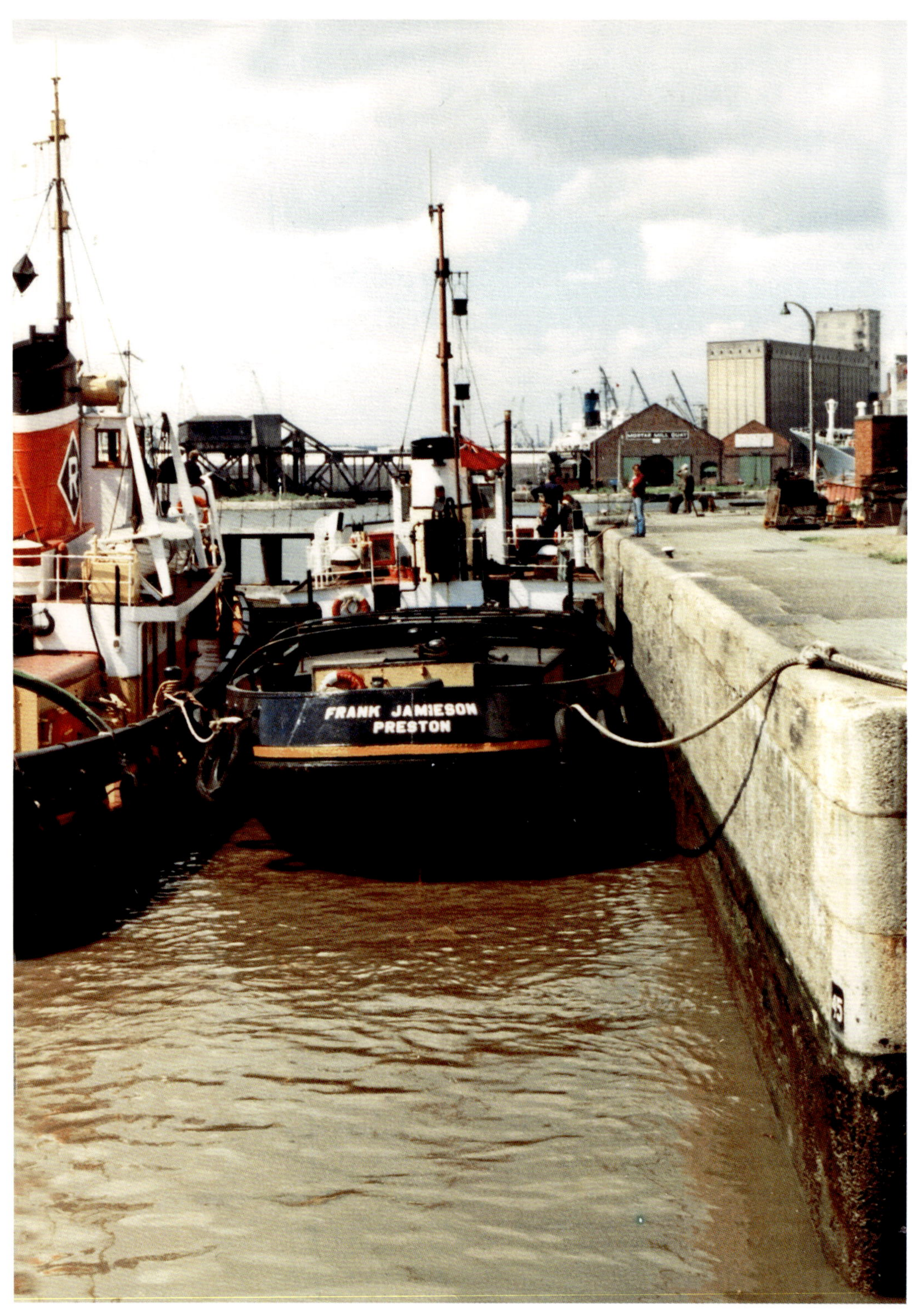

Frank Jamieson (1956/146 grt) arrives at Birkenhead from Preston.

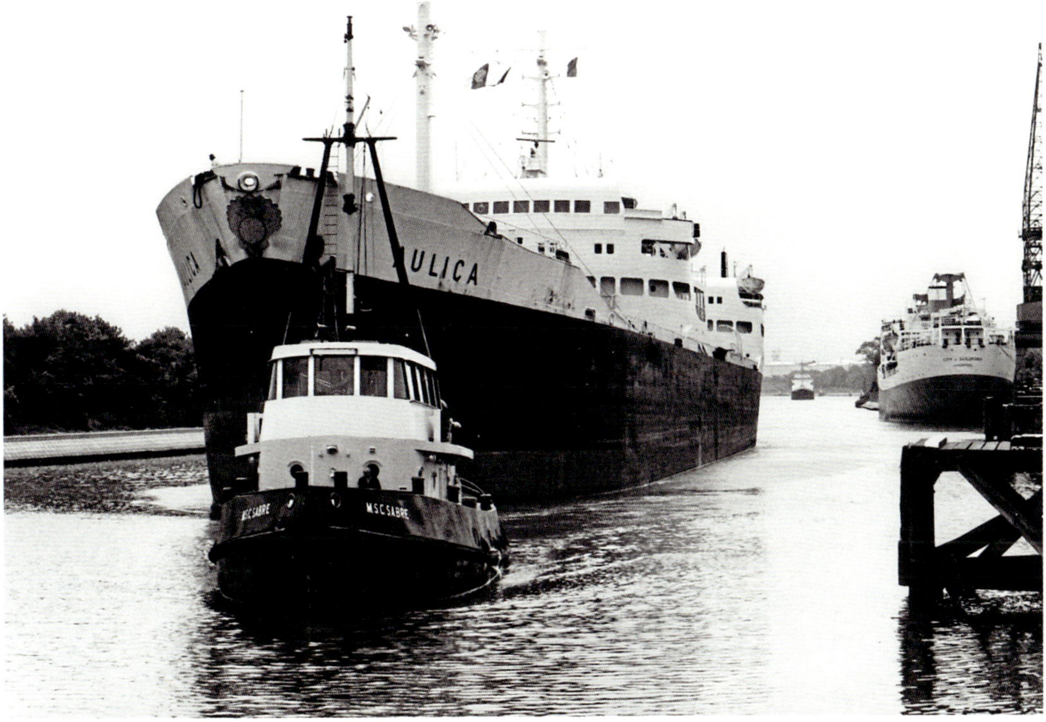

MSC *Sabre* (1956/147 grt) helps navigate the Shell tanker *Aulica* in the Manchester Ship Canal.

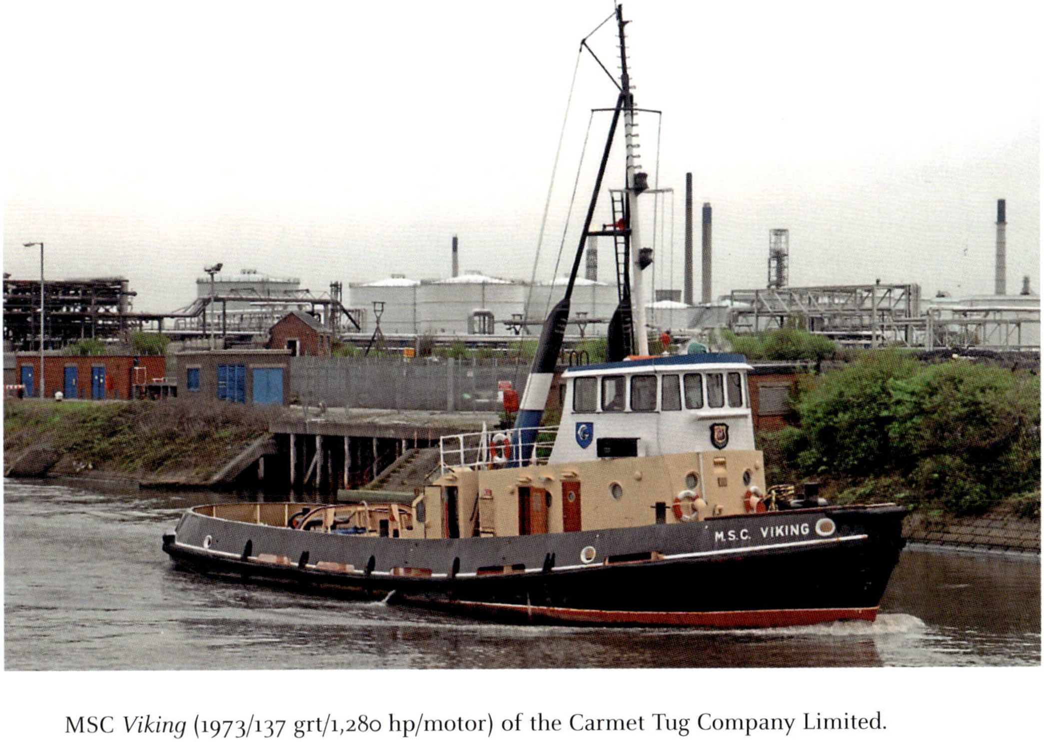

MSC *Viking* (1973/137 grt/1,280 hp/motor) of the Carmet Tug Company Limited.

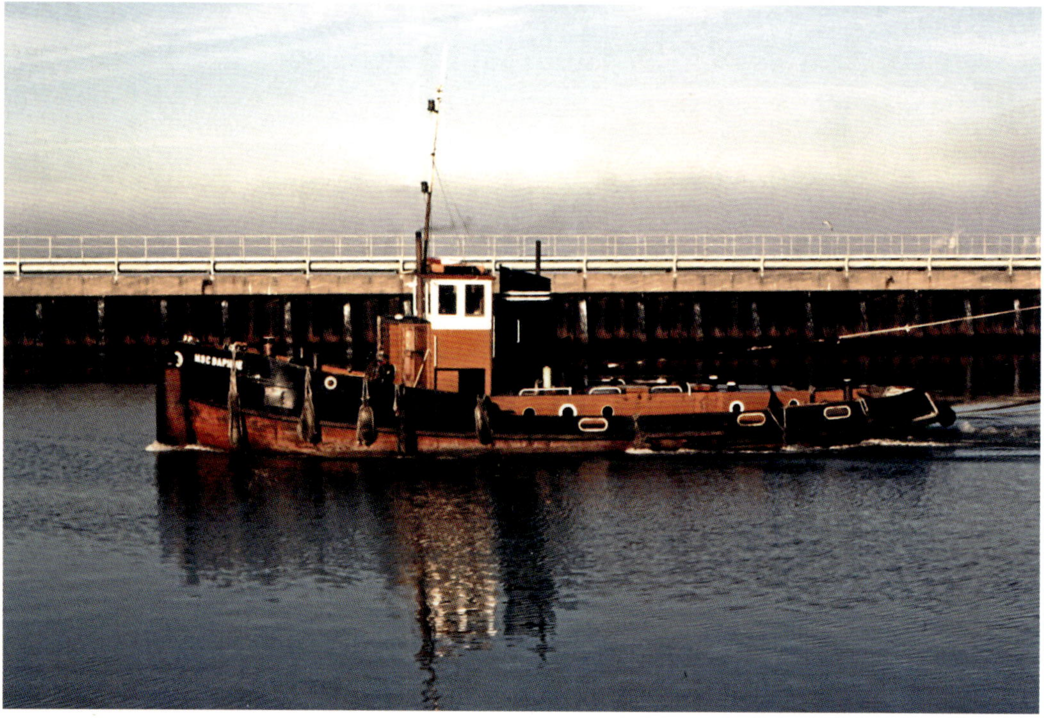

MSC *Daphnie* (1954/30 grt) in the Manchester Ship Canal.

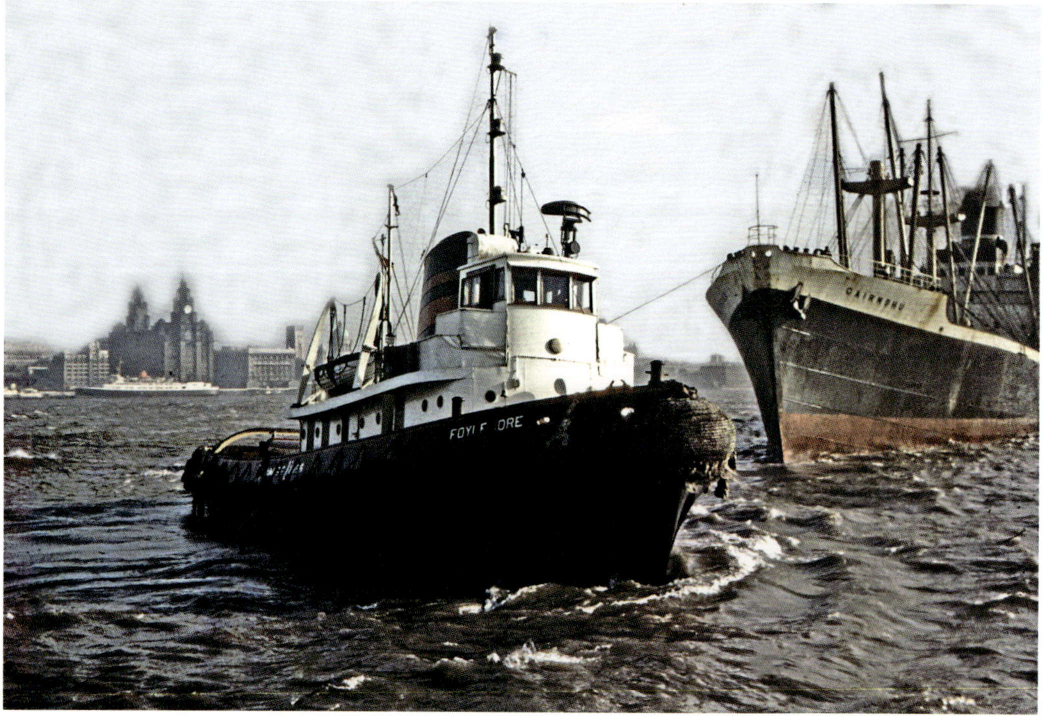

Foylemore at the bow of Cairn Line's *Cairndhu* (1952/7,403 grt) off Alfred Dock.

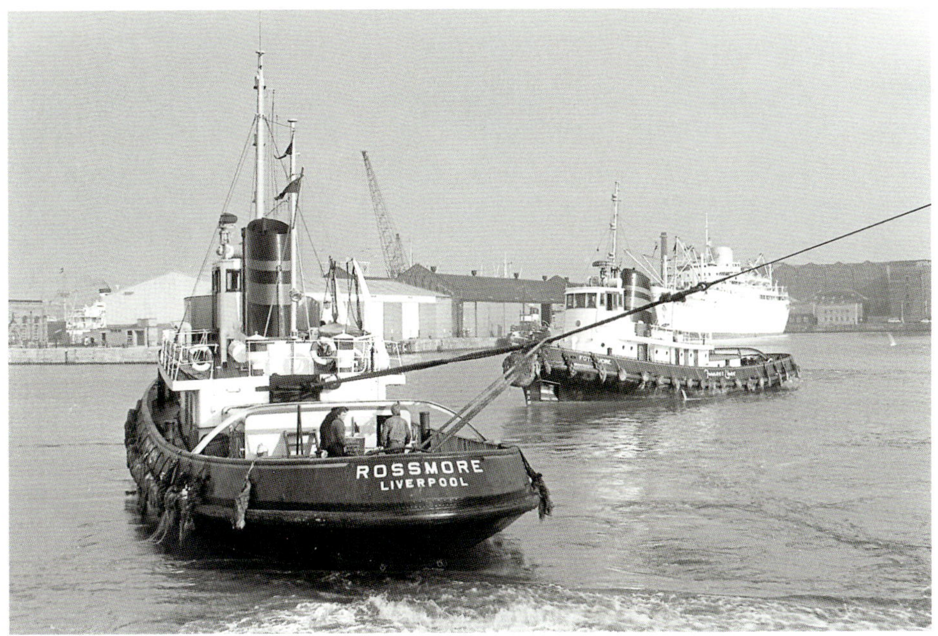

Rossmore (1958/206 grt) and *Foylemore* in Langton Dock with Elder Dempster's *Aureol* (1951/14,083 grt) loading at her berth in Brocklebank Dock.

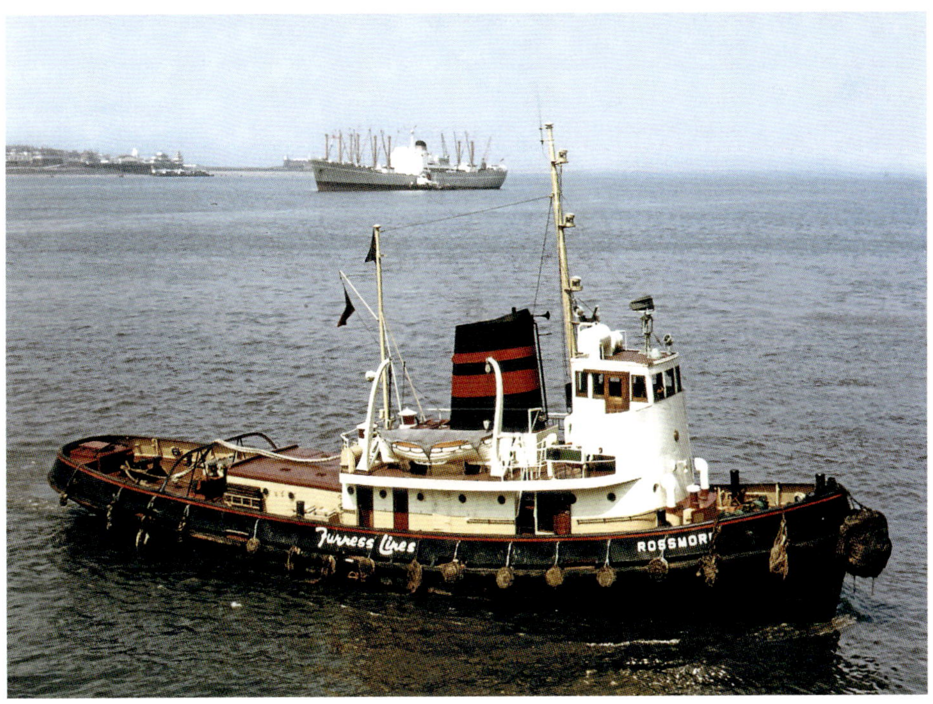

Rossmore (1958/206 grt/1,270 hp) of Johnston Warren Lines Limited. She became *Rossgarth* in 1968 and was sold in 1972. Renamed *Rozi* in 1981 when sold to Tug Malta Limited, she operated for them until 1992, when she was purchased by a local company prior to being sunk as an artificial reef in August that year.

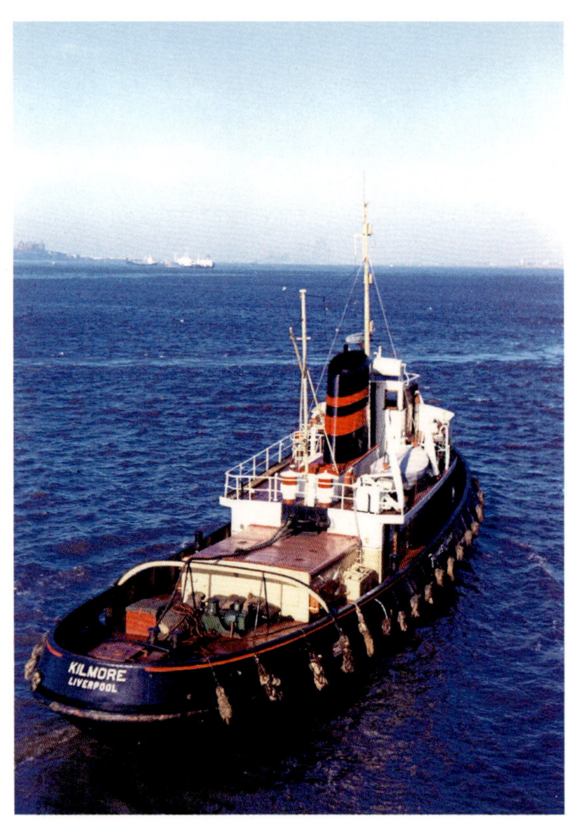

Kilmore (1958/207 grt/1,270 hp) of Johnston Warren Lines Limited. She became *Kilgarth* in 1969, *Aghios Gerassimos* in 1984, *Hellas* in 1999 and *Weisshaupt* in 2003.

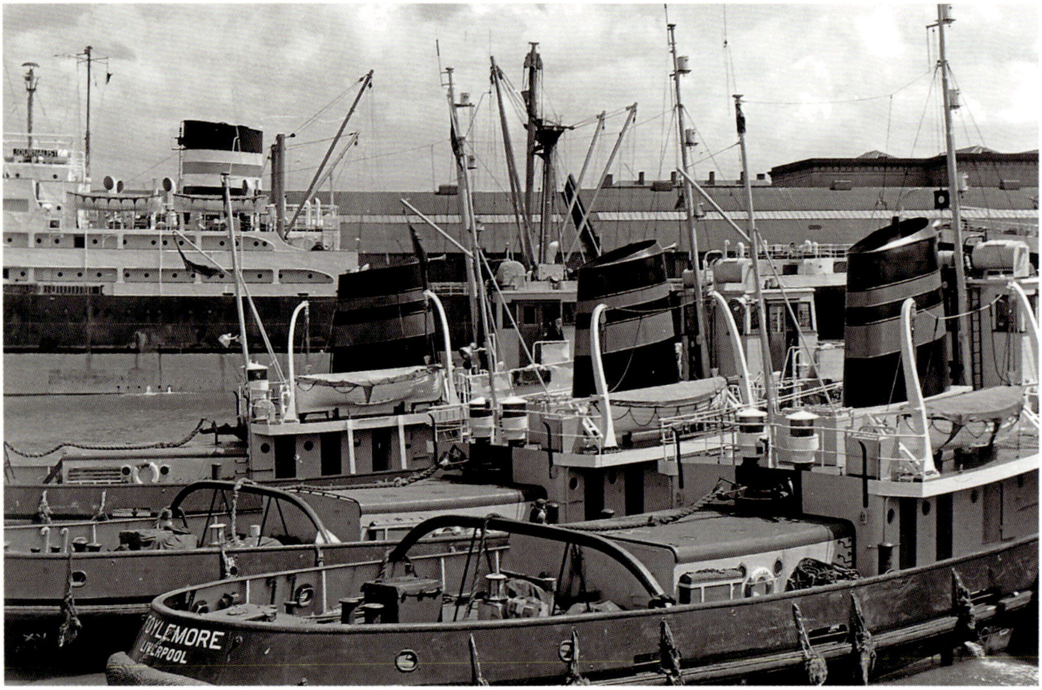

Foylemore, Kilmore and *Rossmore* berthed together in Canada Dock, Liverpool.

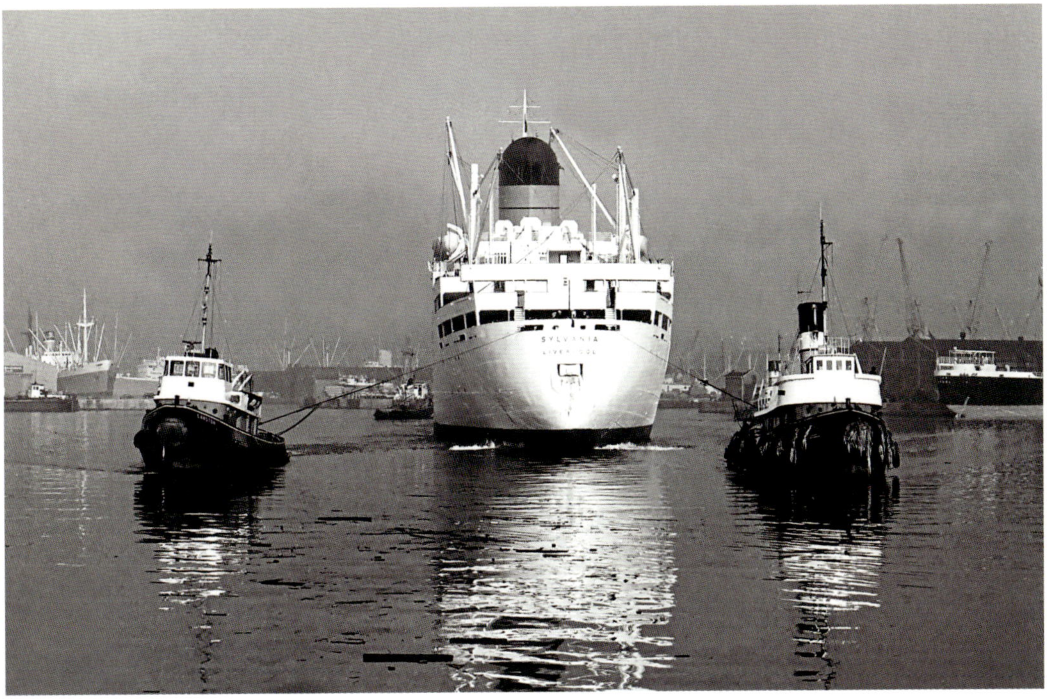

Alexandra tugs in charge of the Cunard liner *Sylvania* (1957/22,017 grt) in Canada Dock, Liverpool.

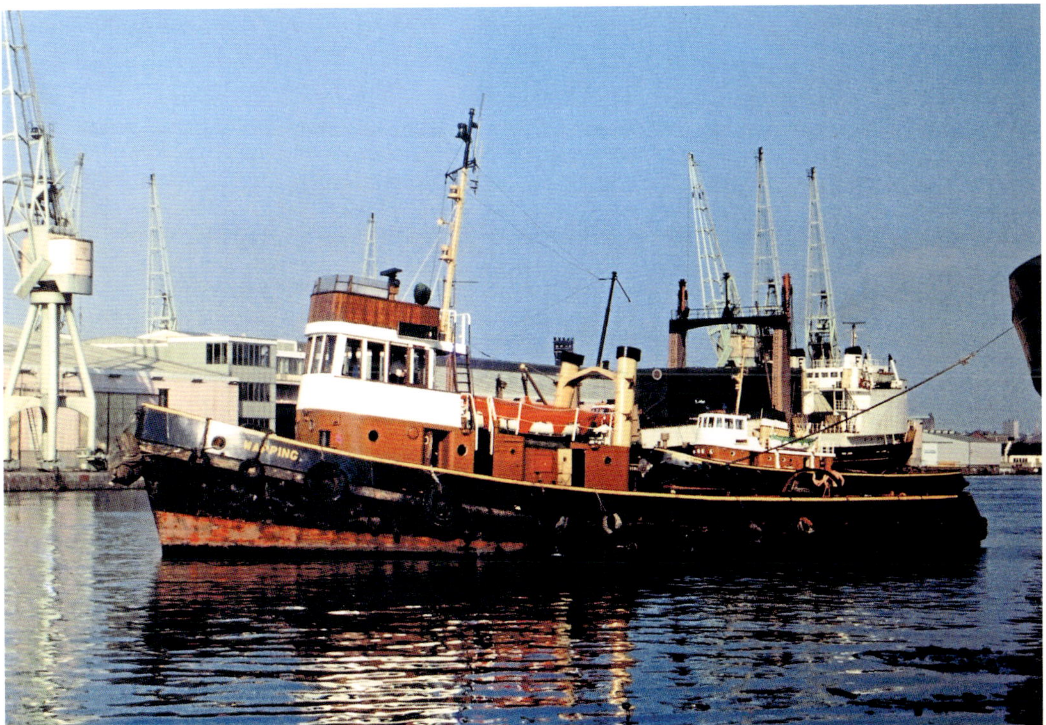

Wapping (1959/166 grt) in Vittoria Dock, Birkenhead.

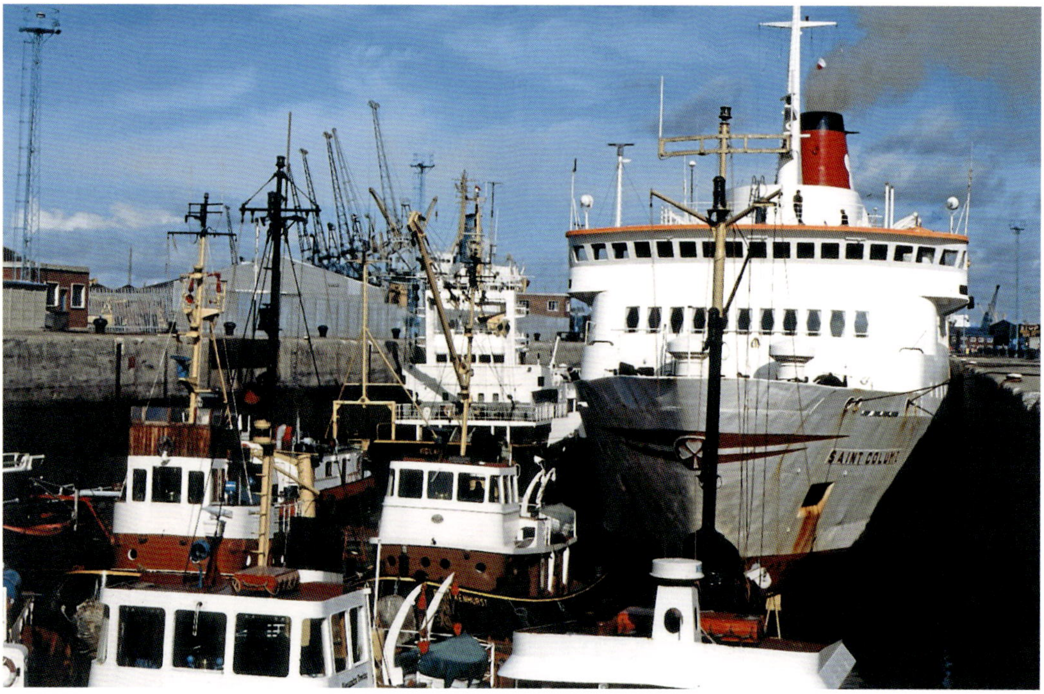

Saint Colum 1, Alexandra and Rea tugs lock out into the Mersey from Langton Dock.

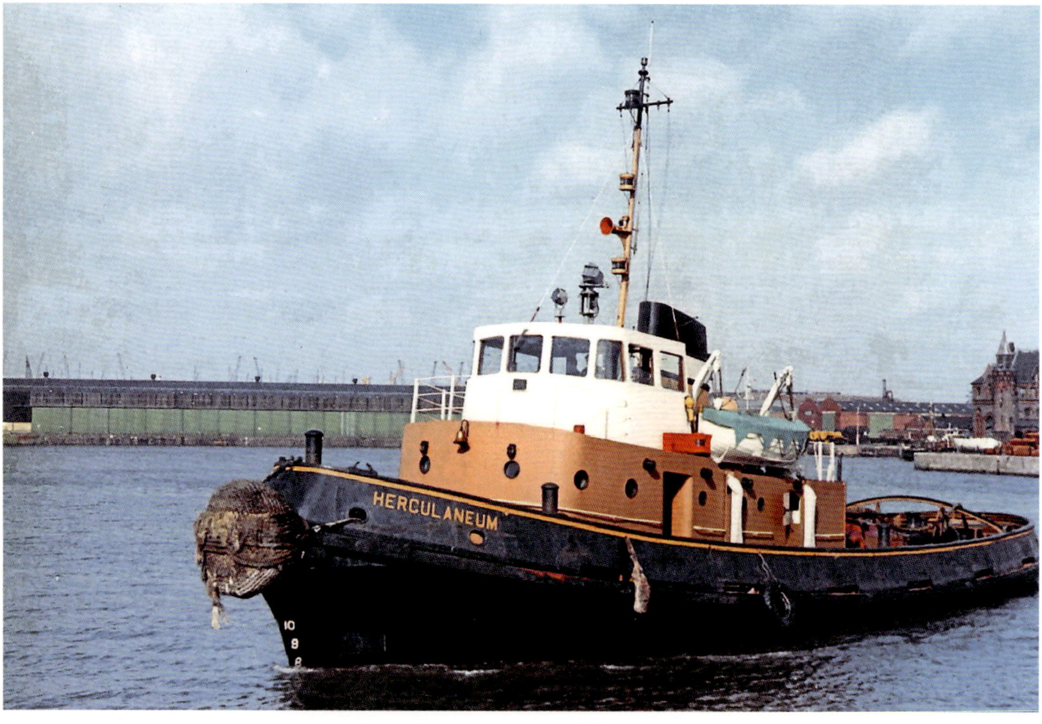

Herculaneum (1962/161 grt/940 hp/motor) of the Alexandra Towing Company Limited. She was sold in 1997, renamed *Atlas* and then *Christos VIII* in 2000.

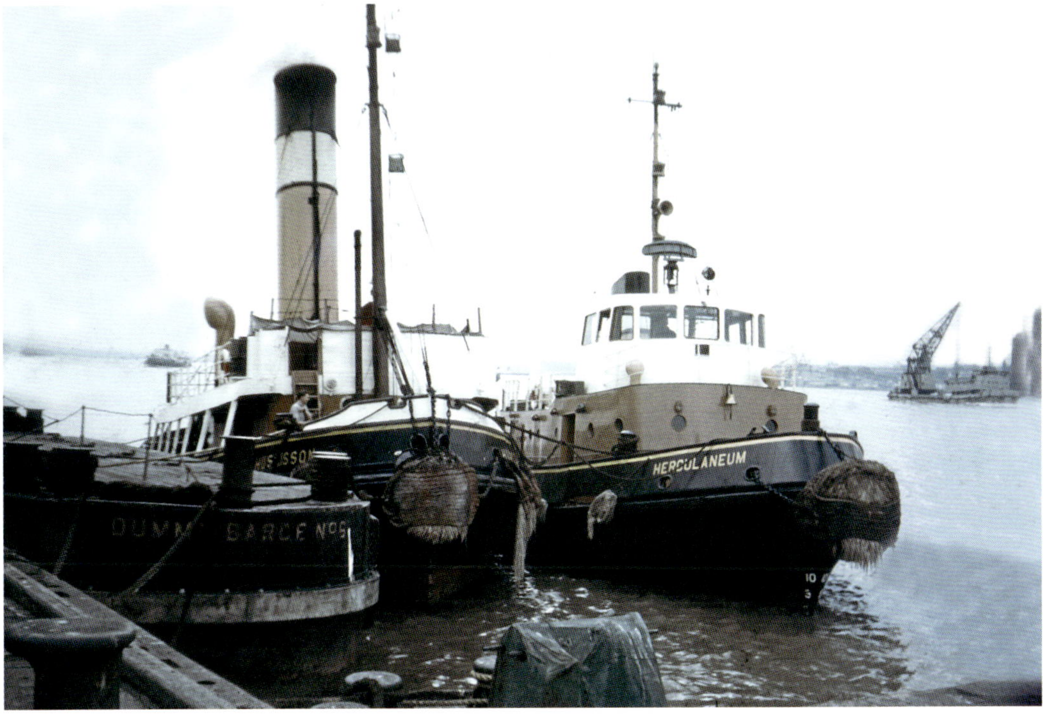

Huskisson (1934/201 grt) and *Herculaneum* (1962/161 grt) berthed at Princes Landing Stage.

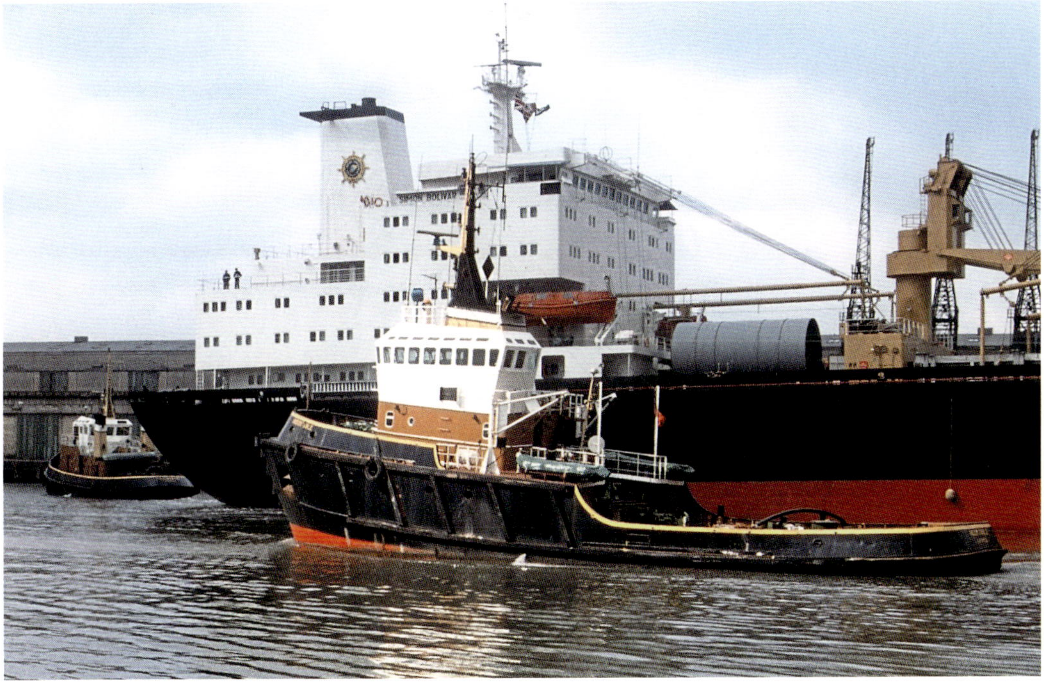

Indomitable (1979/416 grt/3,520 hp/motor) of the Alexandra Towing Company Limited. She was renamed *Hibernia* in 2009.

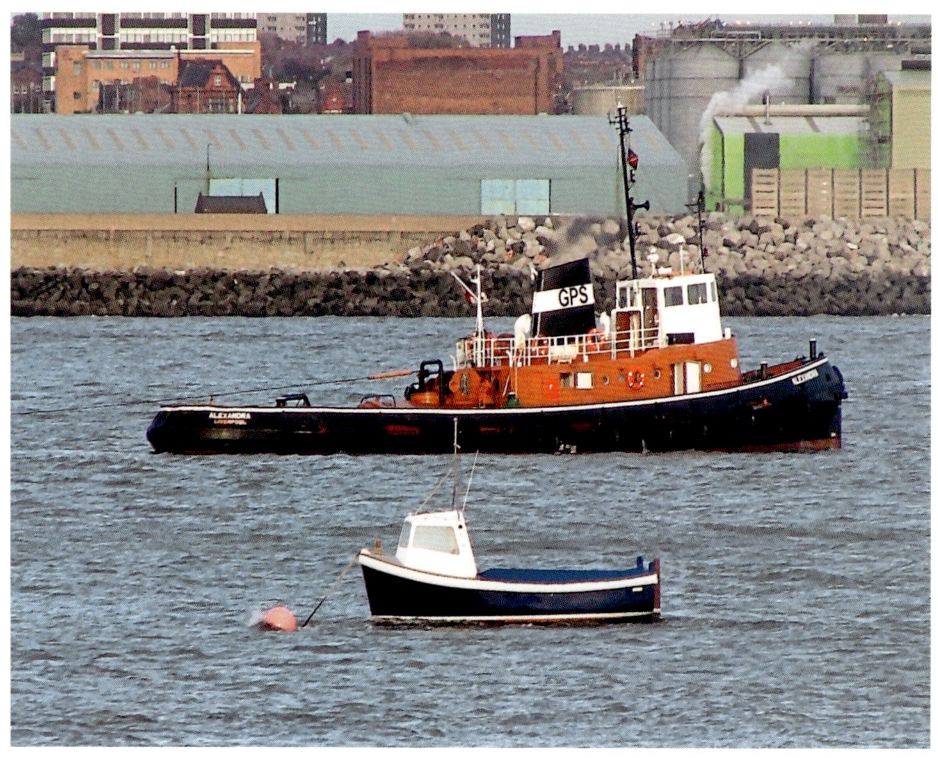

Alexandra (1963/164 grt) in the Mersey again. She was sold to GPS Marine Contractors Limited, West India Dock, London in 1998.

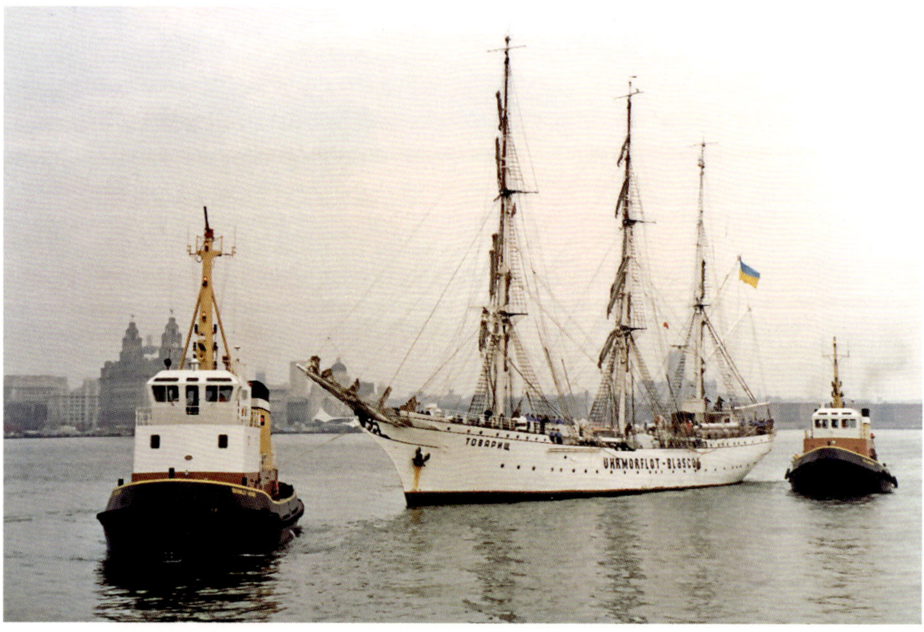

Bramley Moore (1984/336 grt) and *Canada* (1980/282 grt) with the Ukrainian three-masted barque *Tovarisch,* off Alfred Dock, Birkenhead.

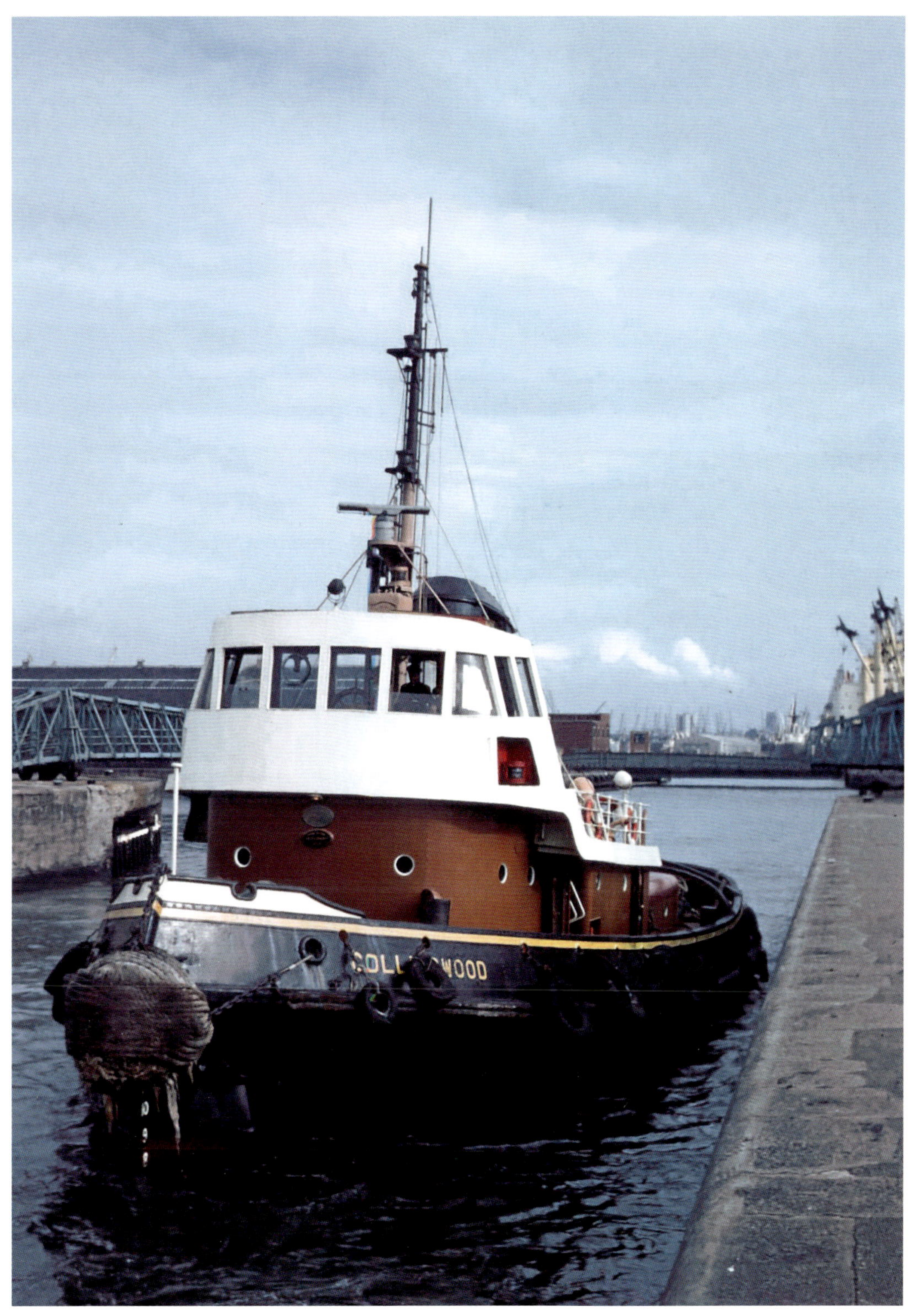

Collingwood (1958/193 grt) was originally the *Heath Cock*.

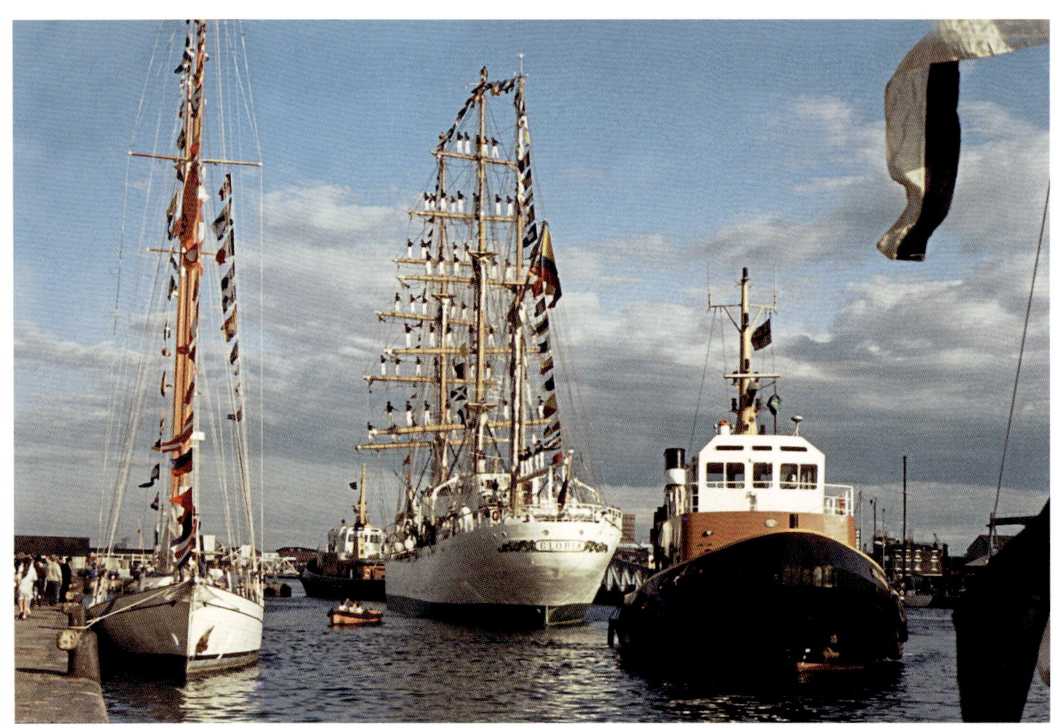

Alexandra tugs towing the *Gloria* into Alfred Dock, Birkenhead. *Gloria* is the official flagship and sail-training ship of the Colombian Navy, and her home port is Cartagena. She was built in Spain in 1968 and has a crew of 176.

Opposite above: Canada (1980/282 grt) delivers *Bramley Moore* (1984/336 grt) to the fitting out berth in the East Float following her launch. *Bramley Moore* is almost identical to the *Sun Thames,* which entered service with the Gravesend fleet in 1982. *Bramley Moore*'s main engines are Ruston diesels rated at 1,722 bhp each. The engines drive twin Voith Schneider propulsion units, giving a bollard pull of 38½ tonnes. *Bramley Moore* became *Smit Liverpool* in 2007 and then *Liverpool* in 2010.

Opposite below: Trafalgar (1998/369 grt) fitting out in the East Float in 1998.

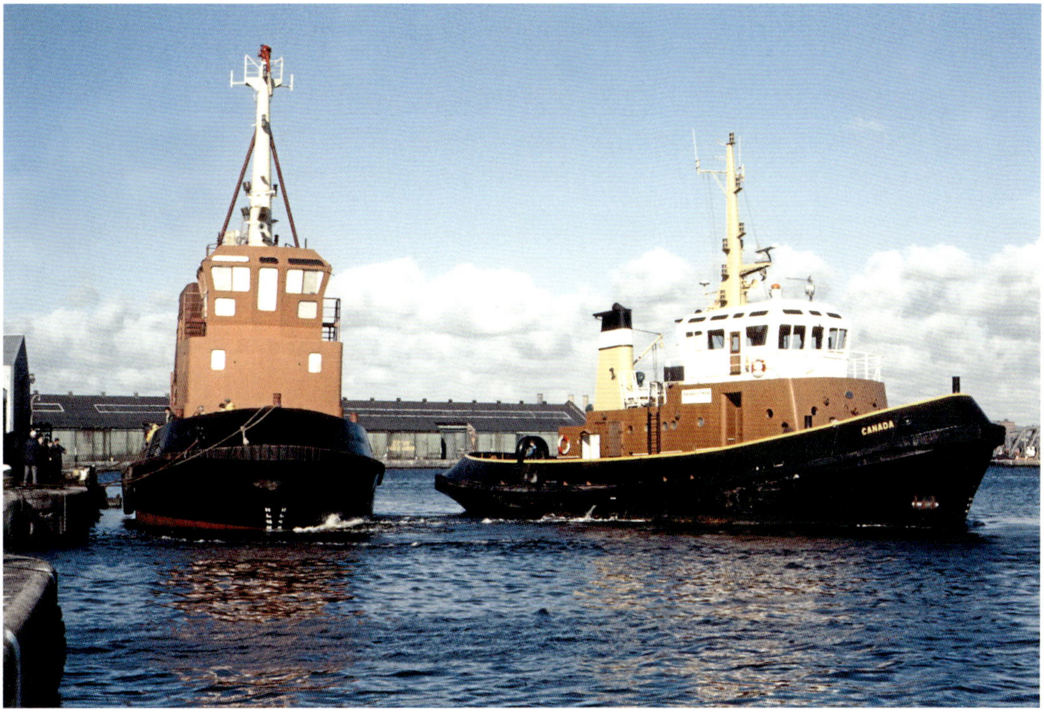

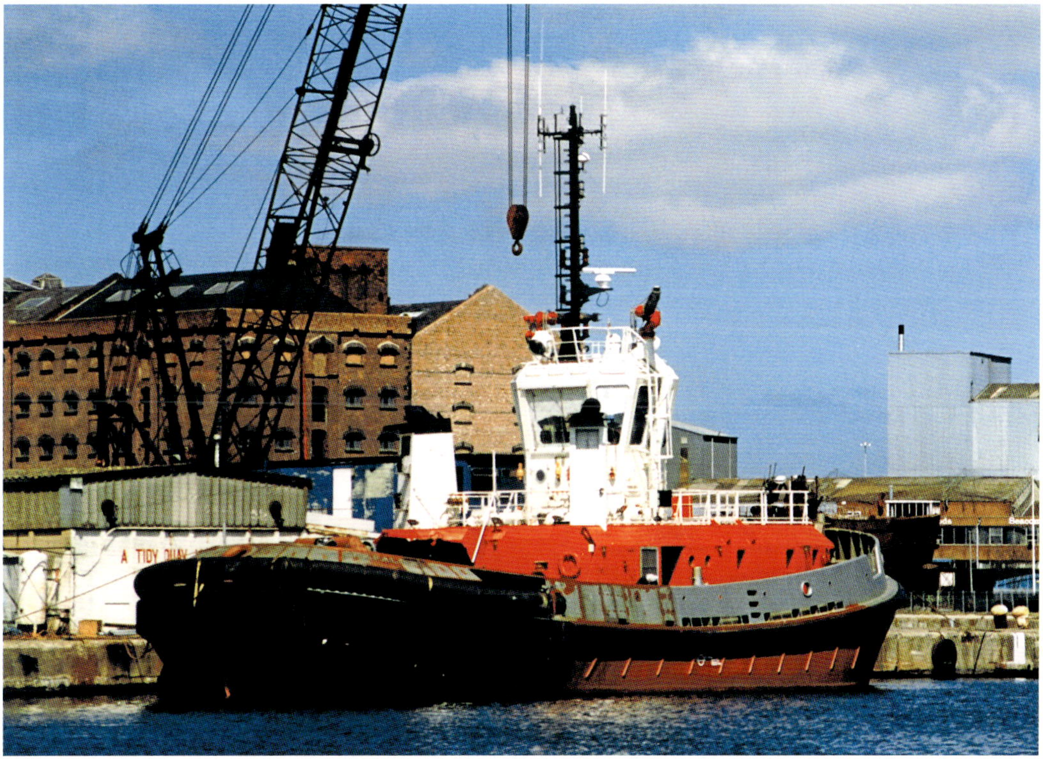

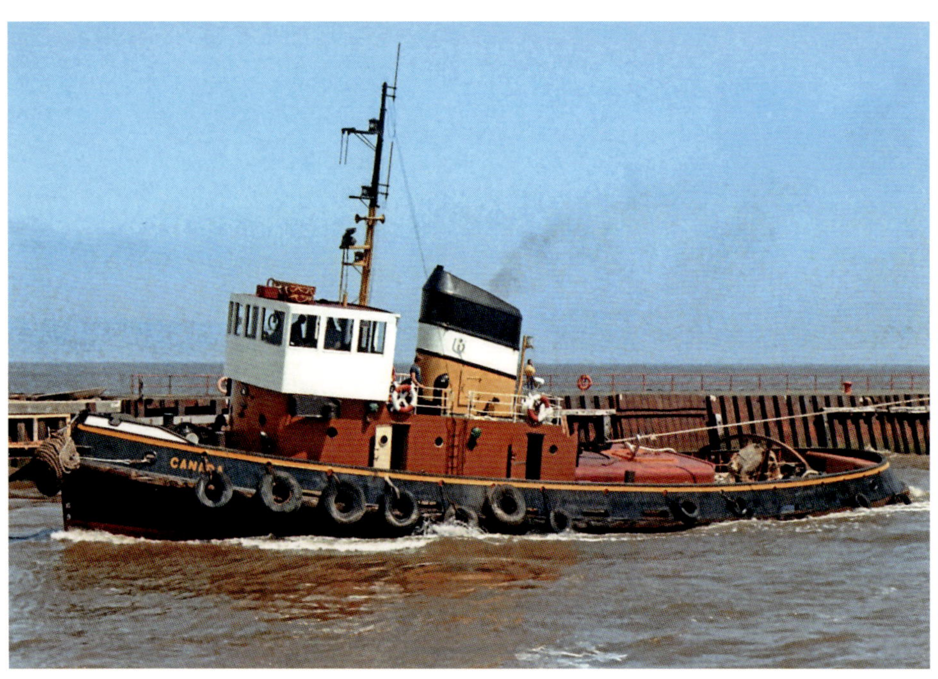

Canada (ex *Pea Cock*) (1960/165 grt/motor) of the Alexandra Towing Company Limited.

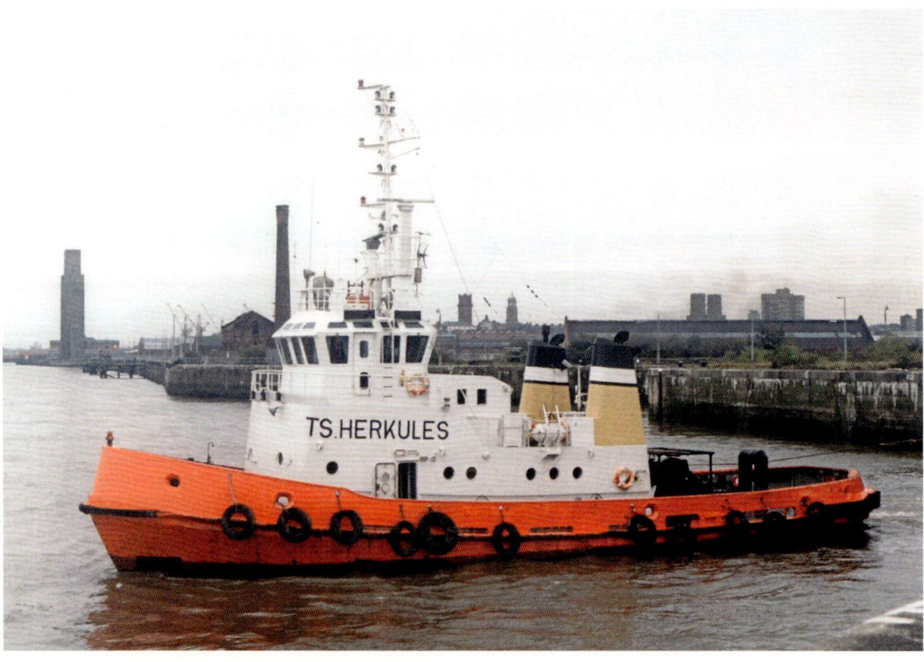

TS Herkules (1977/256 grt) leaving Alfred lock, Birkenhead. The vessel was on charter from the German towage company Hapag-Lloyd Transport & Services from 1988. She became *TS Herkules* in 1990 and was purchased by the Alexandra Towing Company on 6 May 1994 and renamed *Gladstone*. She is a Voith Schneider tractor tug and is powered by two MAK main engines rated at 2,400 bhp, giving a bollard pull of 27½ tonnes.

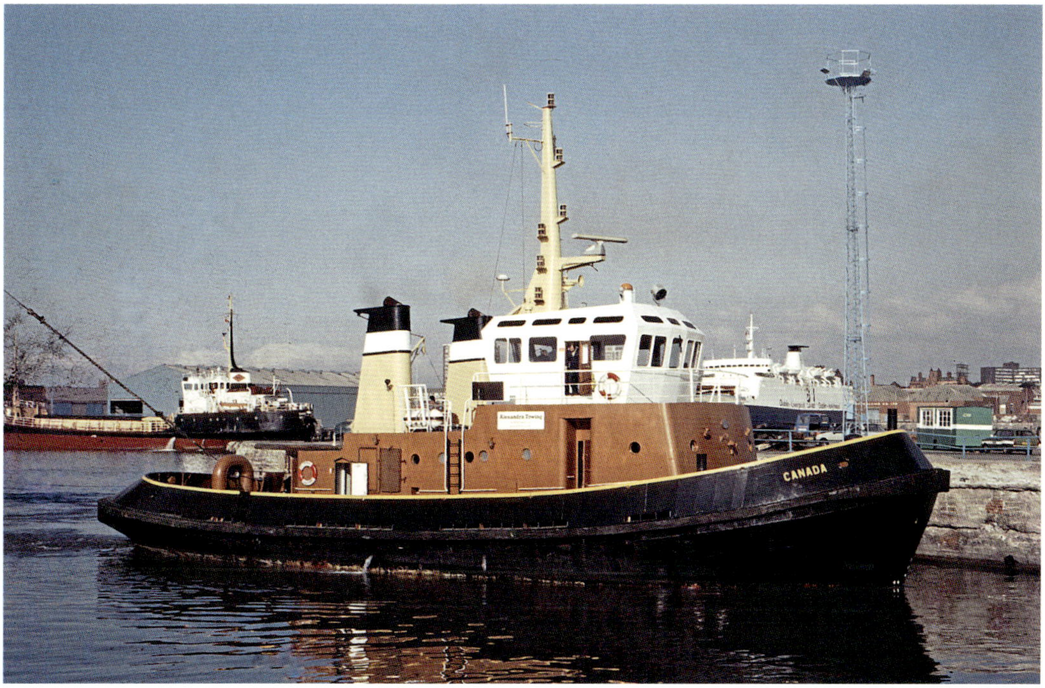

Canada (1980/282 grt/2,640 hp/motor) of the Alexandra Towing Company Limited.

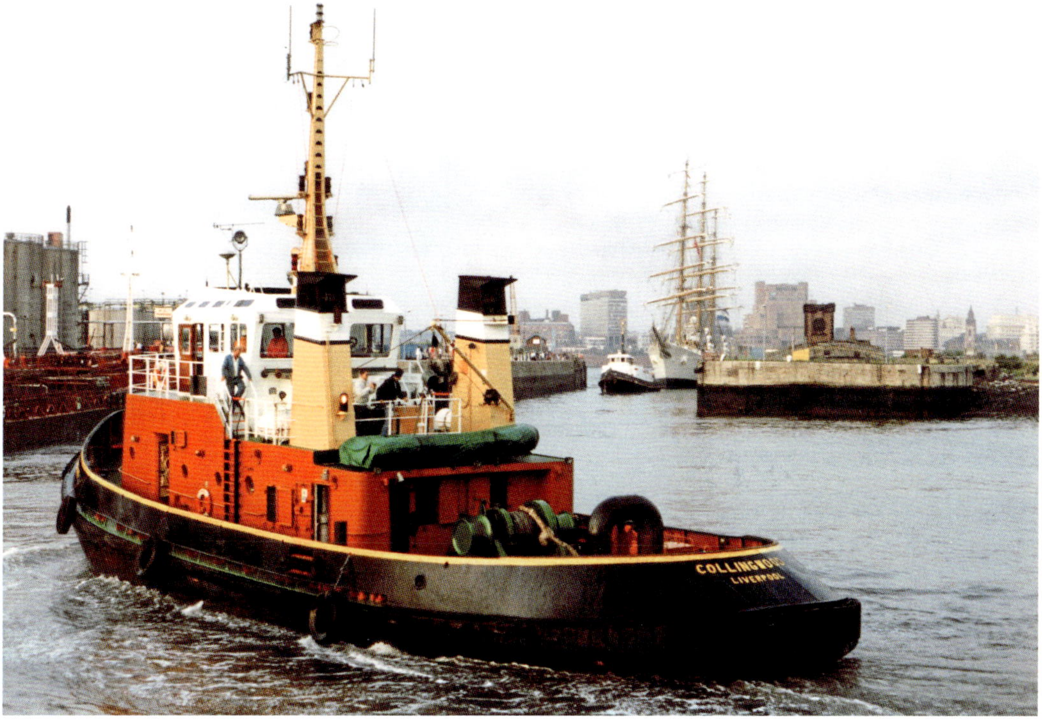

Collingwood (1981/281 grt/2,640 hp/motor) of the Alexandra Towing Company Limited.

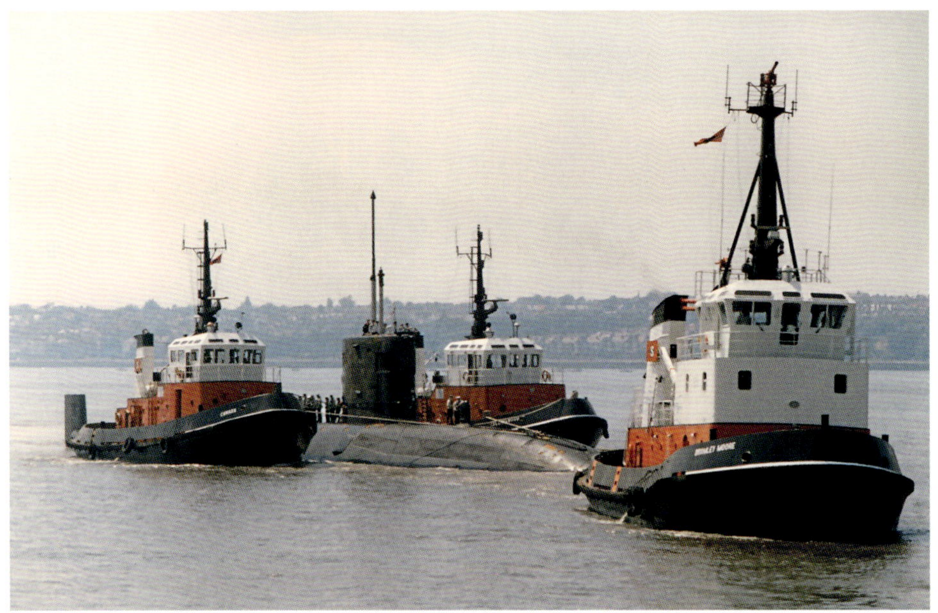

Bramley Moore (1984/336 grt) leads HMS *Triumph* into Gladstone Dock. *Triumph* is a Trafalgar Class nuclear submarine and was the seventh and final vessel of her class. She was laid down by Vickers Shipbuilding & Engineering Limited in 1987 and launched on 16 February 1991. It is anticipated that she will be the last of the Trafalgar class submarines to be decommissioned in 2022.

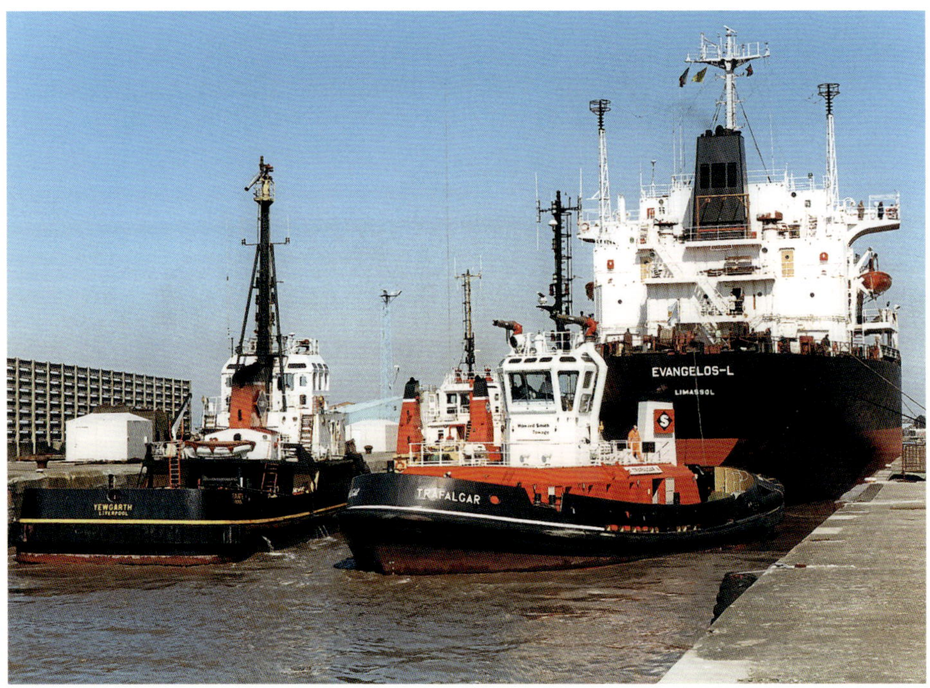

Yewgarth (1985/452 grt), *Willowgarth* (1989/392 grt), *Trafalgar* (1998/369 grt) and *Evangelos-L* in Langton lock.

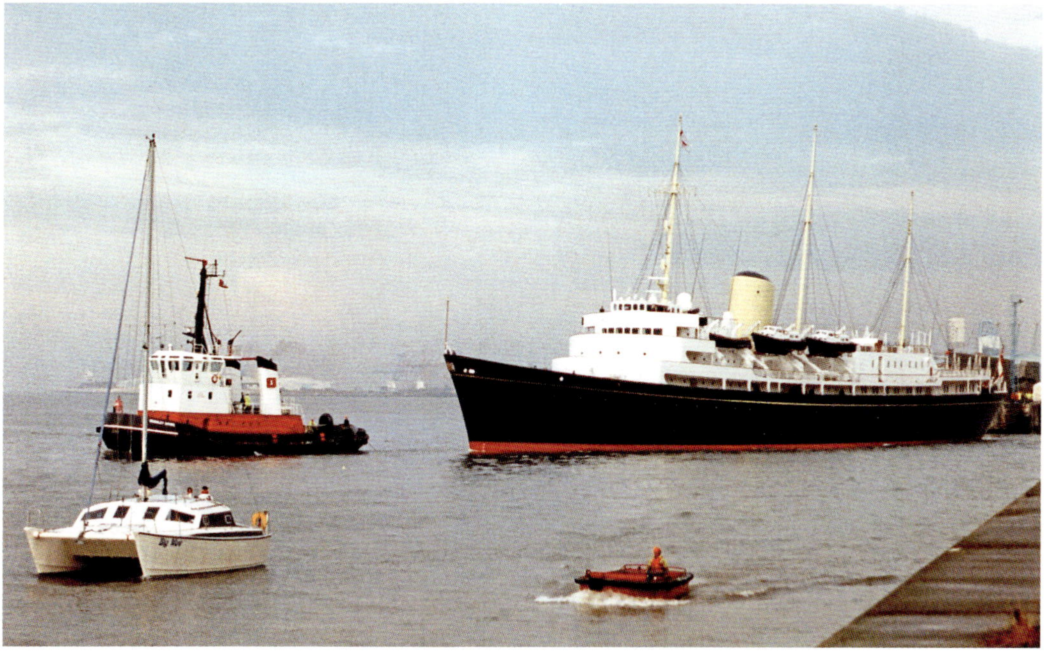

Bramley Moore (1984/336 grt) assists HM Royal Yacht *Britannia* into the Mersey from Langton lock.

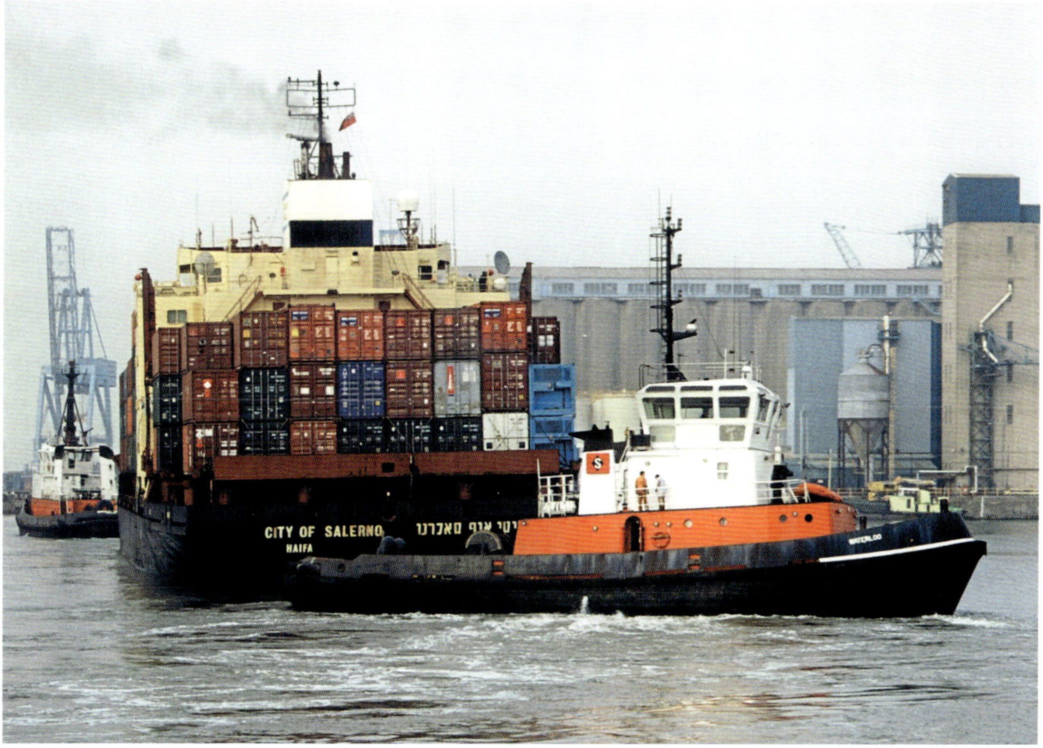

Bramley Moore (1984/336 grt), *City of Salerno* (1983/11,860 grt) and *Waterloo* (1987/298 grt) in Gladstone Dock.

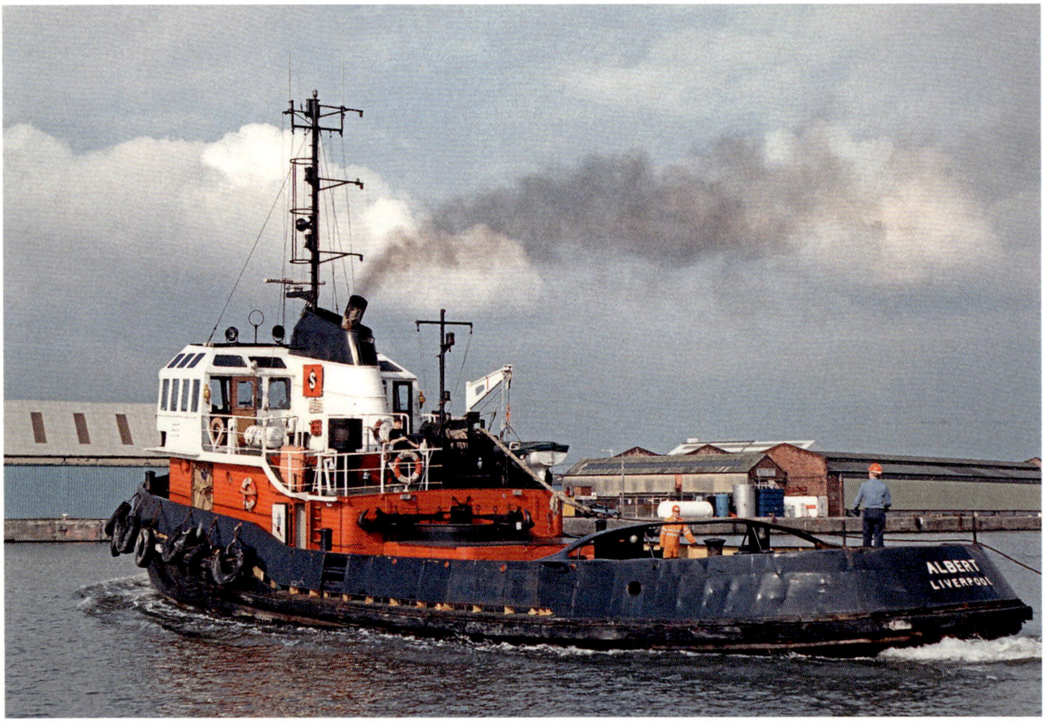

Alfred (1971/272 grt/2,401 hp/motor)of the Howard Smith Towage Limited.

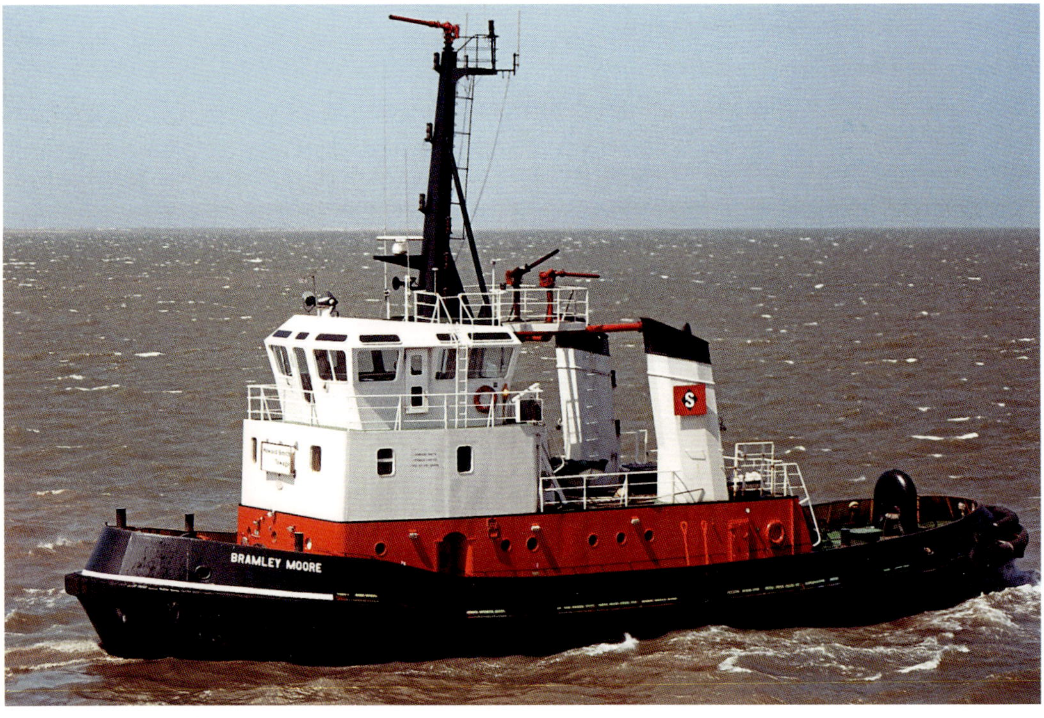

Bramley Moore (1984/336 grt) in Howard Smith livery.

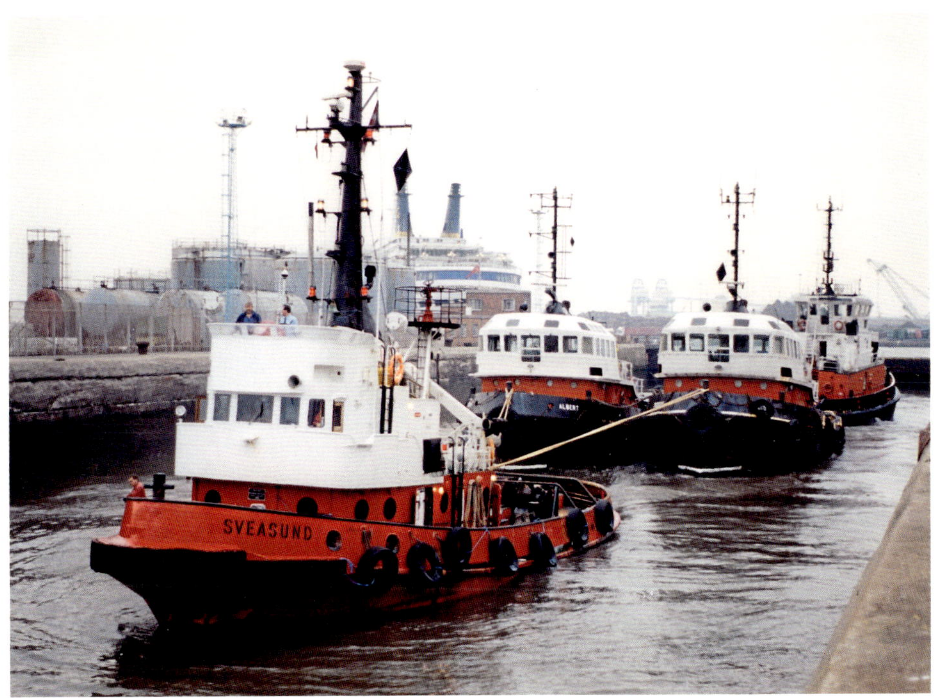

The tug *Sveasund* tows *Crosby* (1972/272 grt) and *Albert* (1971/272 grt) out of Langton lock following their sale to Portuguese interests.

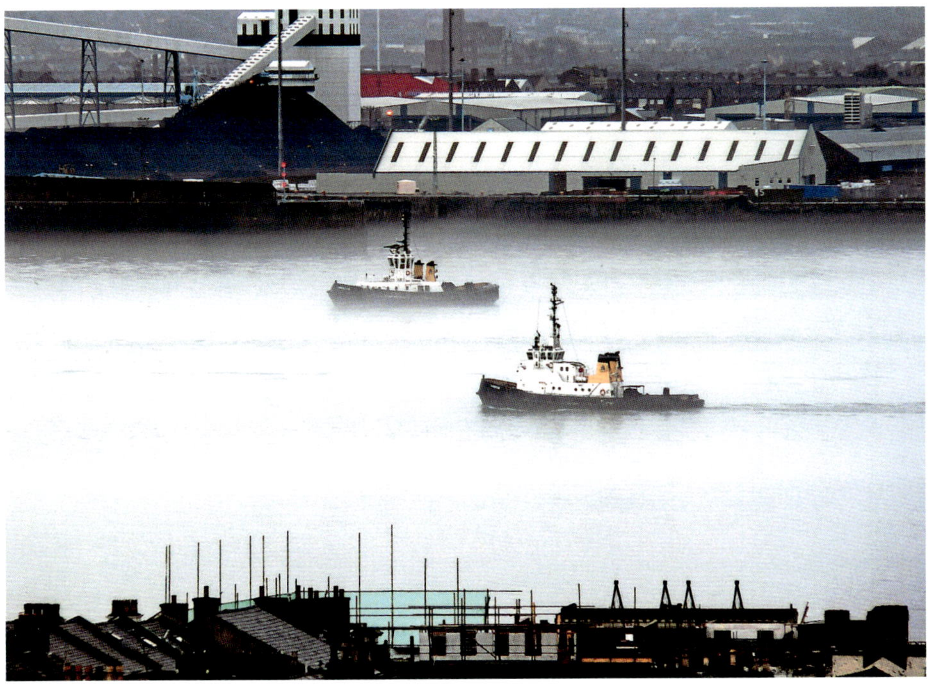

Trafalgar (1998/369 grt) and *Gladstone* (1977/256 grt) off Gladstone Dock in a Mersey sea mist.

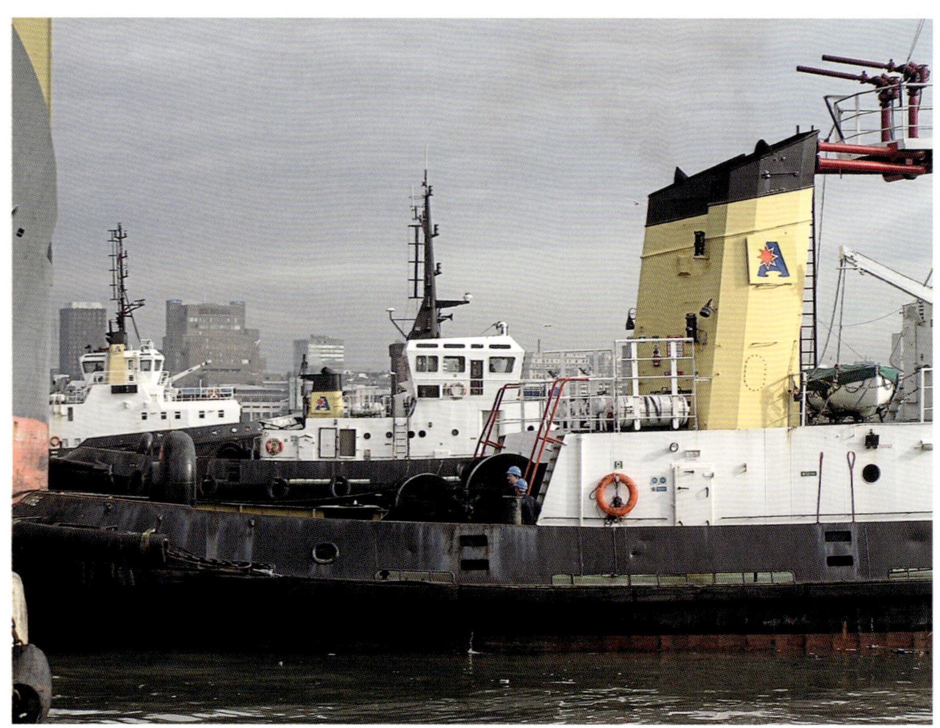

Adsteam vessels in Alfred Dock, Birkenhead.

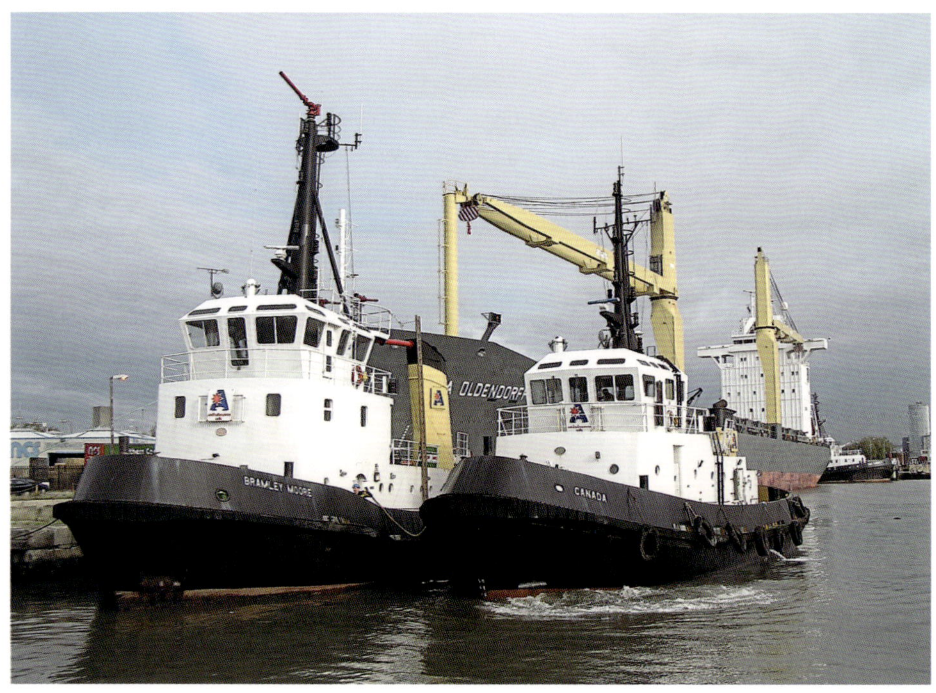

Bramley Moore (1984/336 grt) and *Canada* (1980/282 grt) at the bow of an Oldendorff vessel at Alfred Dock, Birkenhead.

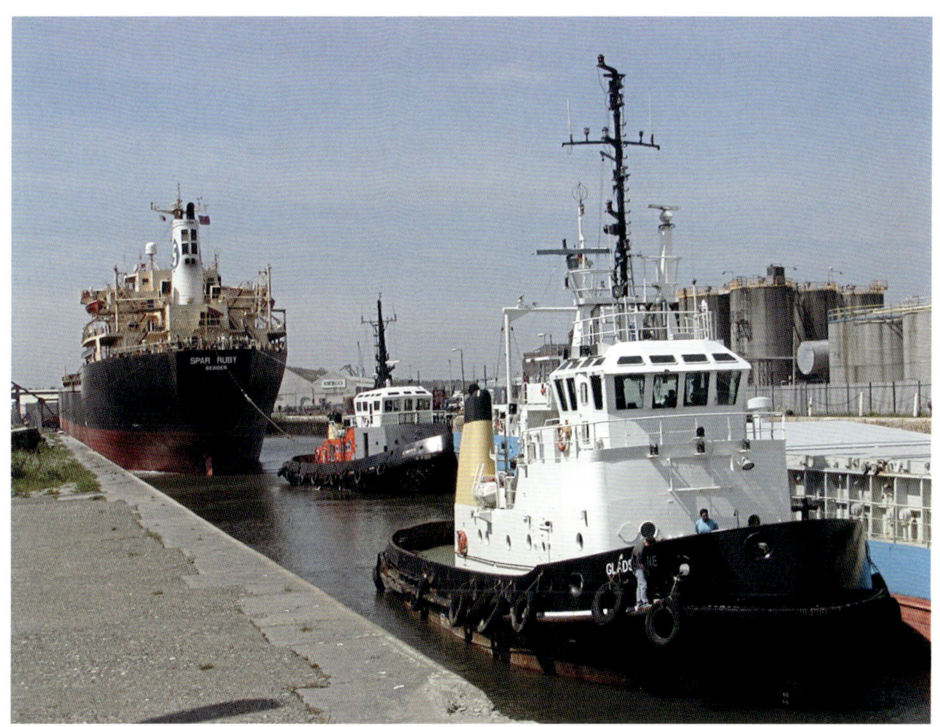

Gladstone (1977/256 grt) and *Canada* (1980/282 grt) working with the *Spar Ruby* at Birkenhead.

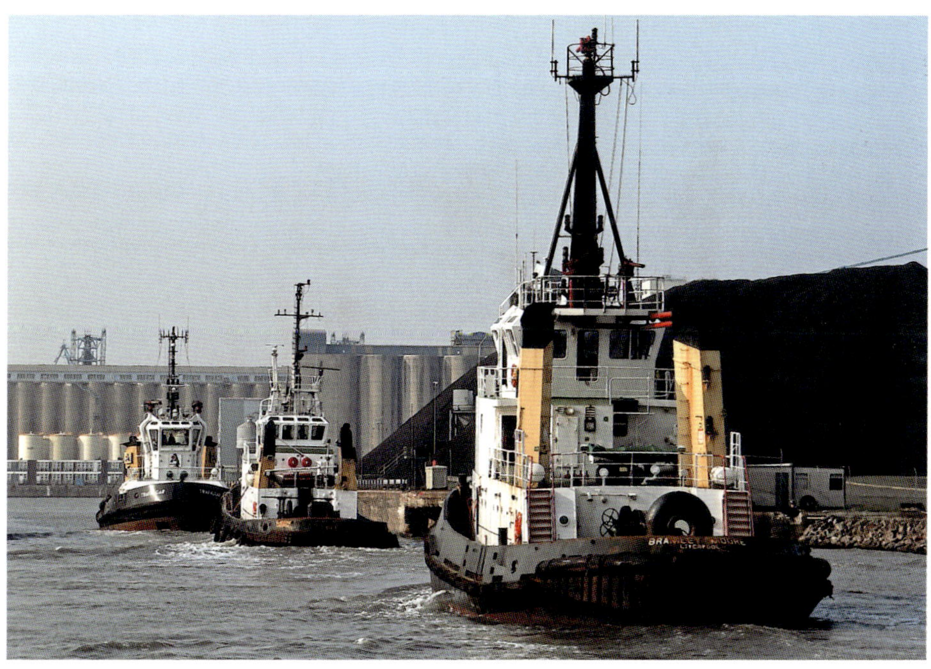

Trafalgar (1998/369 grt), *Gladstone* (1977/256 grt) and *Bramley Moore* (1984/336 grt) on their way to Gladstone lock to begin their towing duties in the river.

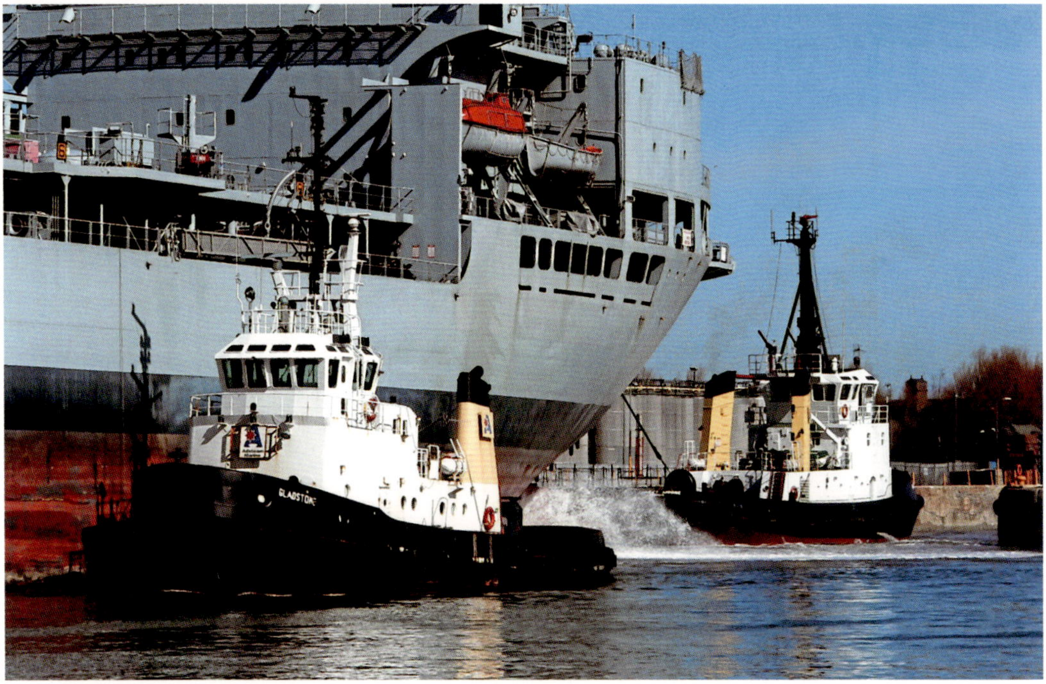

Gladstone (1977/256 grt) and *Bramley Moore* (1984/336 grt) in Alfred Dock.

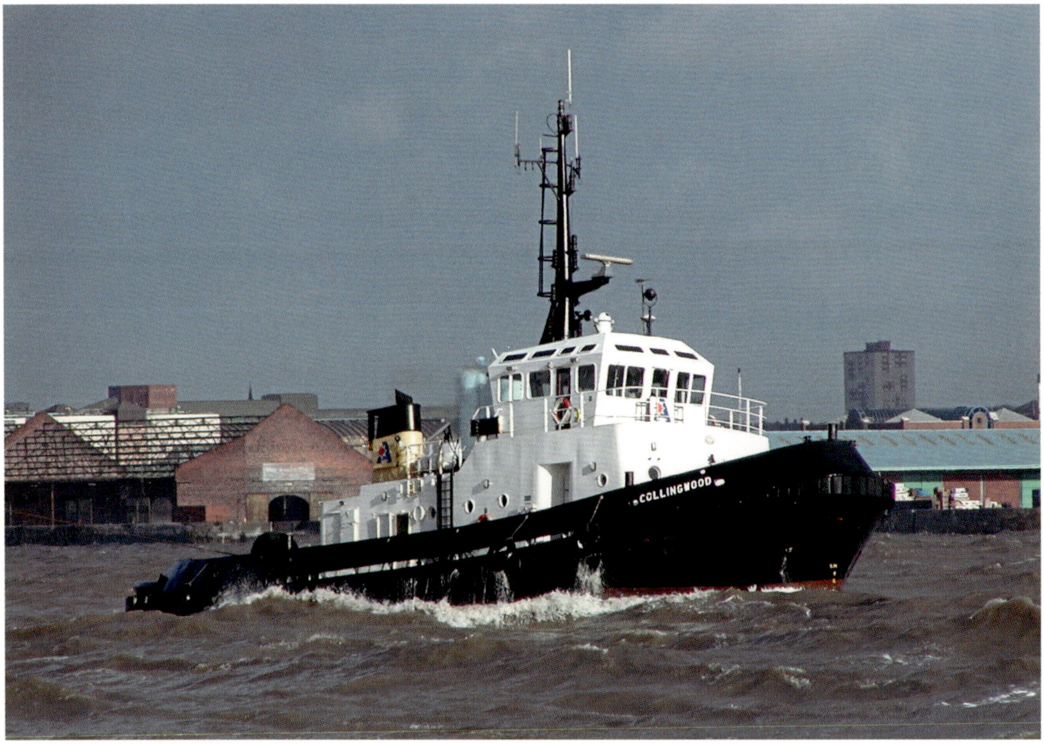

Collingwood (1981/281 grt) deals with a heavy swell in the river.

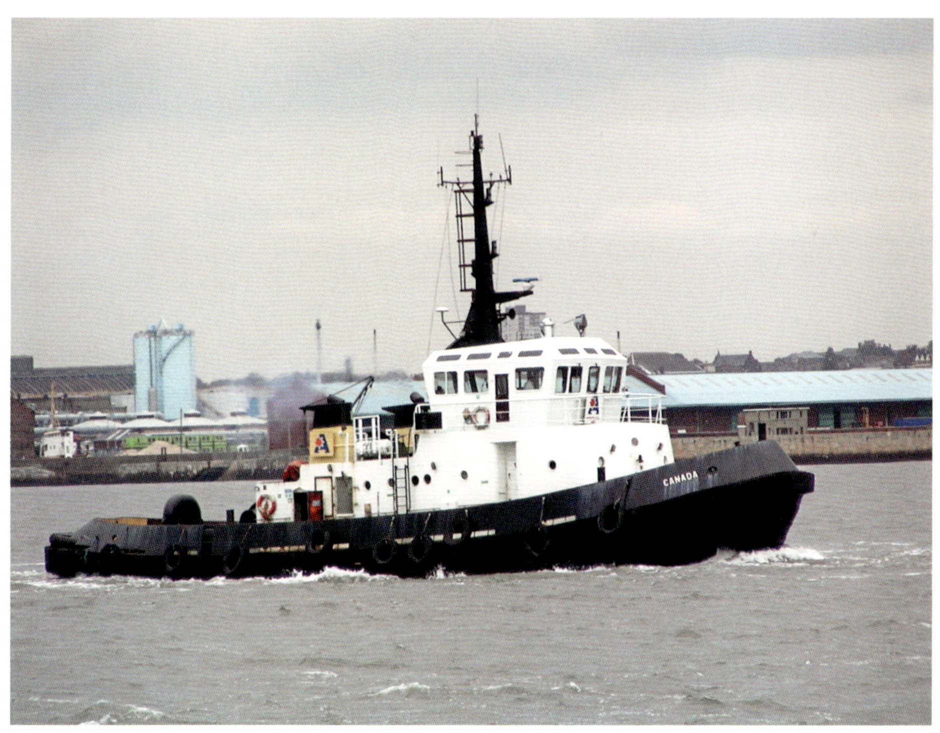

Canada (1980/282 grt) off Sandon Dock in the River Mersey.

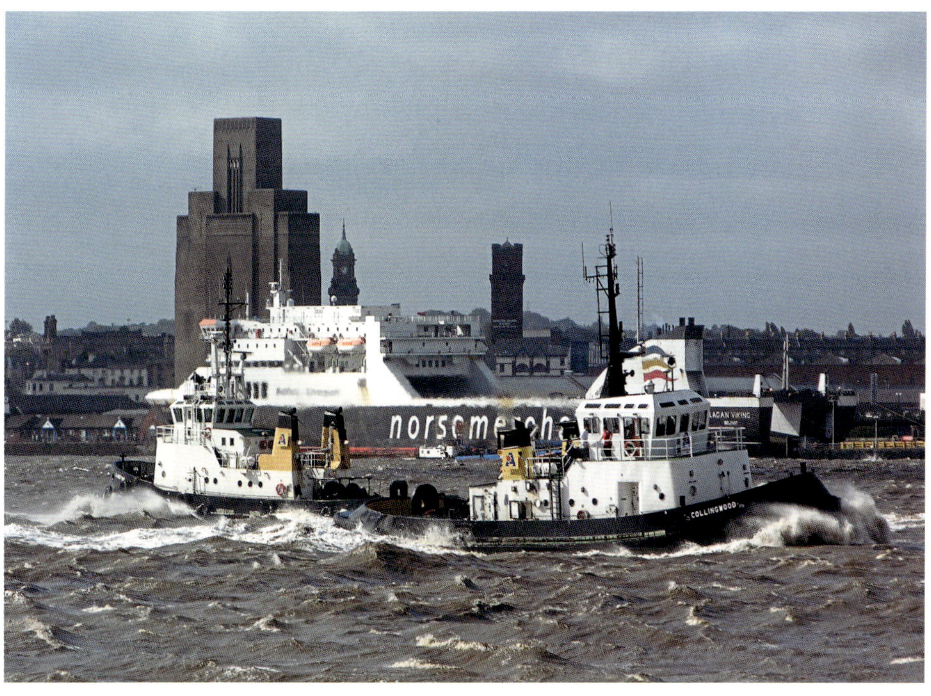

Gladstone (1977/256 grt) and *Collingwood* (1981/281 grt) pass *Lagan Viking,* berthed at Twelve Quays at Birkenhead.

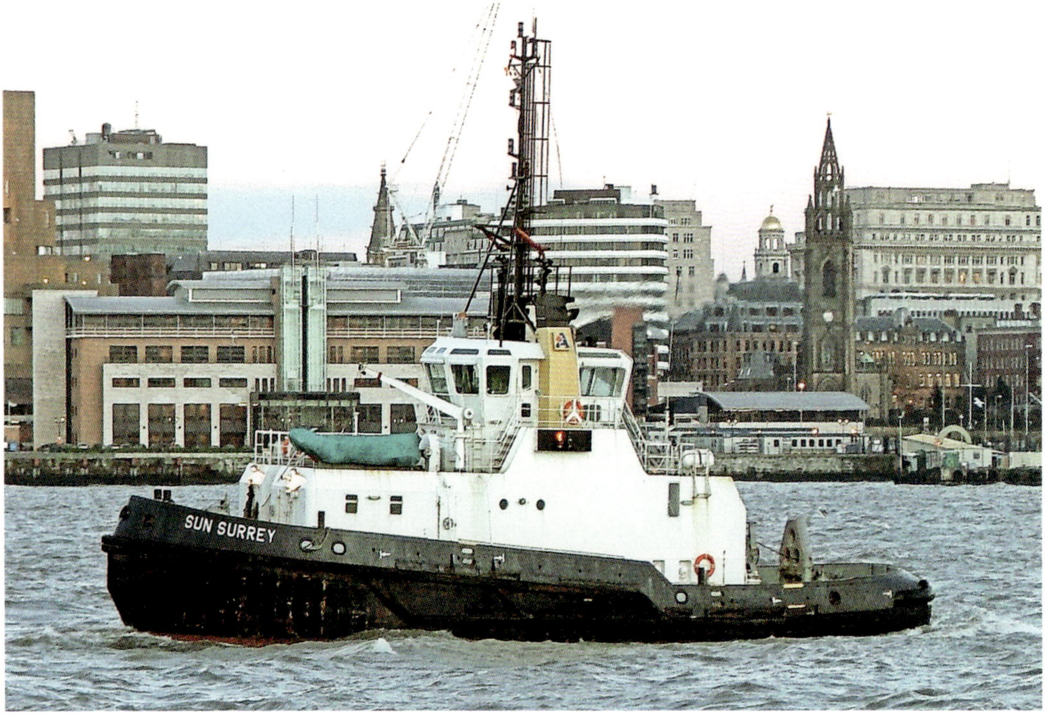

Sun Surrey (1992/399 grt) off the Pier Head, Liverpool.

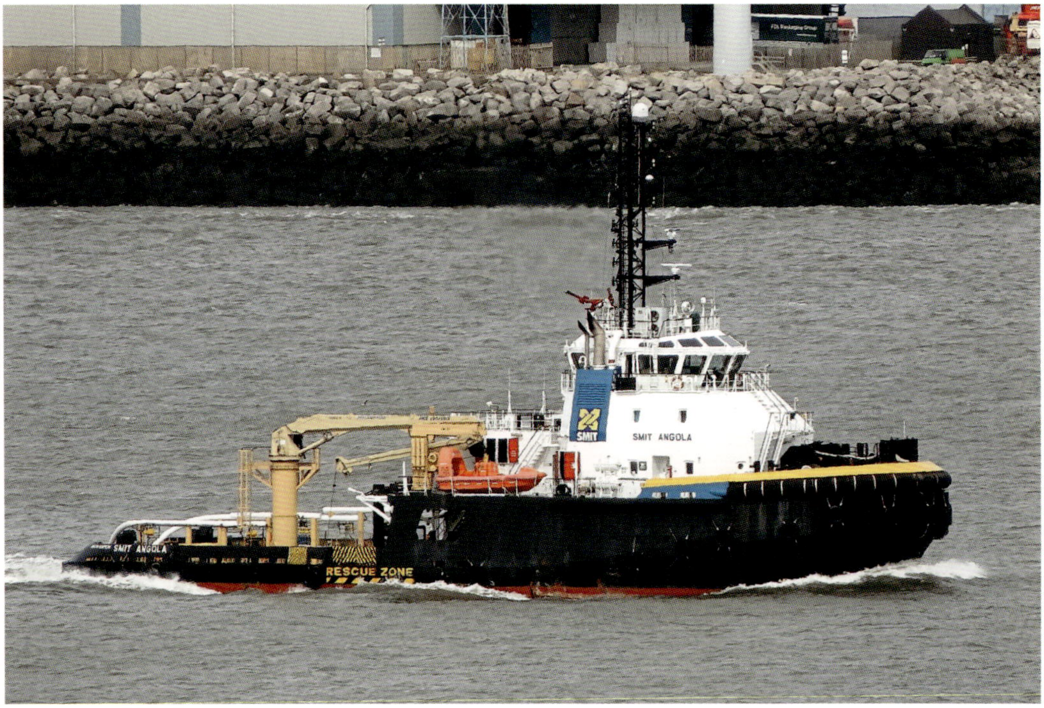

Smit Angola (2010/1,438 grt/motor) of Smit Singapore Pte.

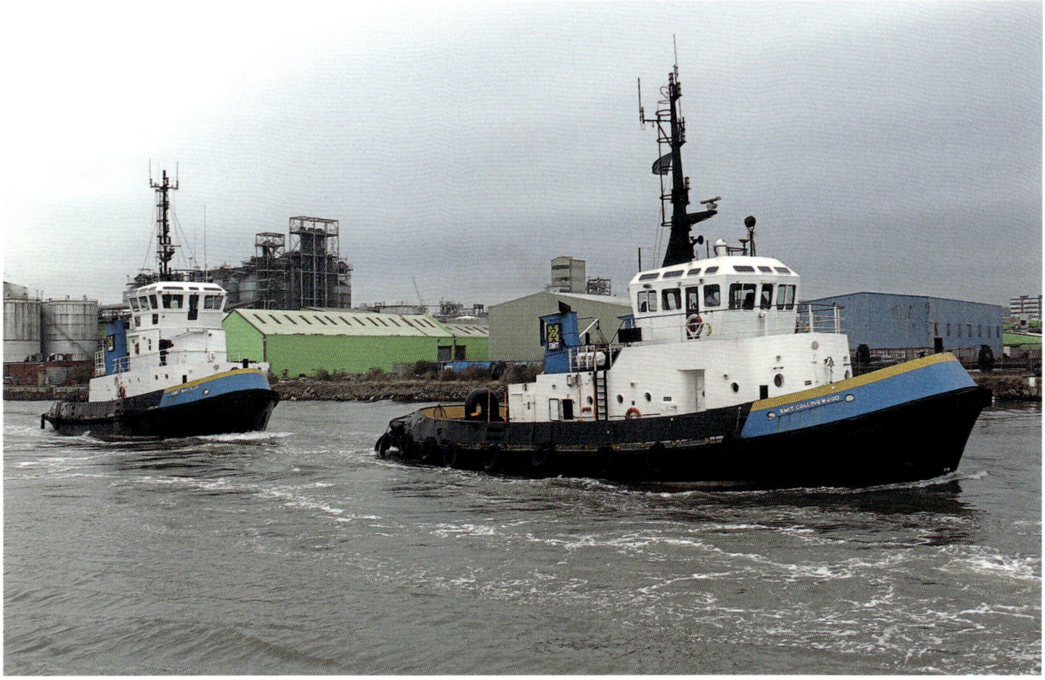

Smit Collingwood (1981/281 grt) and *Smit Waterloo* (1987/298 grt) in Langton Dock.

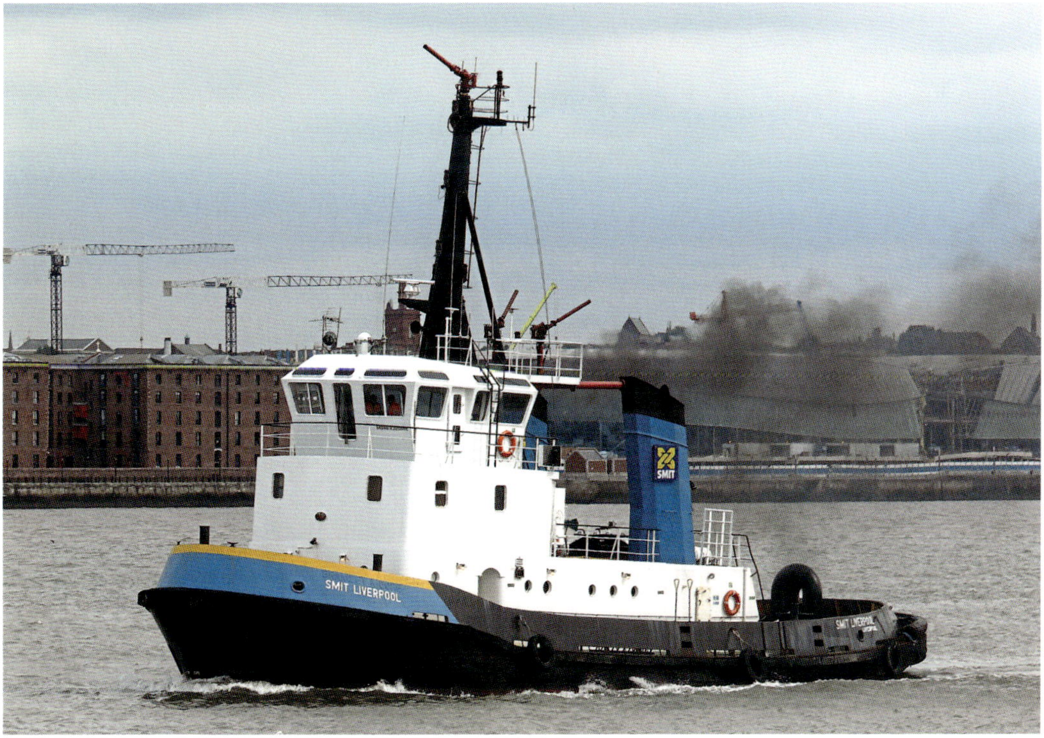

Smit Liverpool was originally the *Bramley Moore* and was renamed in 2007.

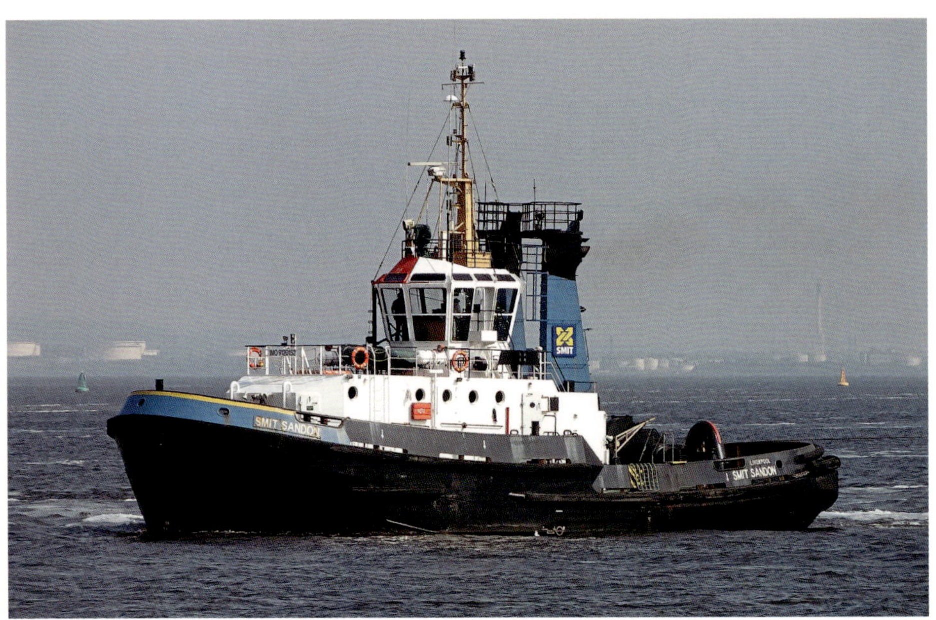

Smit Sandon (1996/398 grt) was built as *Schelde 20* and renamed in 2009.

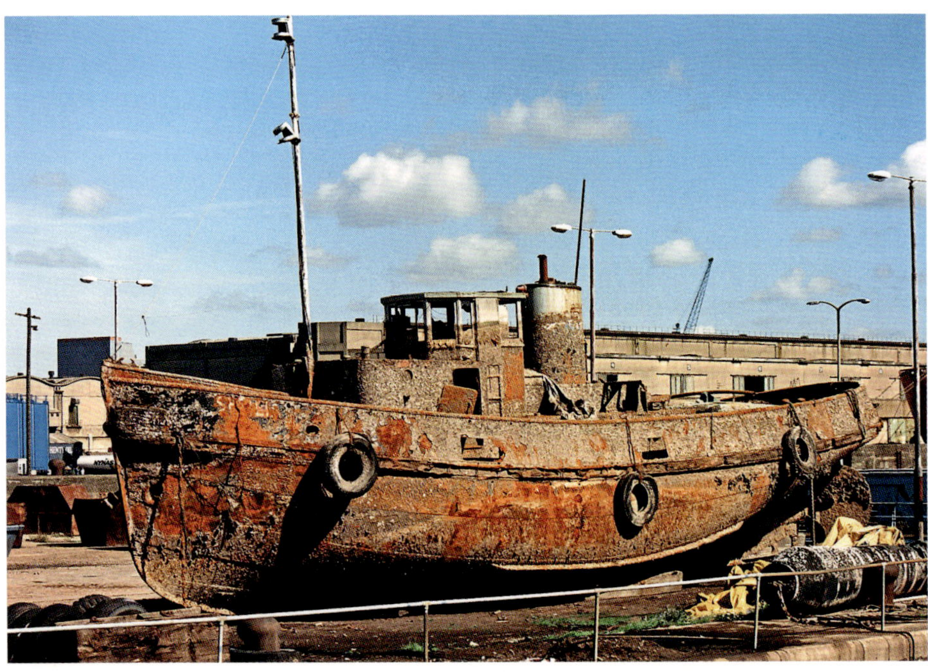

Wachtel was built in Hamburg in 1940 and it is reported that she assisted the battleship *Bismark* from the quay, when she sailed on her final voyage. During the Second World War she operated at Wilhelmshaven, and became *Sheilia* at the end of hostilities. For several years she was based at Milford Haven and later moved to Liverpool. In 1998 she sank in Sandon Dock, but was not raised until August the following year. She is seen here on the quayside at Sandon Dock, where she remained for some time until she was transferred to Holyhead by a preservation trust.

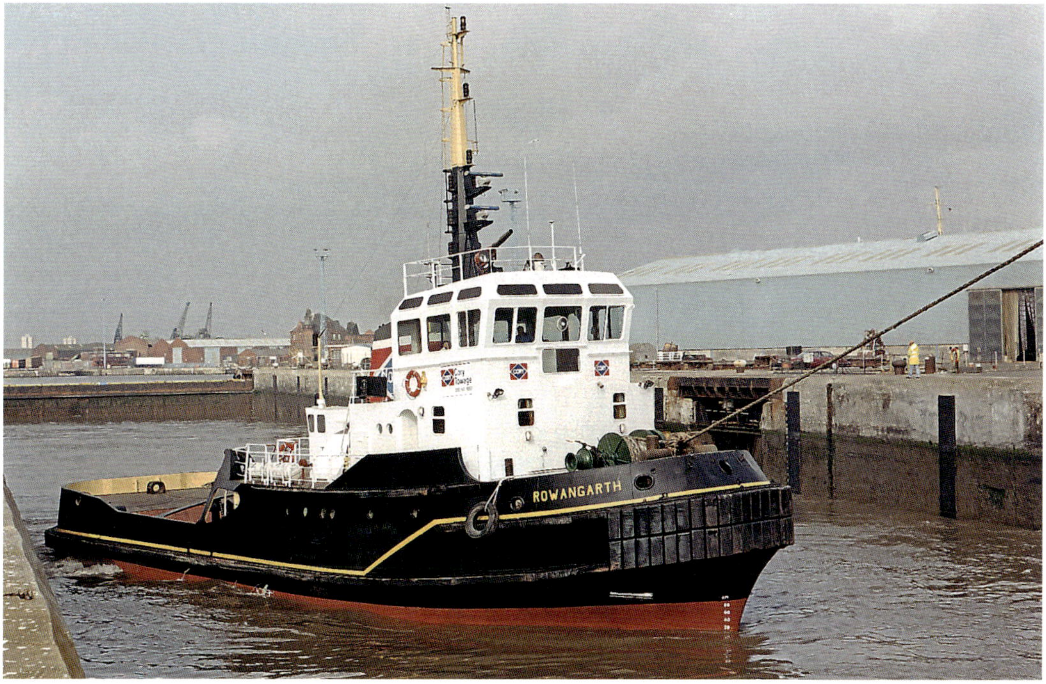

Rowangarth (1981/382 grt/3,200 hp/motor) of Cory Tugs.

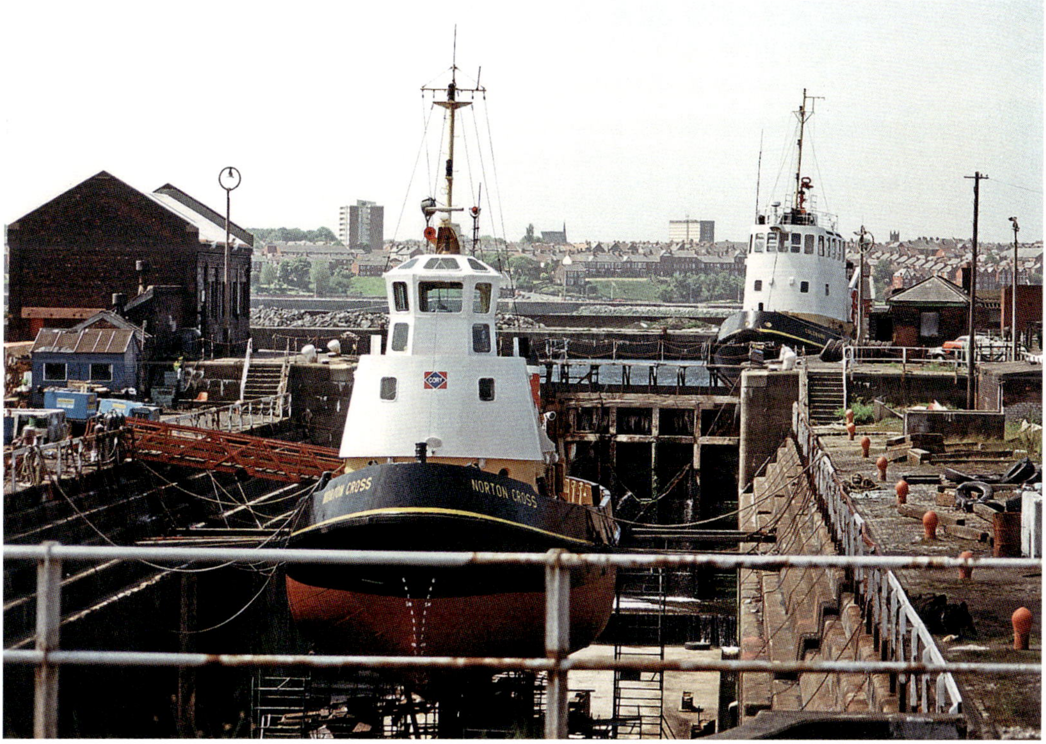

Norton Cross (1984/216 grt) and *Coleraine* (1970/245 grt) in Clarence Dock.

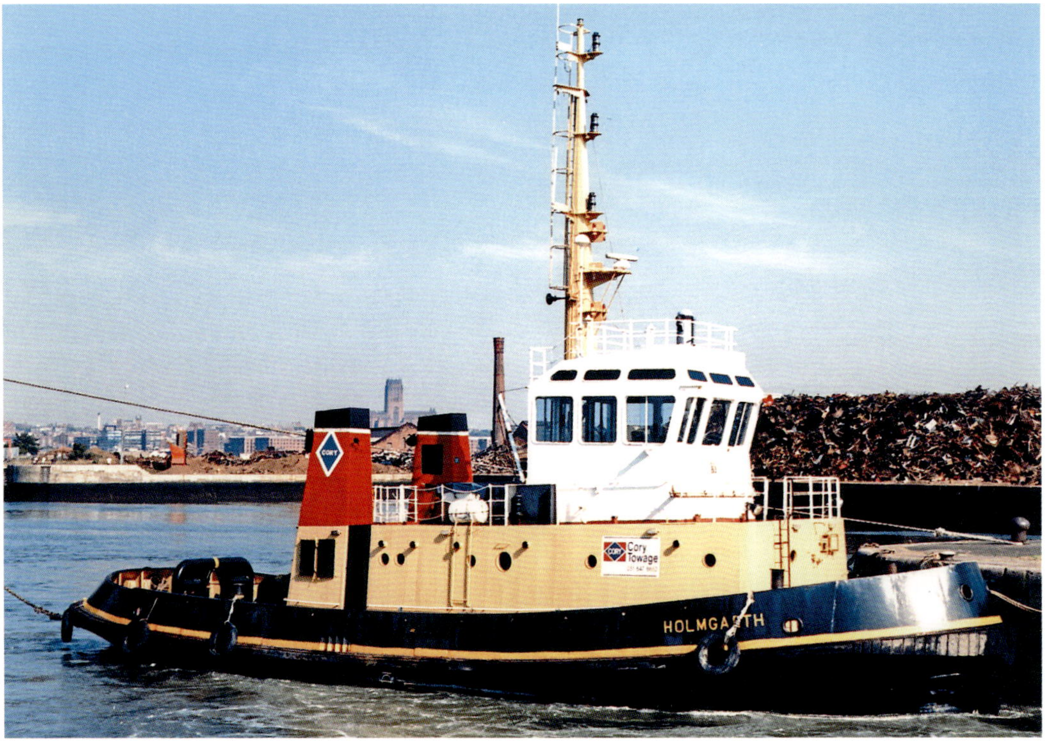

Holmgarth (1979/223 grt/2,190 hp/motor) of Cory Towage Limited.

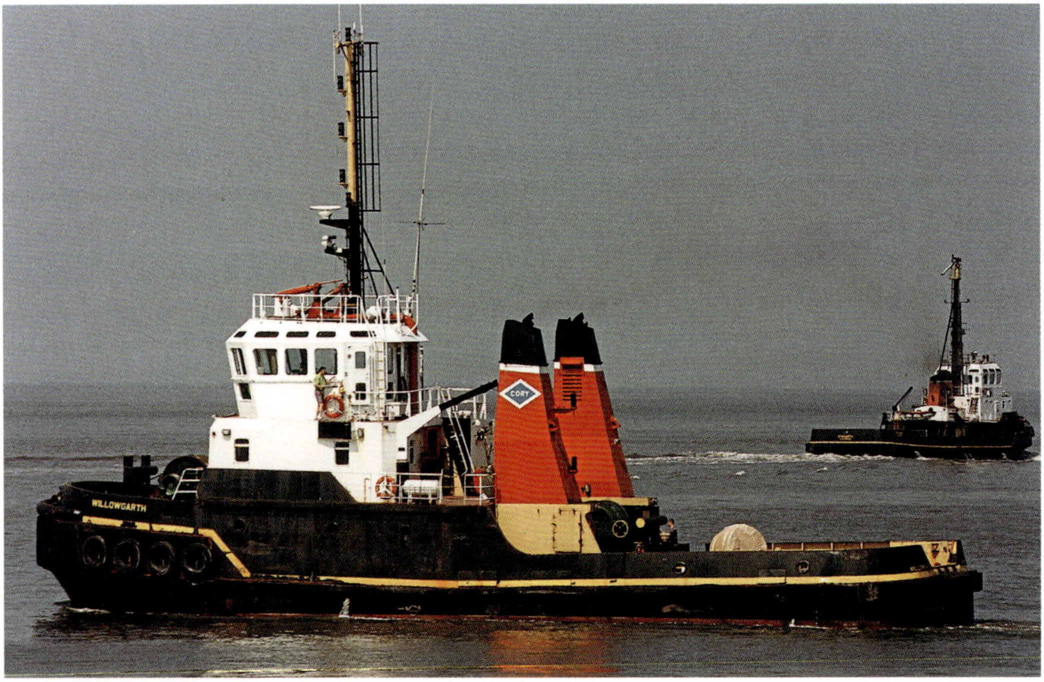

Willowgarth (1989/392 grt/3,400 hp/motor) of Cory Towage Limited.

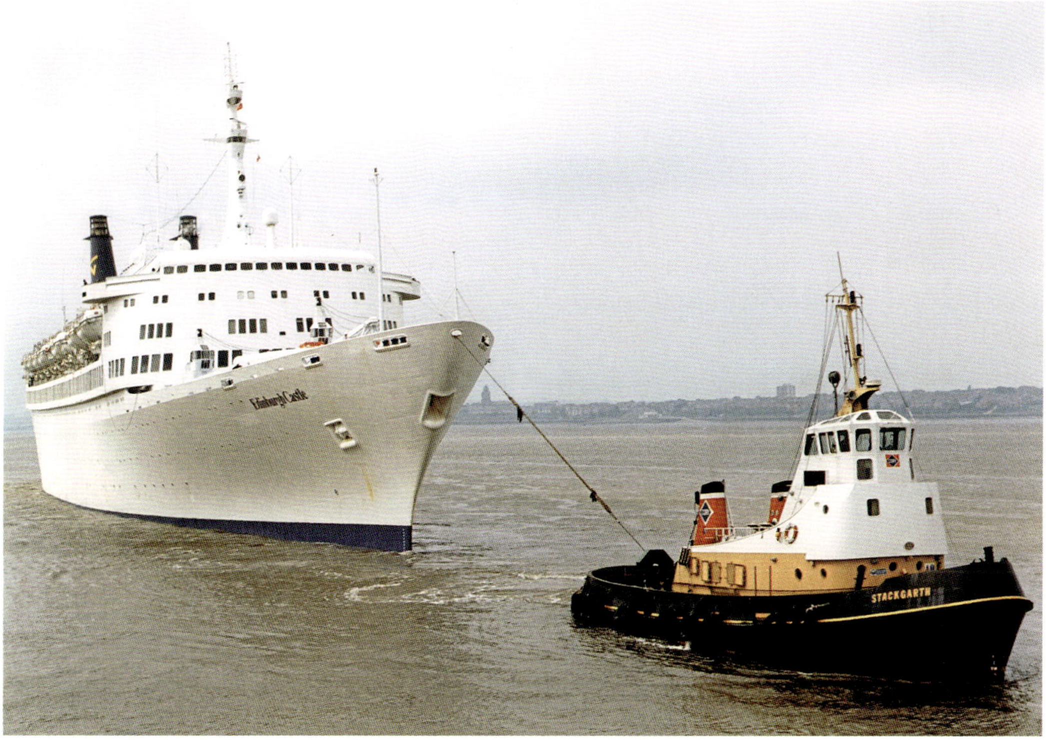

Stackgarth (1985/216 grt) leads the *Edinburgh Castle* (1966/30,567 grt) into Langton lock. She was built as *Eston Cross*, becoming *Stackgarth* in 1994.

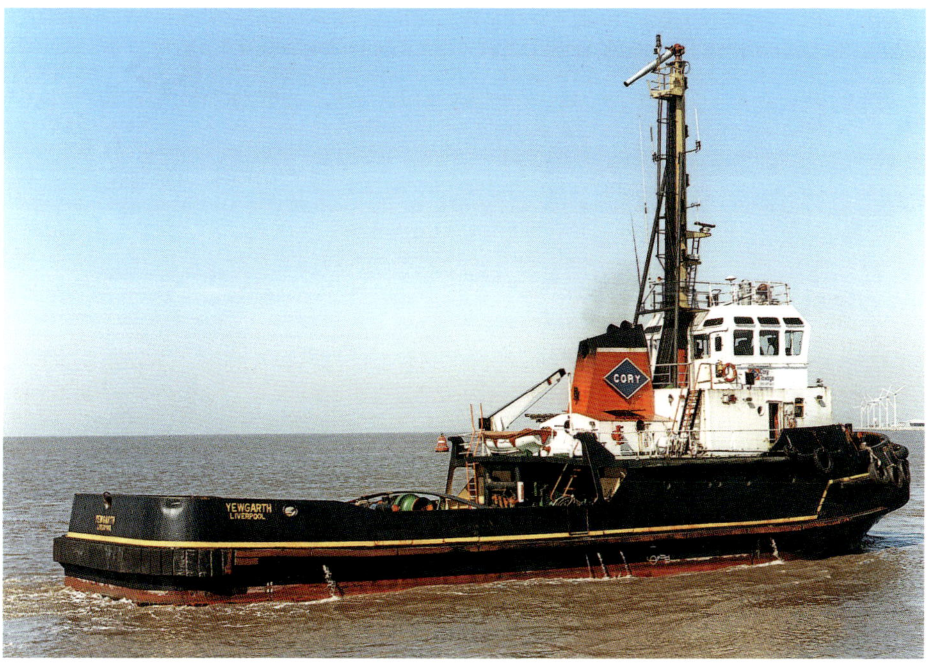

Yewgarth (1985/452 grt/4,000 hp/motor) of Cory Towage Limited.

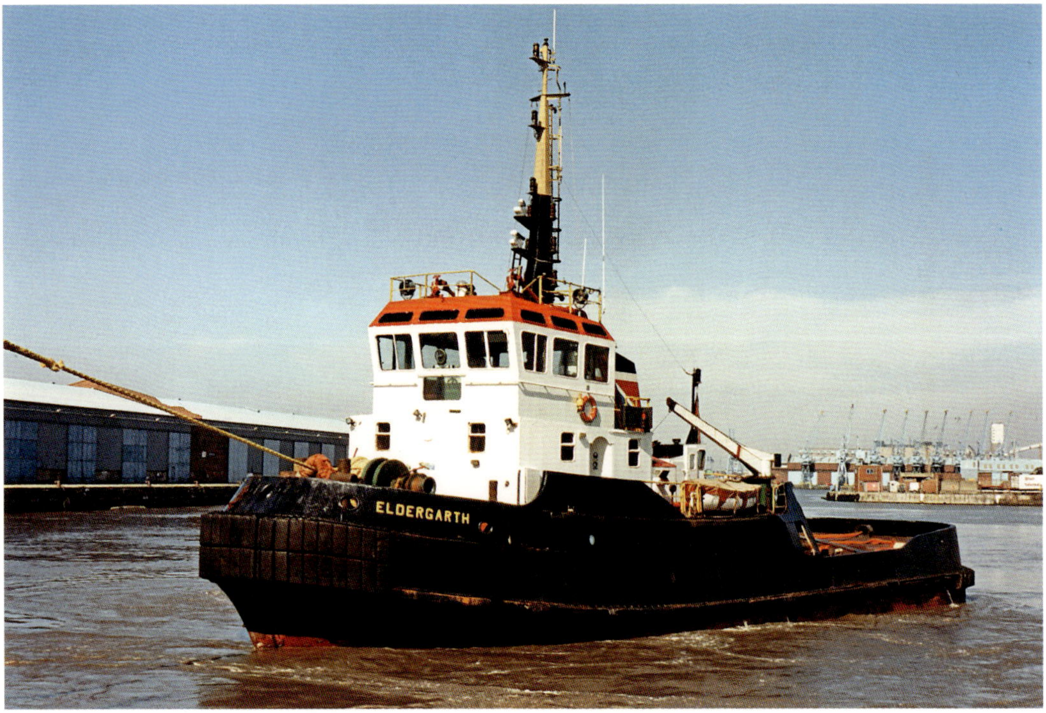

Eldergarth (1981/382 grt/3,200 hp/motor) of Cory Towage Limited. She was renamed *Shannon* in 1999.

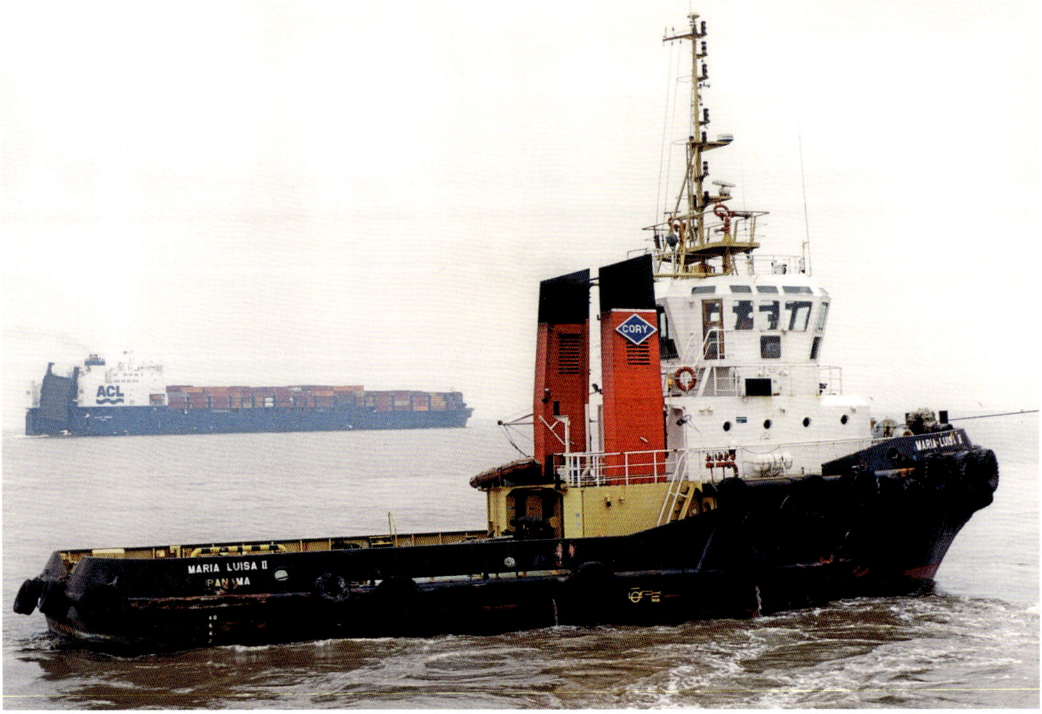

Cory Towage Limited vessel *Maria Luisa II* (1987/376 grt) in the Mersey.

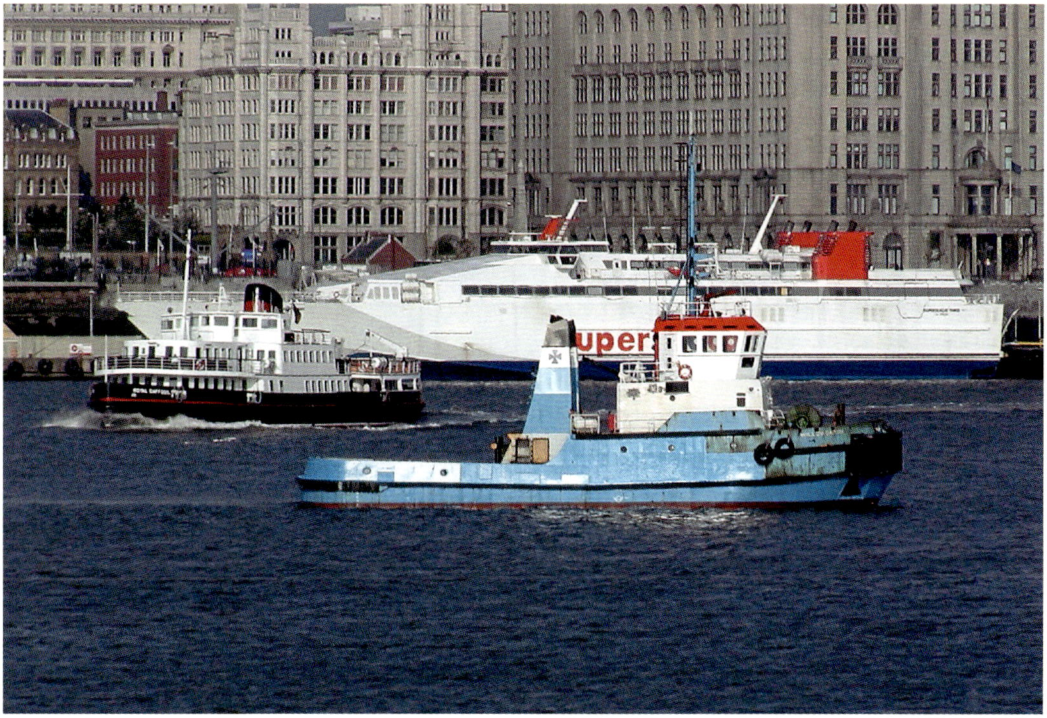

Willowgarth (1989/392 grt), *Royal Daffodil* and *Superseacat Three* in the River Mersey, off the Pier Head.

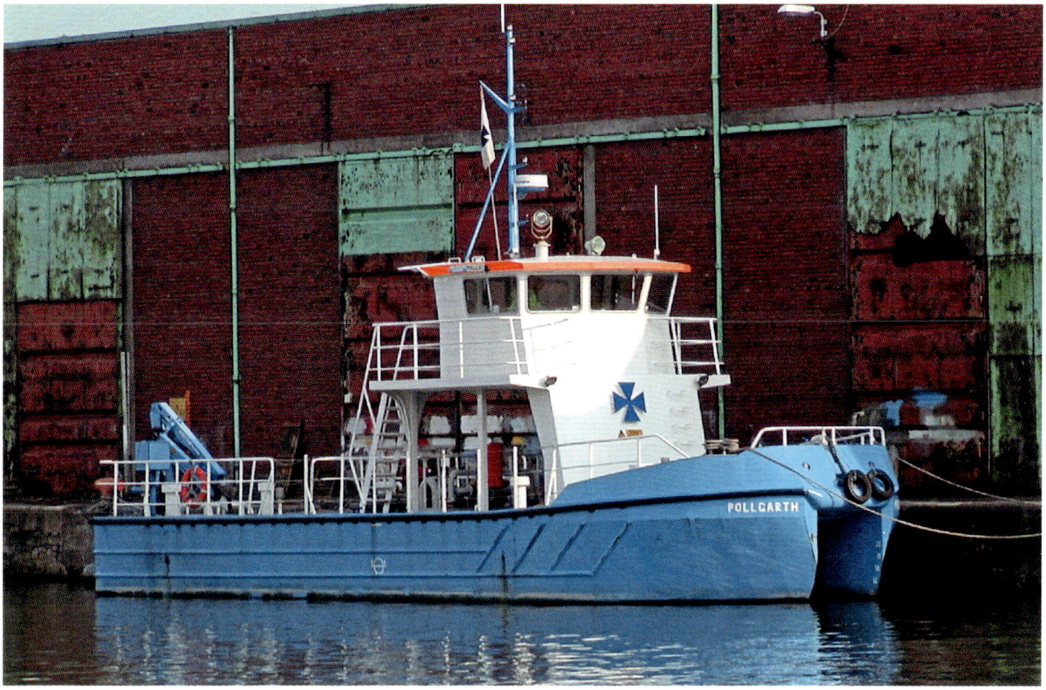

The pollution control vessel *Pollgarth* (1999/35 grt) is operated by Svitzer Marine Limited.

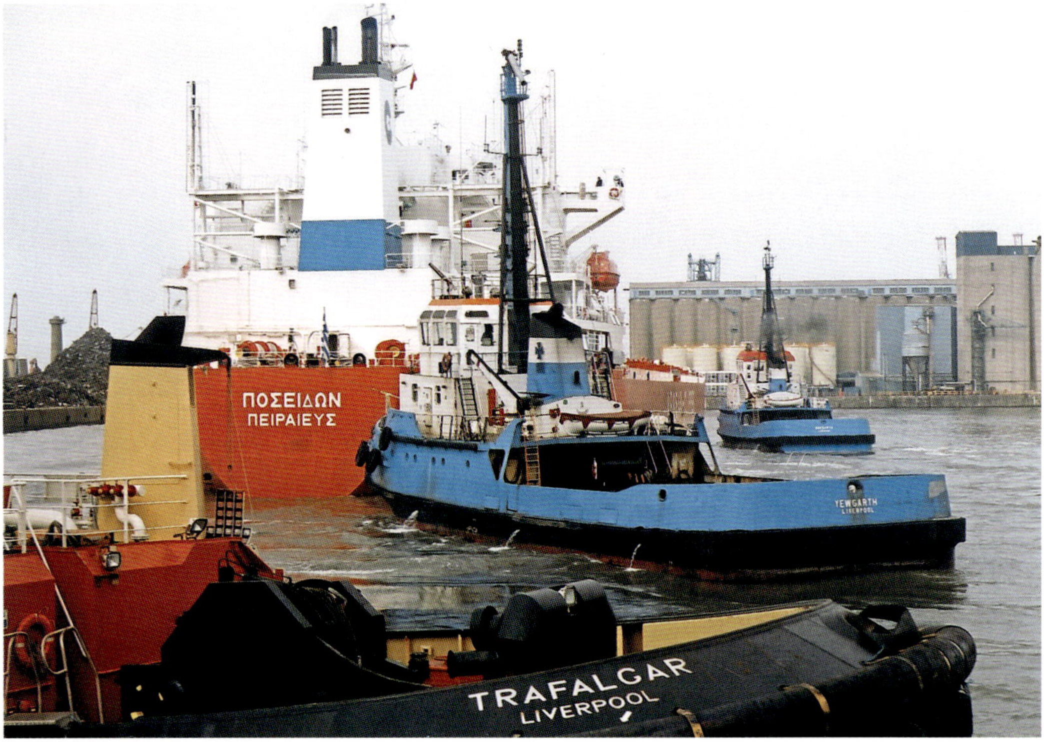

Yewgarth (1985/452 grt), and *Trafalgar* (1998/369 grt) and *Oakgarth* (1984/452 grt) on duty in Gladstone Dock.

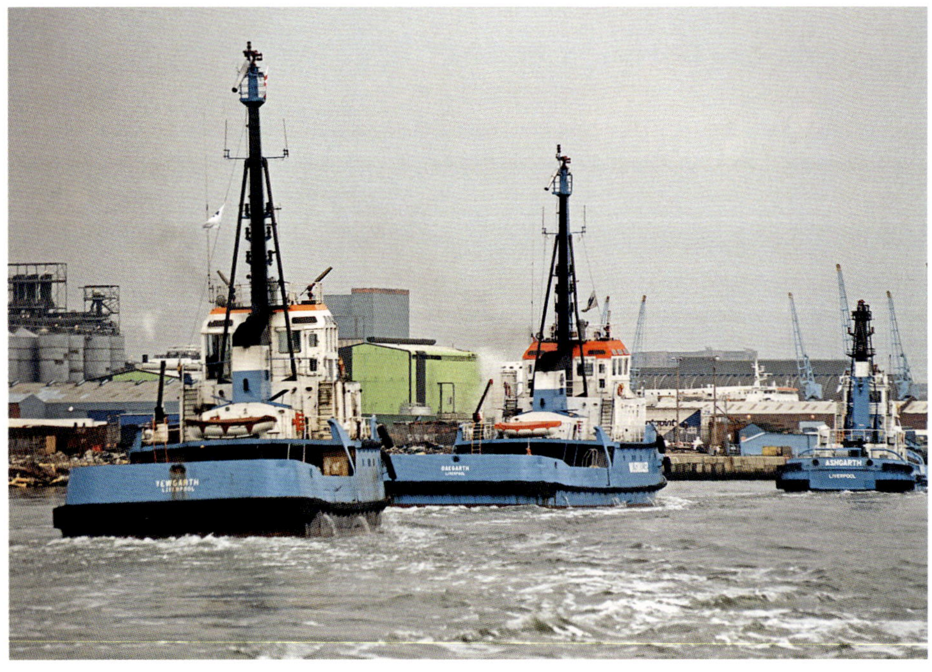

Yewgarth (1985/452 grt), *Oakgarth* (1984/452 grt) and *Ashgarth* (1992/307 grt) in Langton Dock.

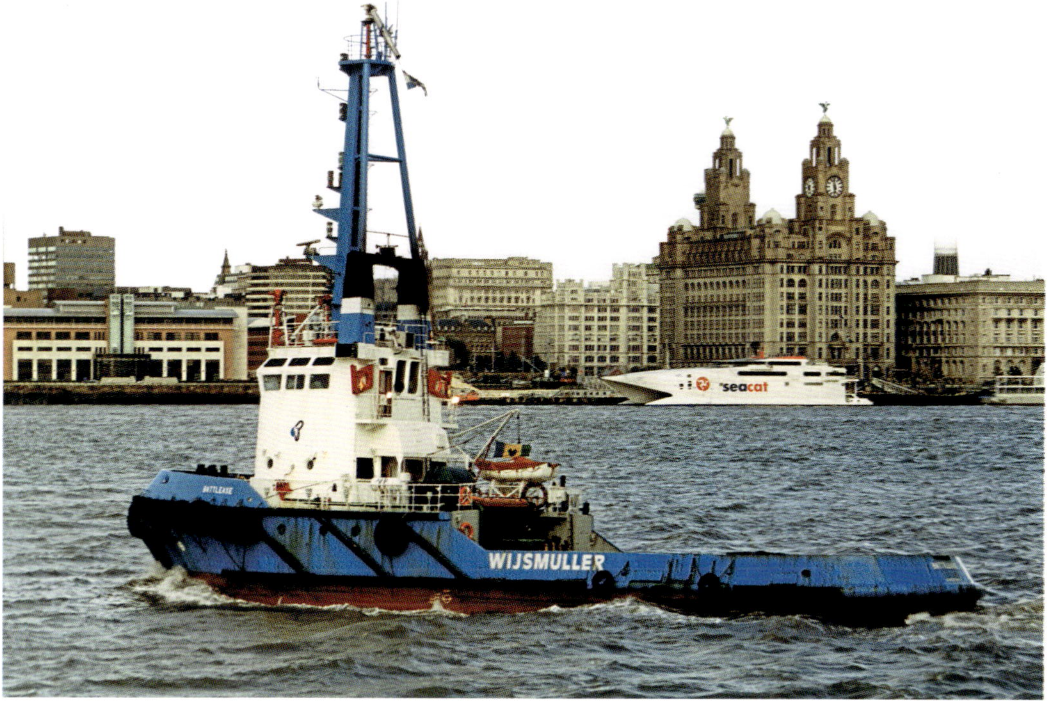

Battleaxe (1978/423 grt) leaving Alfred Dock. She was built as *Lyrie*, becoming *Elsie* in 1996 and *Battleaxe* in 1998.

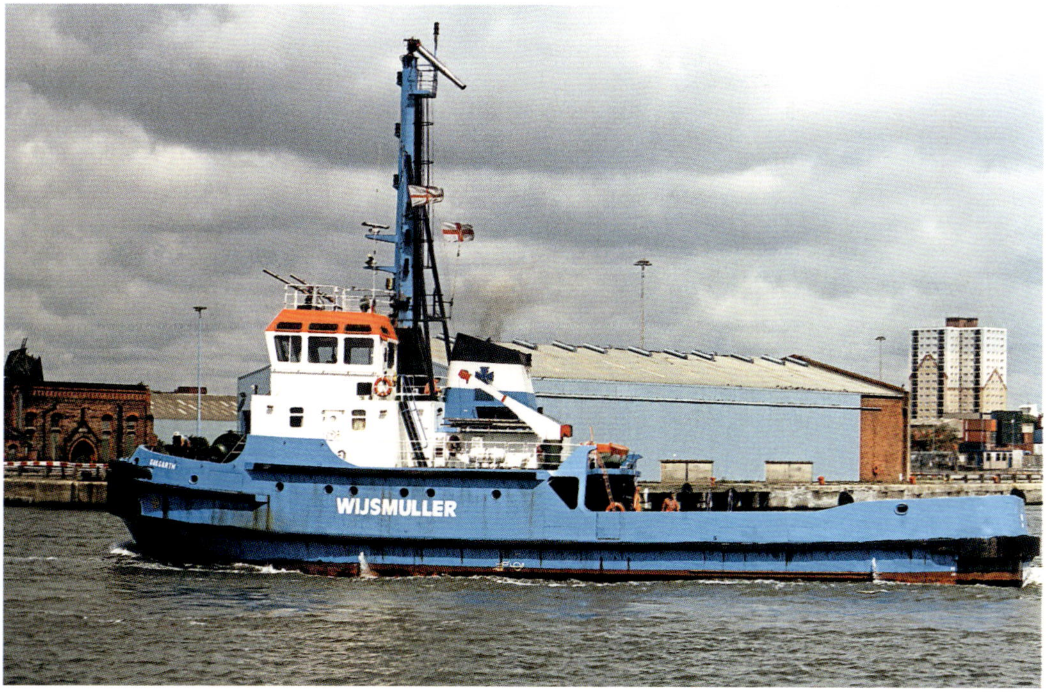

Oakgarth (1984/452 grt/4,000 hp/motor) of Wijsmuller.

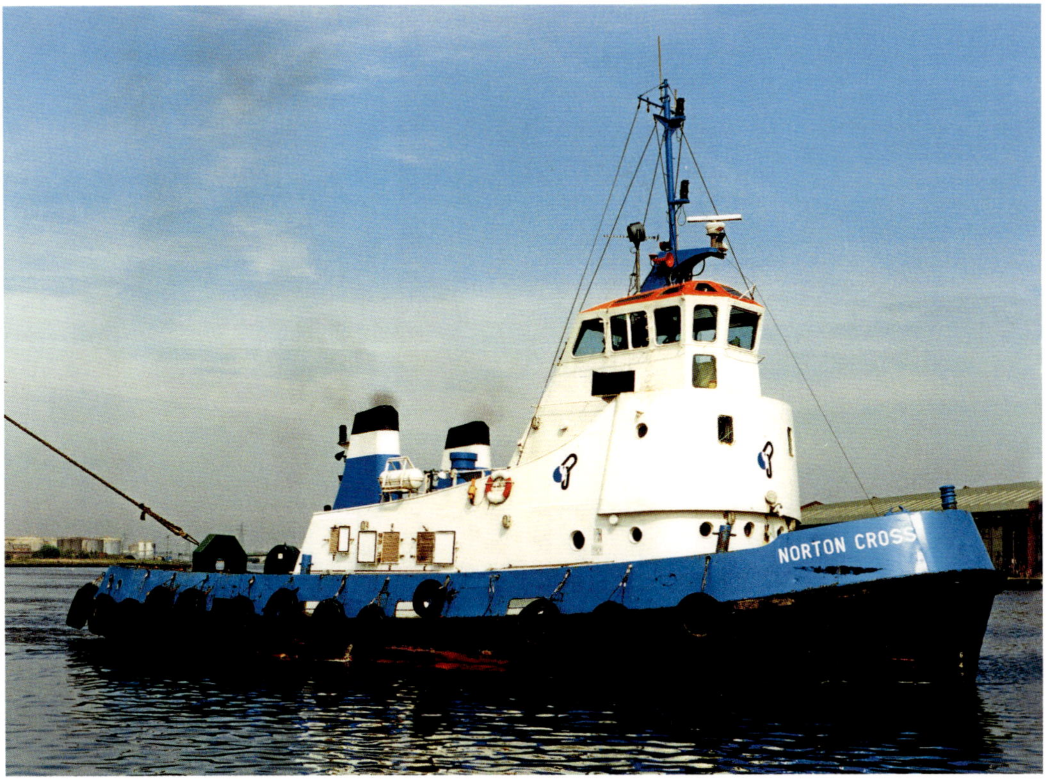

Norton Cross (1984/216 grt/3,400 hp/motor) of Wijsmuller.

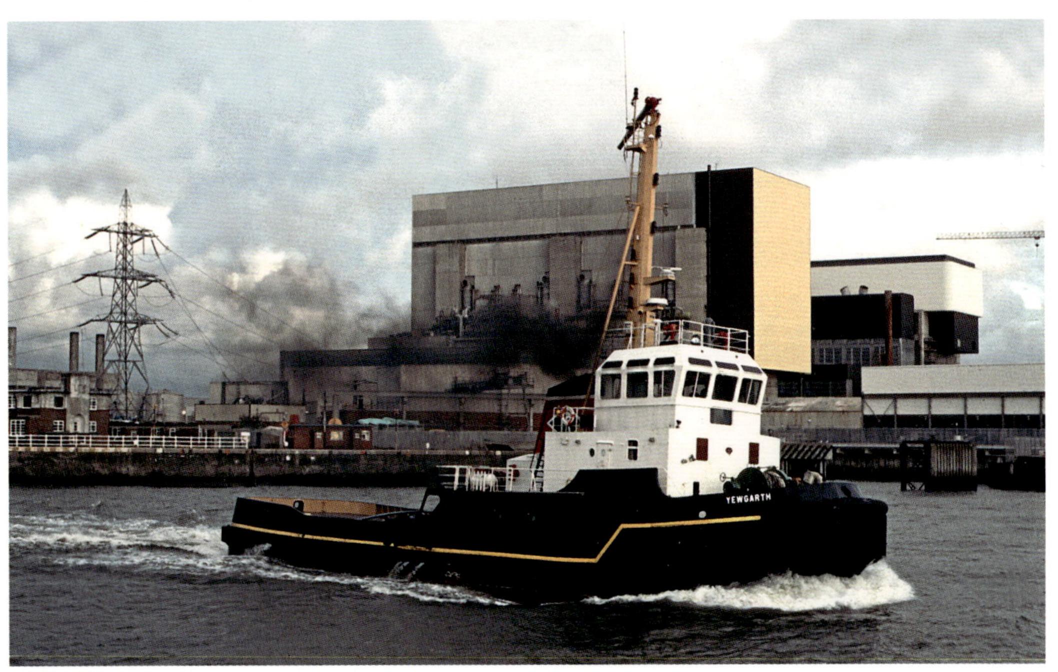

Yewgarth (1985/452 grt) completes towing duties at Heysham and is seen returning back to Liverpool.

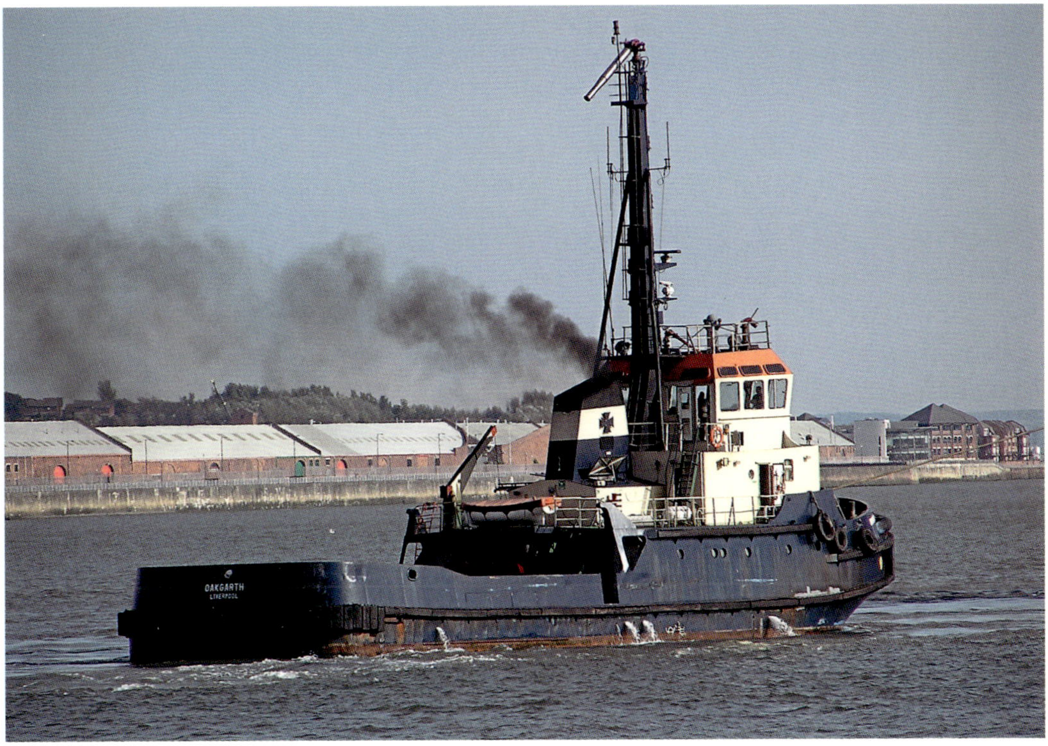

Oakgarth (1984/452 grt/4,000 hp/motor) of Svitzer Marine Limited.

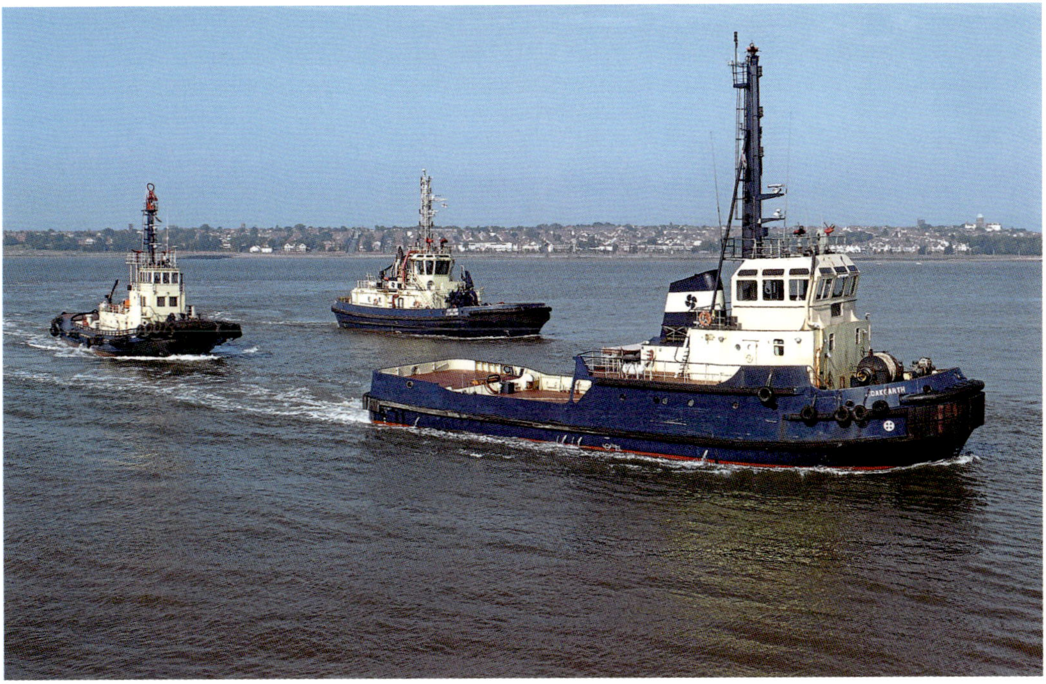

Ashgarth (1992/307 grt), *Svitzer Stanlow* (2006/656 grt) and *Oakgarth* (1984/452 grt) in the river.

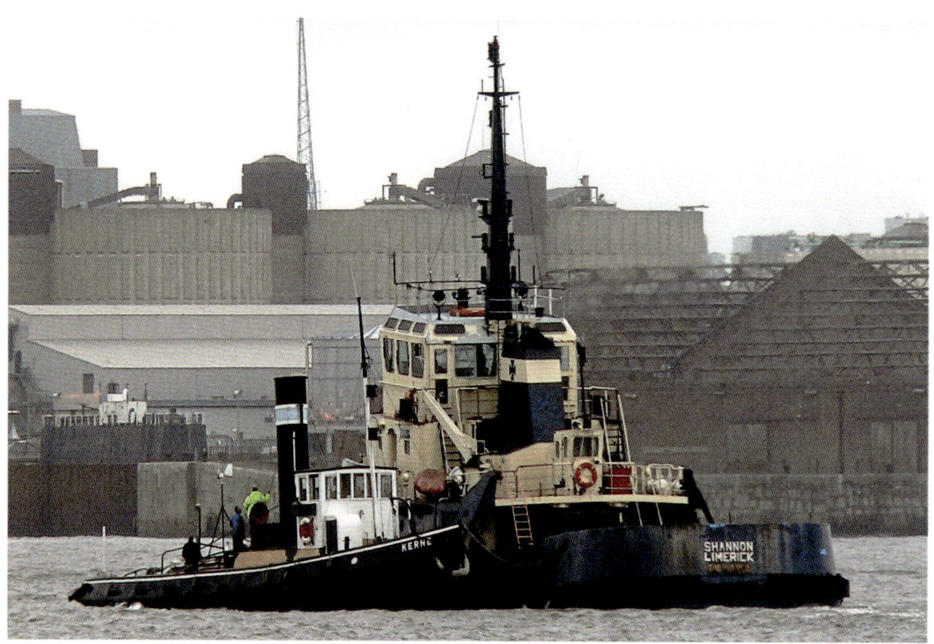

Kerne (1913/63 grt) and *Shannon* (1981/382 grt) in the Mersey, off Sandon Dock. *Kerne* was built by the Montrose Ship Building Company at Montrose and was originally the Naval tug *Terrier*. She was sold to J. P. Knight in 1948 and brought to the Mersey by the Liverpool Lighterage Company Limited. She was retired in 1971 and purchased by the North Western Steam Ship Company for restoration.

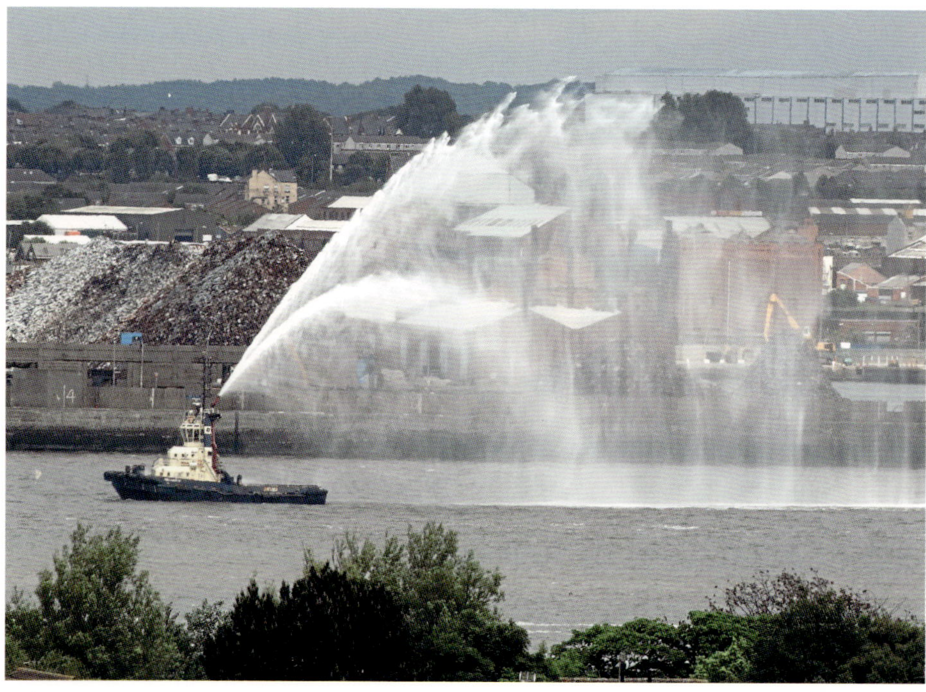

Millgarth (1997/374 grt) tests her firefighting equipment in the river off Langton Dock.

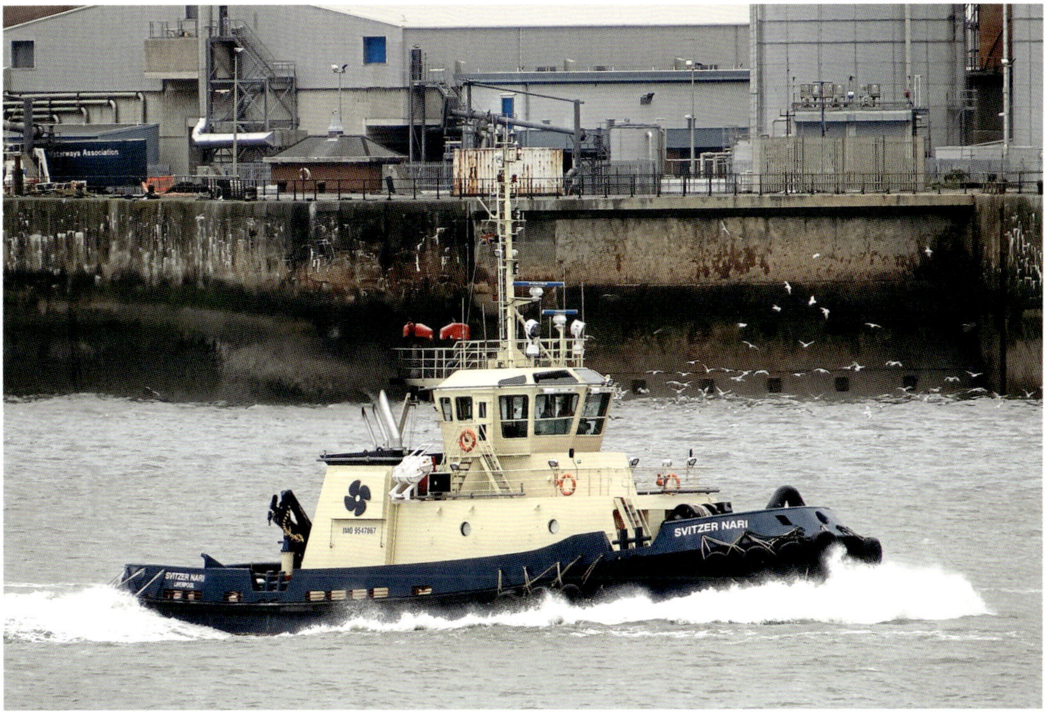

Svitzer Nari (2010/381 grt) was built as *Stevns Battler* and was renamed in 2011.

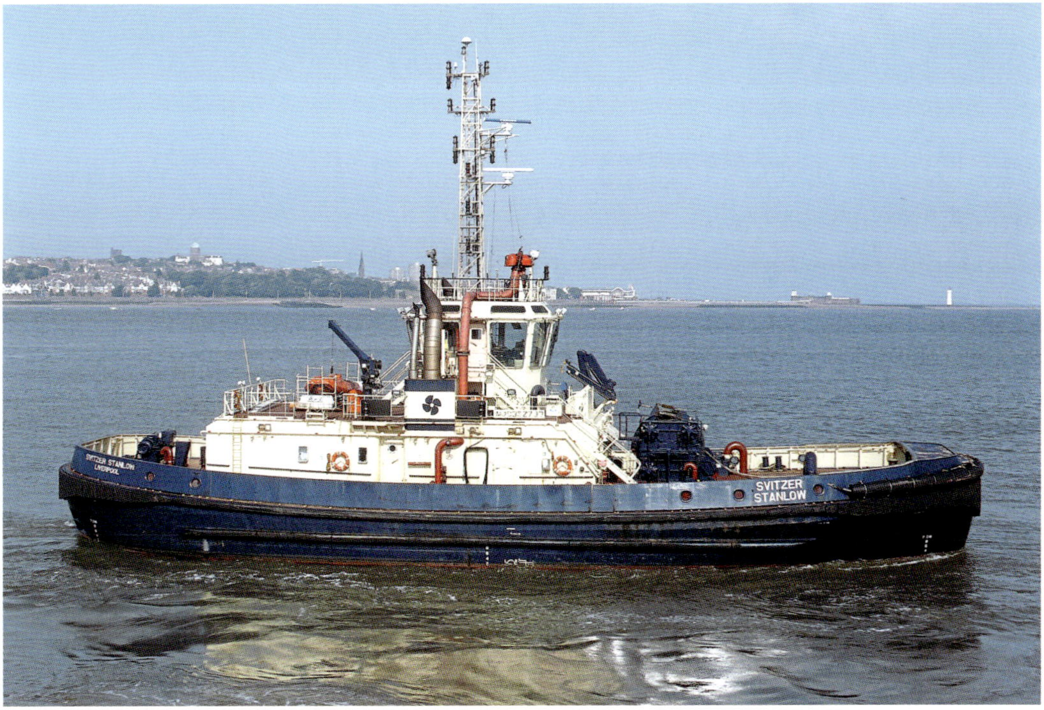

Svitzer Stanlow (2006/656 grt) in the river off Langton Dock.

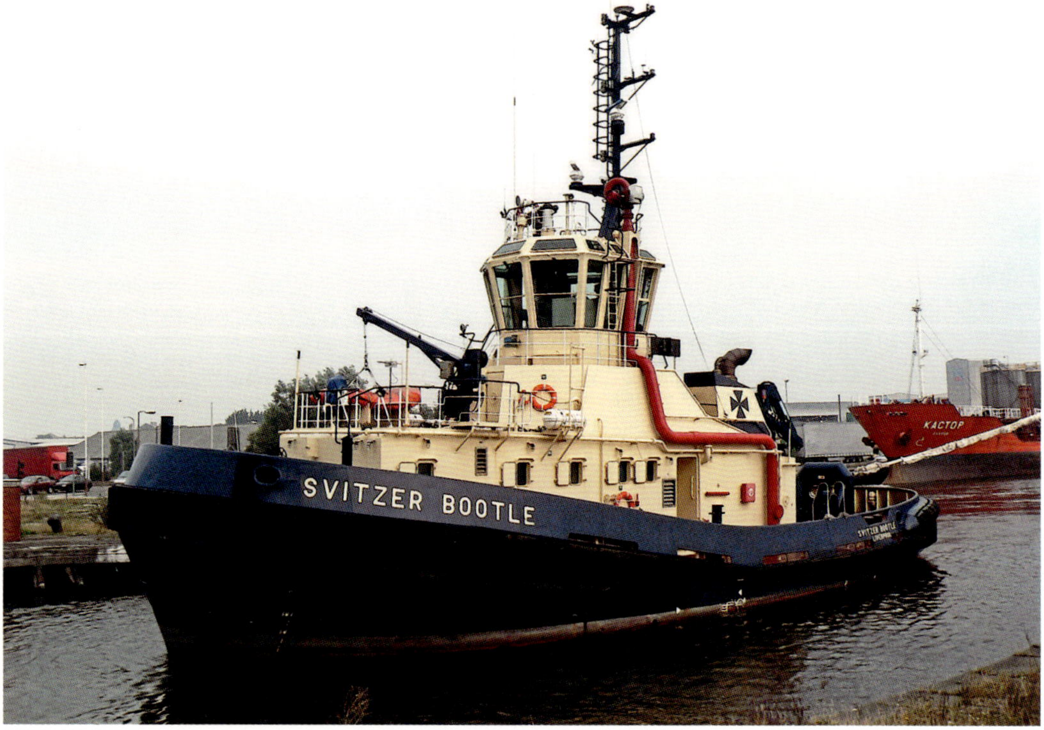

Svitzer Bootle (2004/366 grt/4,338 hp/motor) of Svitzer Marine Limited.

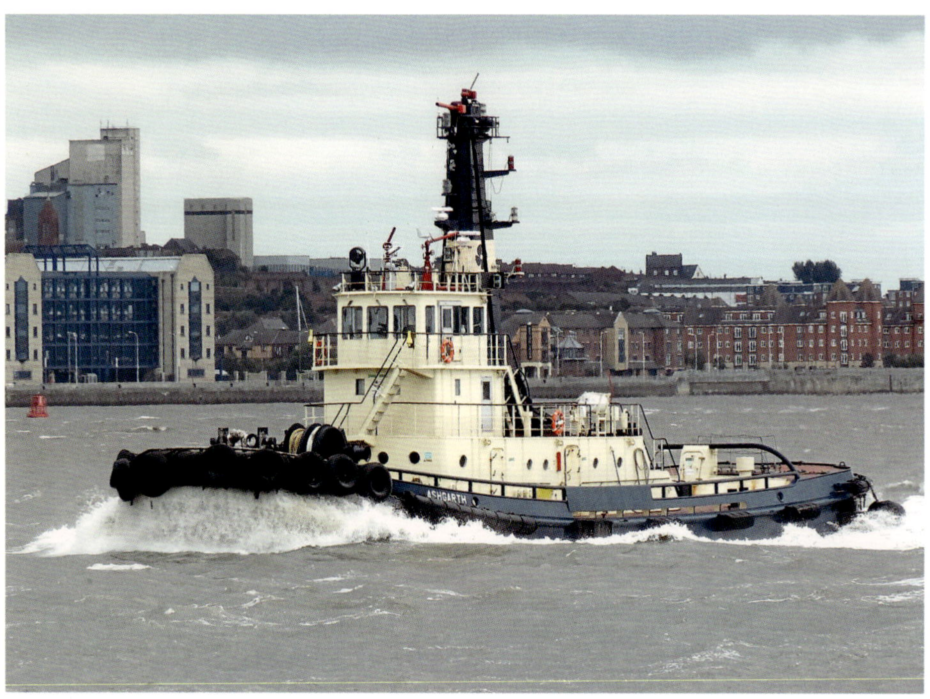

Ashgarth (1992/307 grt/3,660 hp/motor) of Svitzer Marine Limited.

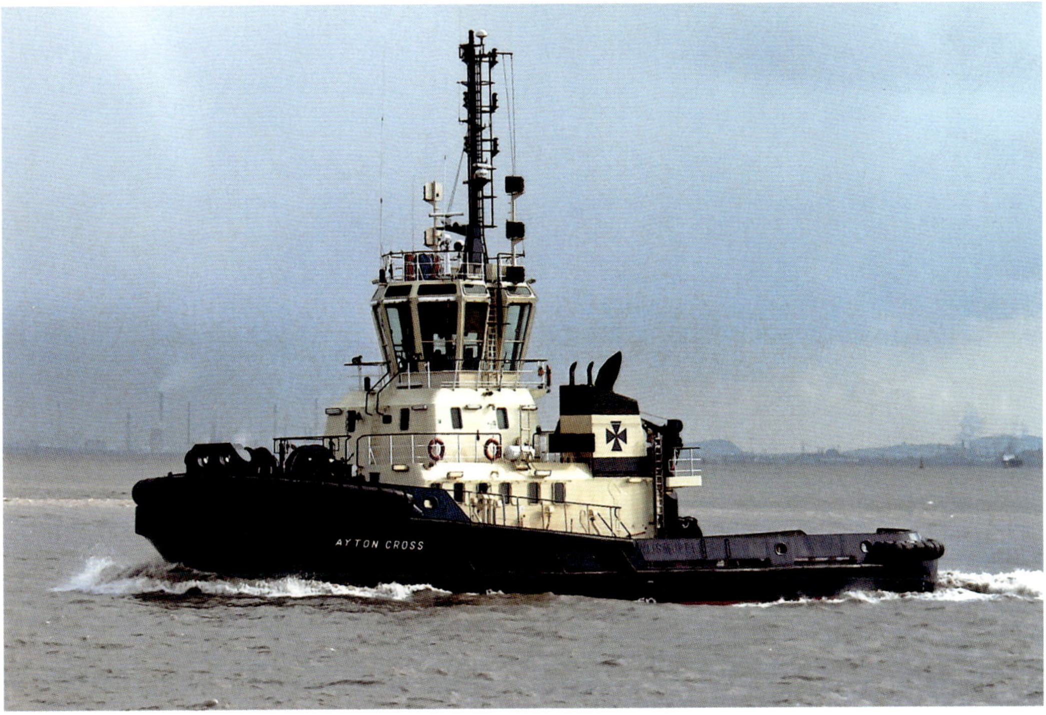

Ayton Cross (2000/433 grt/4,400 hp/motor) of Svitzer Marine Limited.

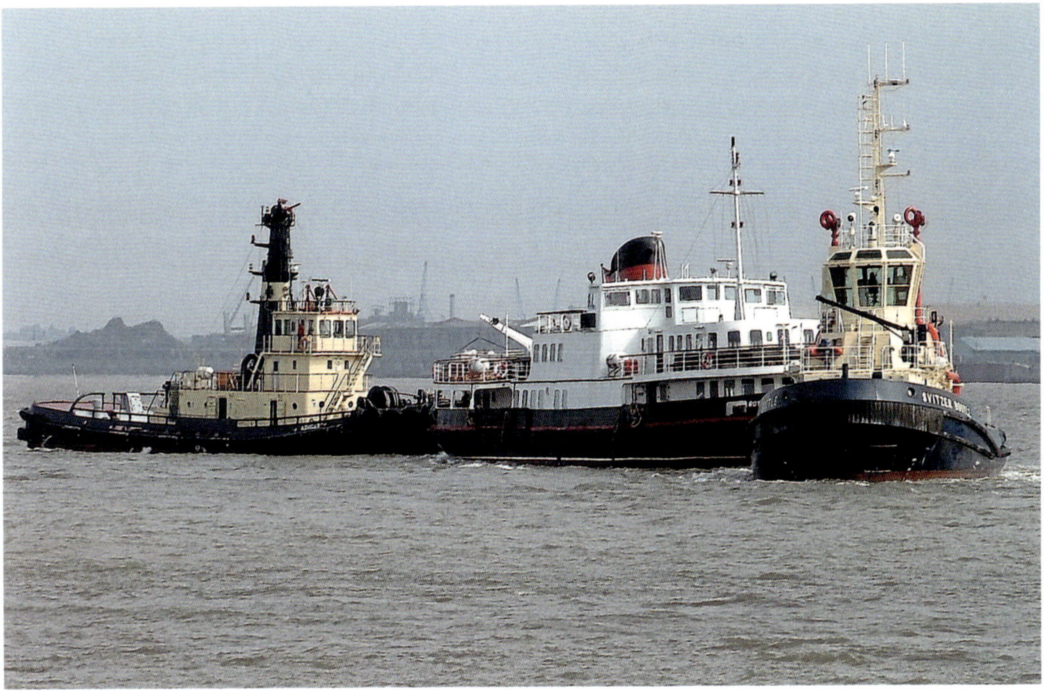

Ashgarth (1992/307 grt)and *Svitzer Bootle* (2004/366 grt) tow the Mersey ferry *Royal Daffodil* from dry dock into Birkenhead docks.

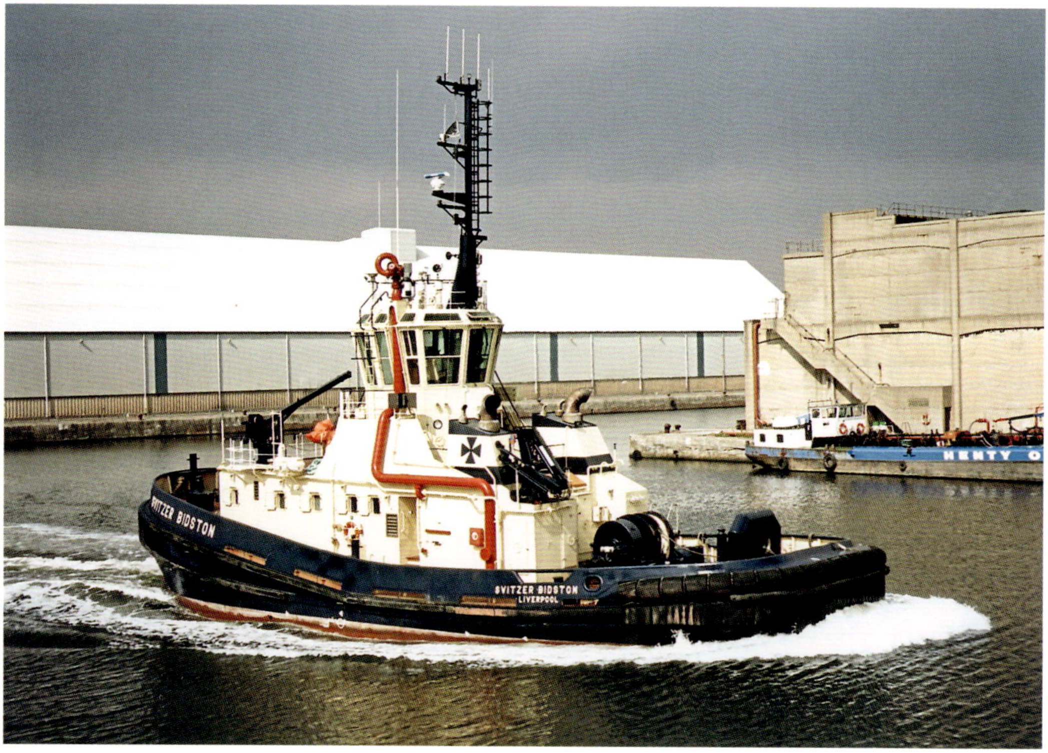

Svitzer Bidston (2004/366 grt/4,338 hp/motor) of Svitzer Marine Limited.

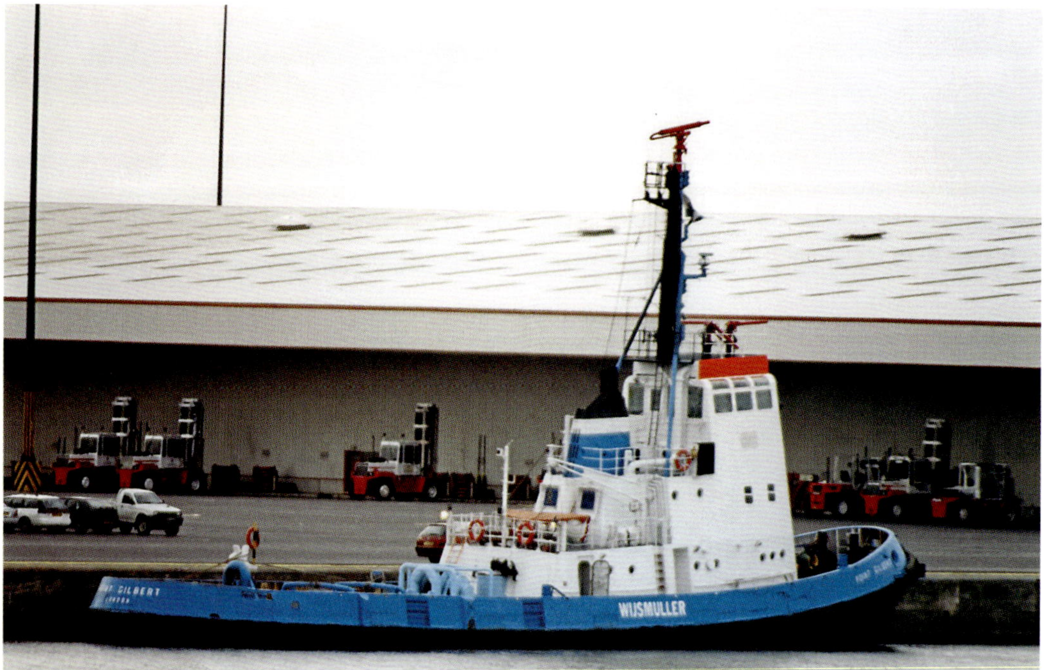

Point Gilbert (1972/339 grt/3,310 hp/motor) of Wijsmuller.

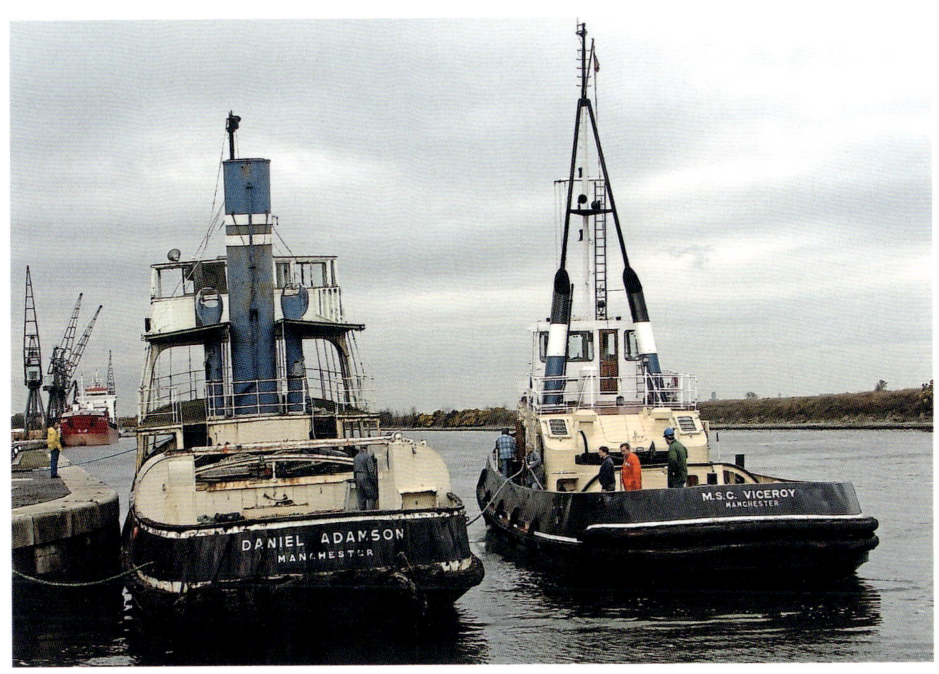

Daniel Adamson (1903/175 grt) and MSC *Viceroy* (1975/137 grt) in the Manchester Ship Canal.

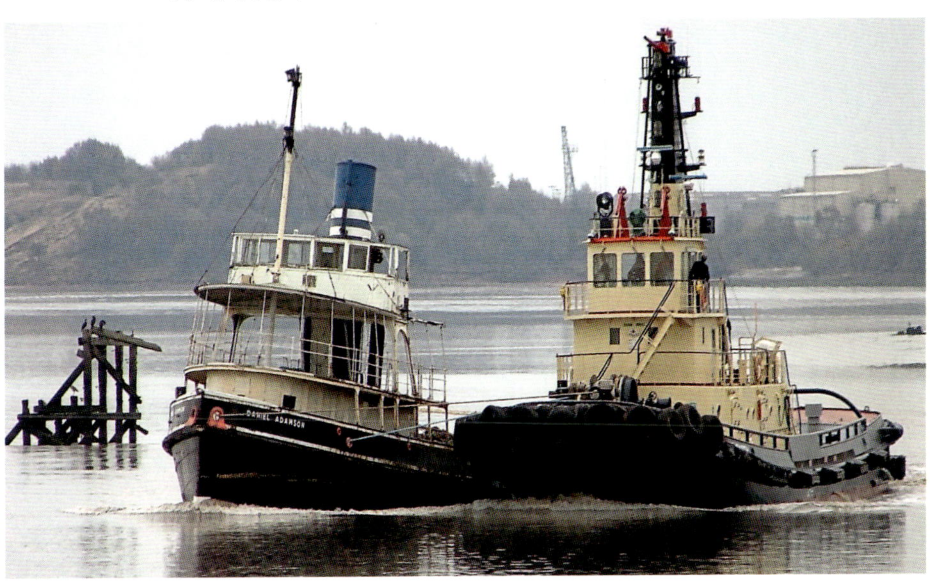

Daniel Adamson is towed from Eastham to Liverpool by the *Ashgarth*. *Daniel Adamson* was built by the Tranmere Bay Development Company, at Birkenhead, as *Ralph Brocklebank*, a tug/tender for the Shropshire Union Canal and Railway Company. She was used for many years towing barges between Ellesmere Port and Liverpool Docks. In 1921 she was owned by the Manchester Ship Canal Company, modified eight years later and rebuilt in 1936, becoming the *Daniel Adamson*. She was retired in 1984 and berthed at the Ellesmere Port Boat Museum. A preservation society was formed in 2004 and it is hoped that she will return to passenger duties on the Mersey when work is completed on her hull, accommodation and engines.

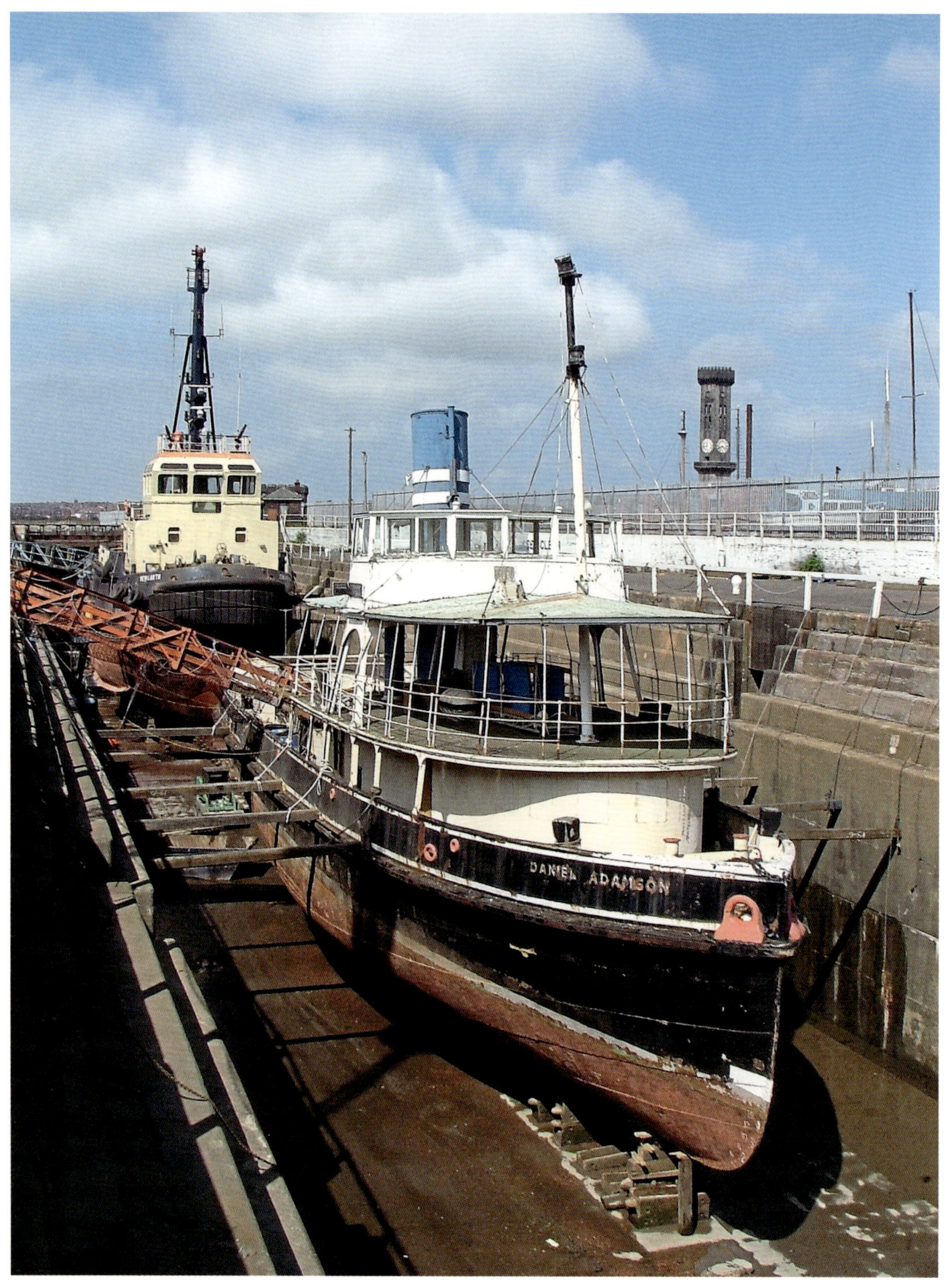

Daniel Adamson in Clarence Dry Dock.

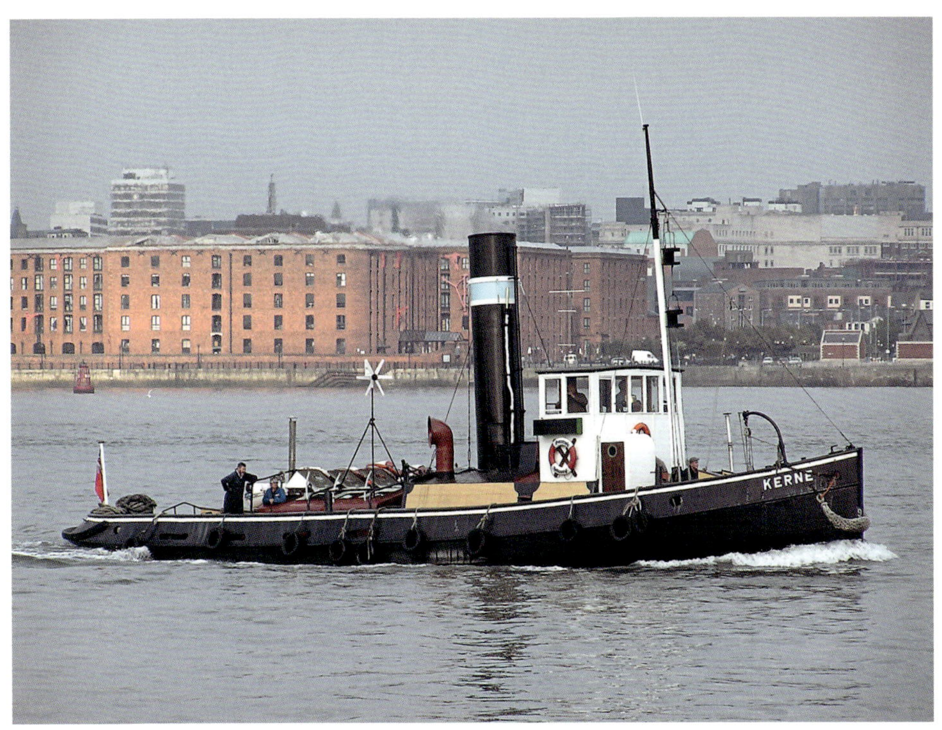

Kerne off Cammell Laird's shipyard, heading towards the Manchester Ship Canal at Eastham.

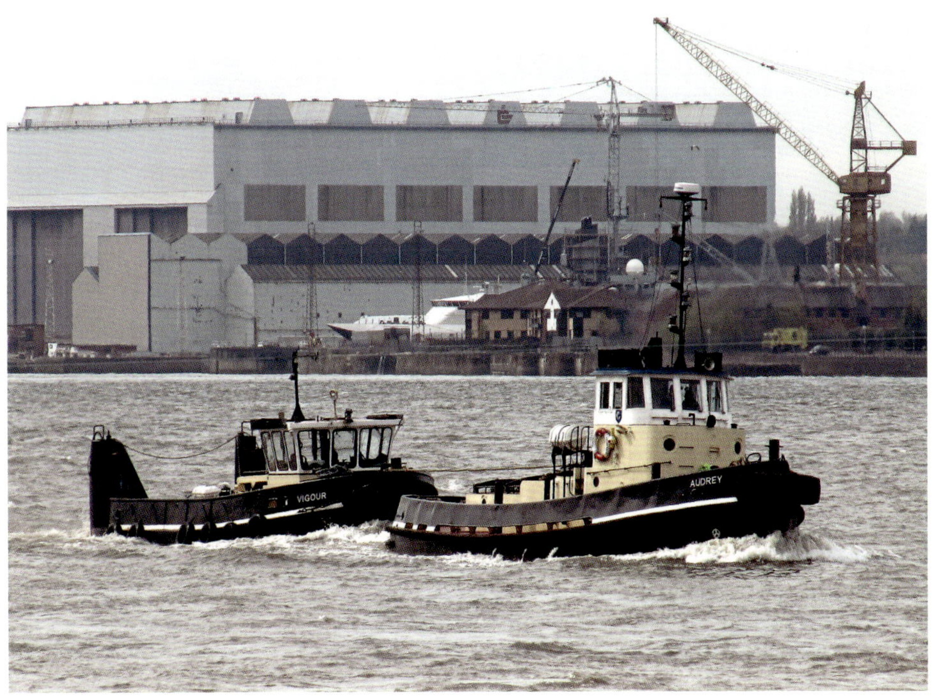

The Carmet Tug Company's vessels *Audrey* (1961/38 grt) and *Vigour* (1966/33 grt) off Woodside.

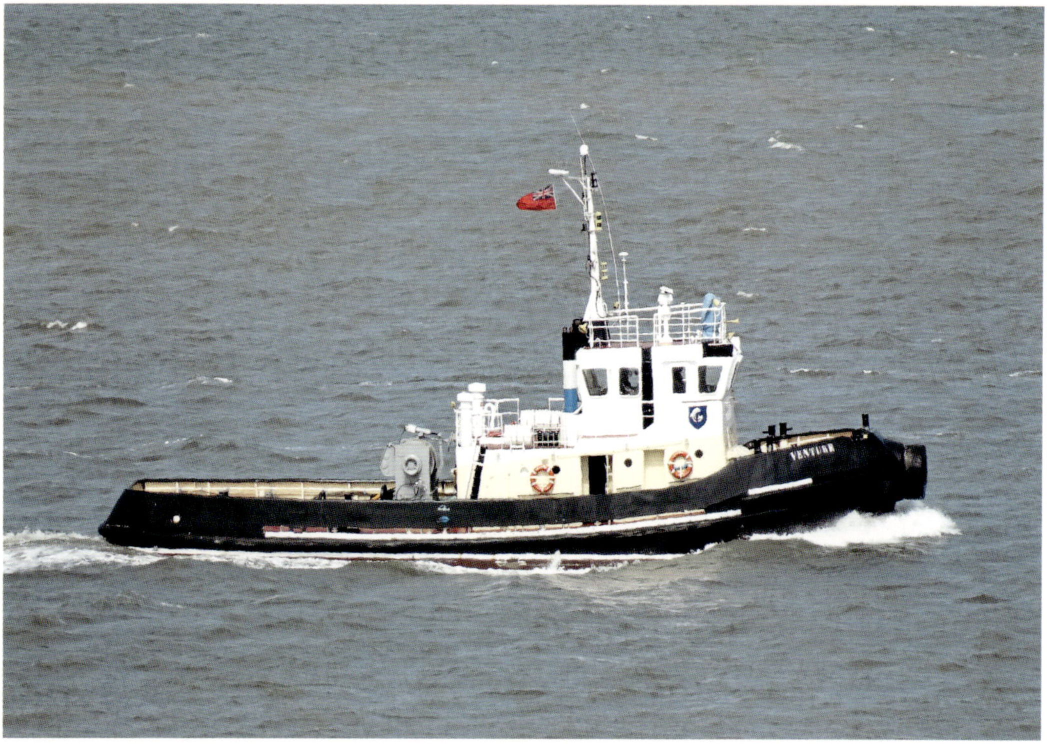

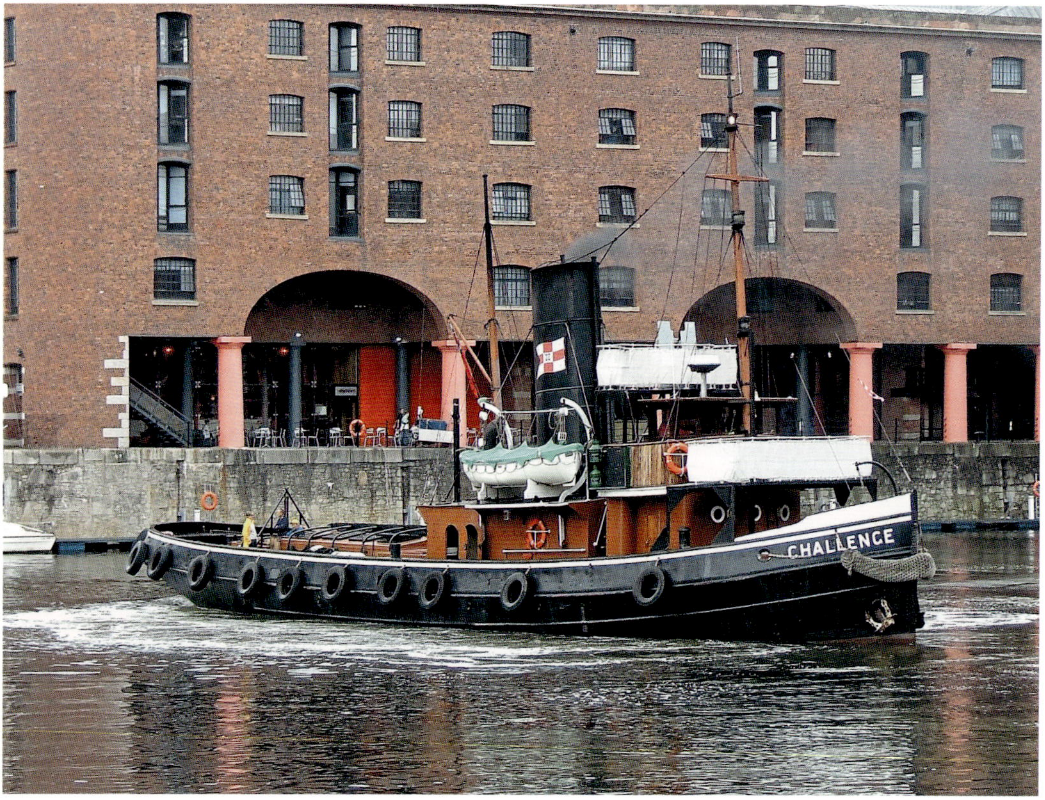

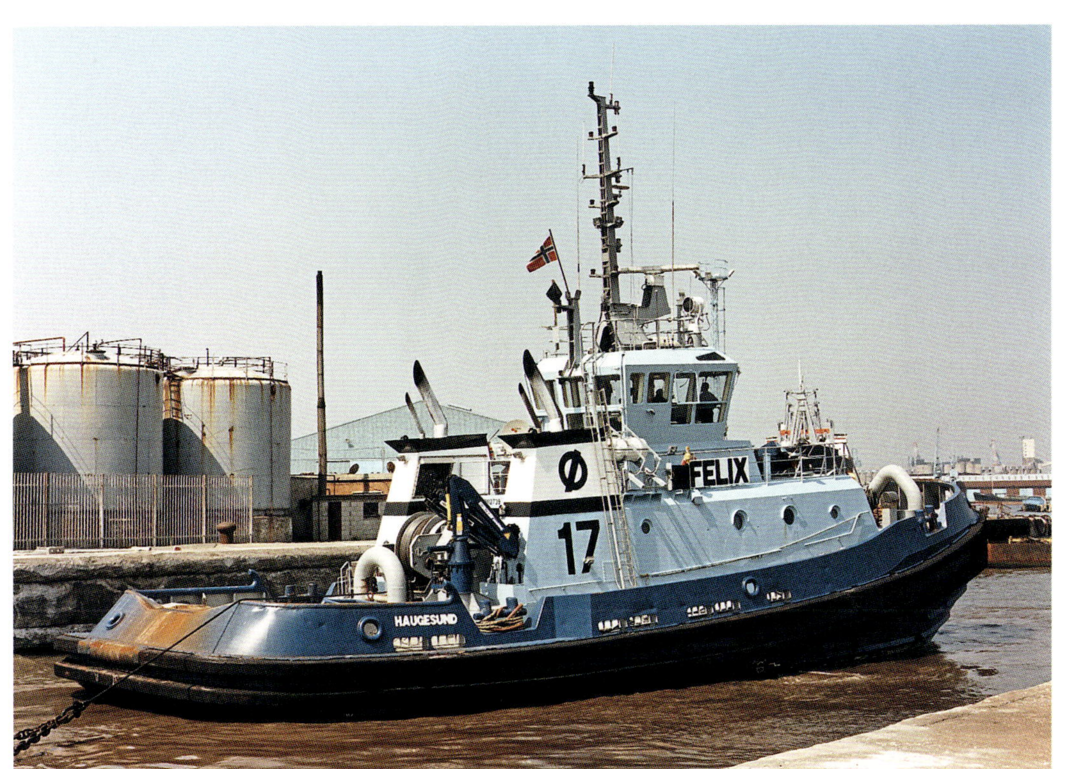

Felix (1995/397 grt) arriving at Langton Dock. She is owned by Ostensjo Reden of Norway.

Opposite above: Venture (1977/105 grt/1,650 hp/motor) Carmet Tug Company Limited.

Opposite below: The preserved tug *Challenge* in Albert Dock. She was built in 1931 for the Elliott Steam Tug Company, London by Alexander Hall at Aberdeen. She was converted to oil burning in 1964 and withdrawn from service with London Tugs Limited in 1971. *Challenge* holds the distinction of being the last steam tug to work on the Thames, and was bought for preservation in 1973.

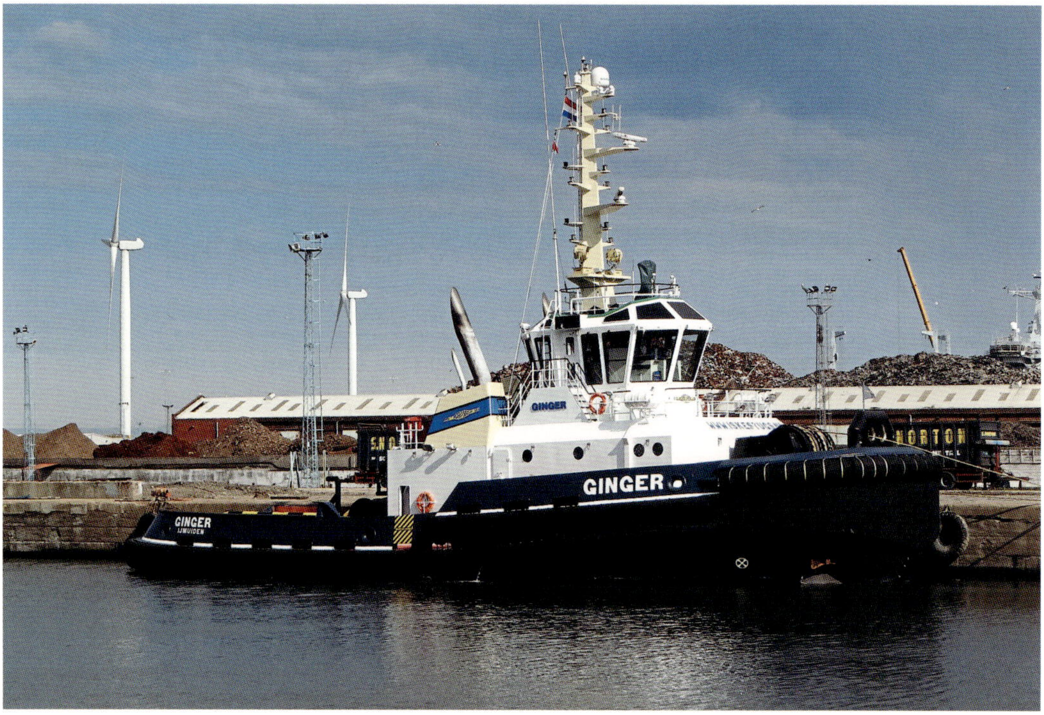

Ginger (2010/487 grt) berthed in Canada Dock. She is owned by the Dutch company Iskes Towing & Salvage (Ginger Tugs NV).

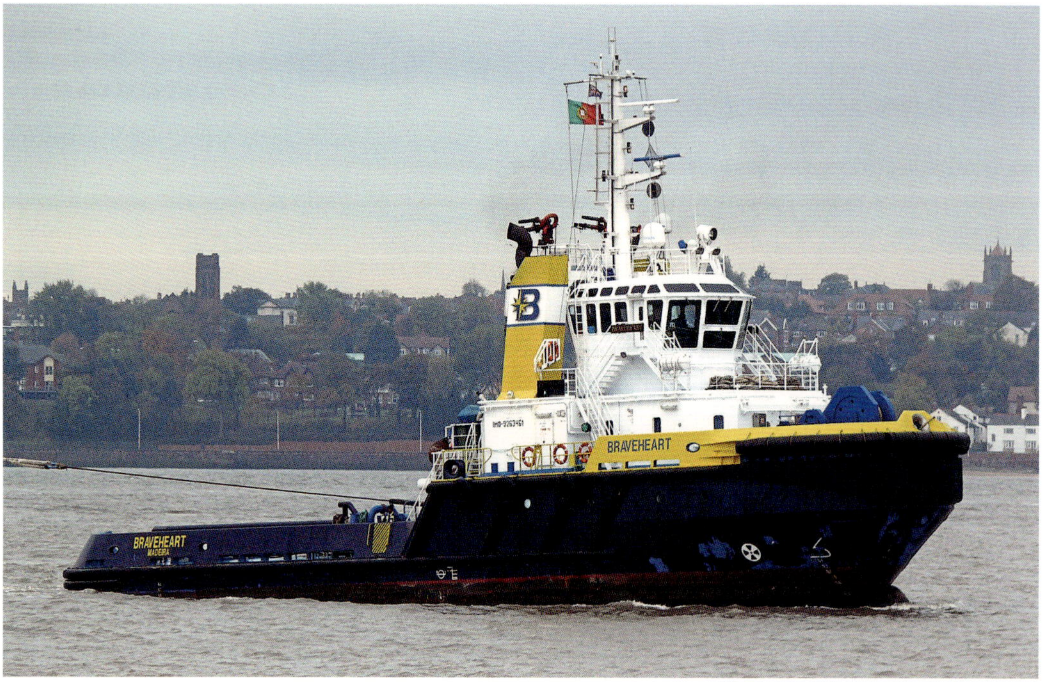

Braveheart (2003/866 grt) is owned by Barry Towage & Offshore, Madeira.

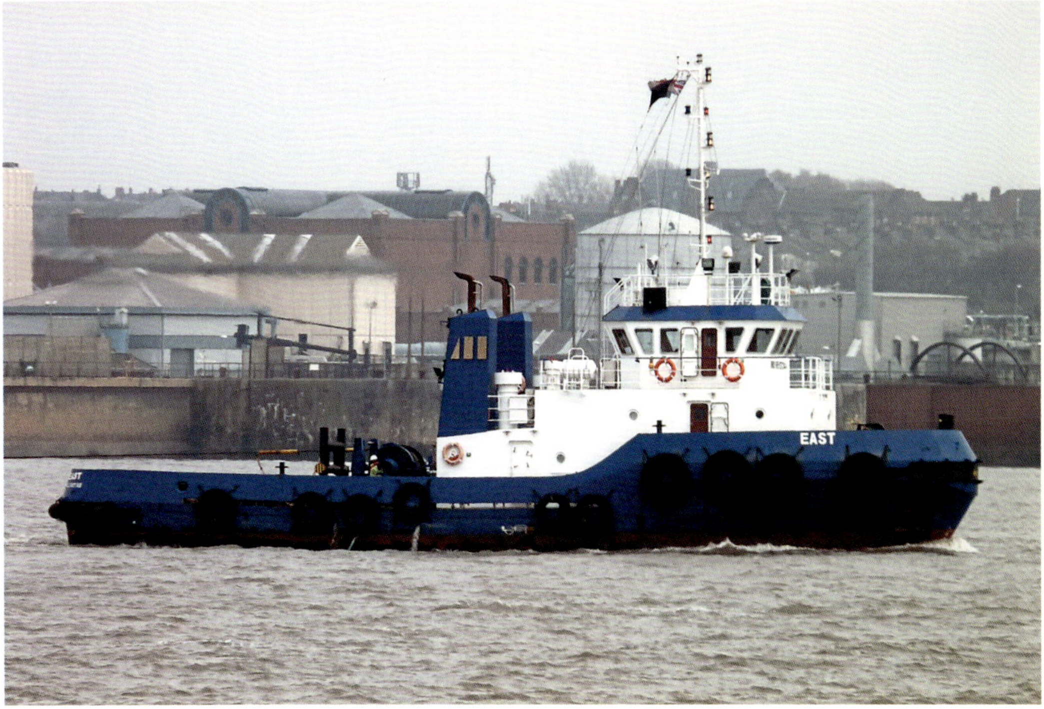

East (2009/259 grt) in the river, opposite Sandon Dock.

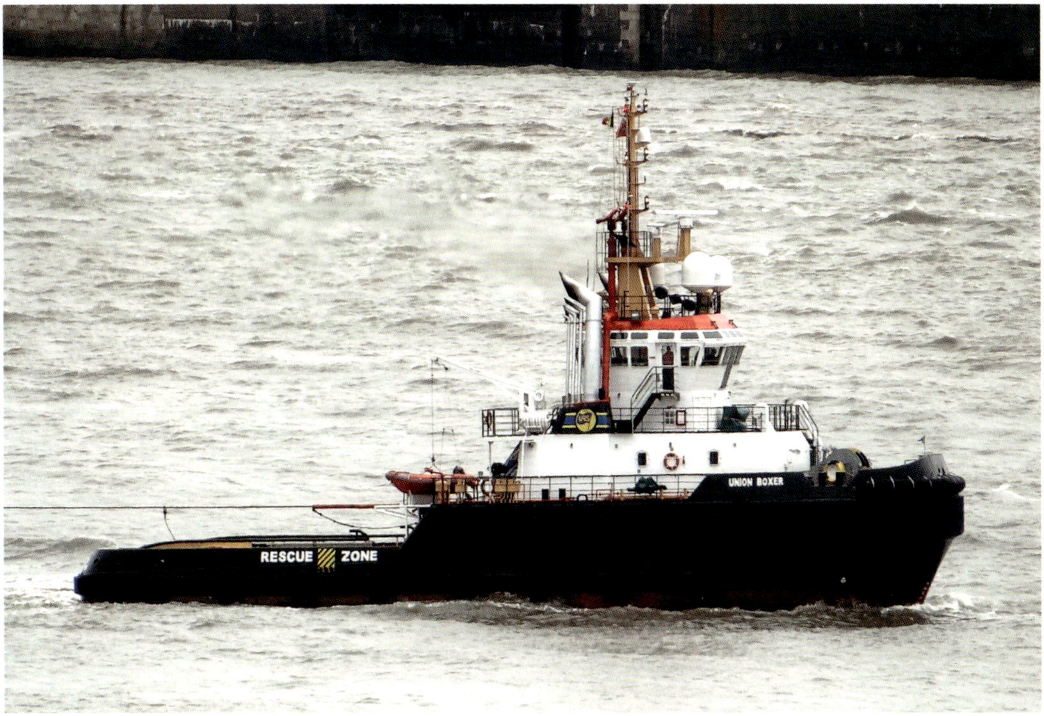

Union Boxer (2010/810 grt) She is a tug/supply ship owned by Caixa D'Estalvis.

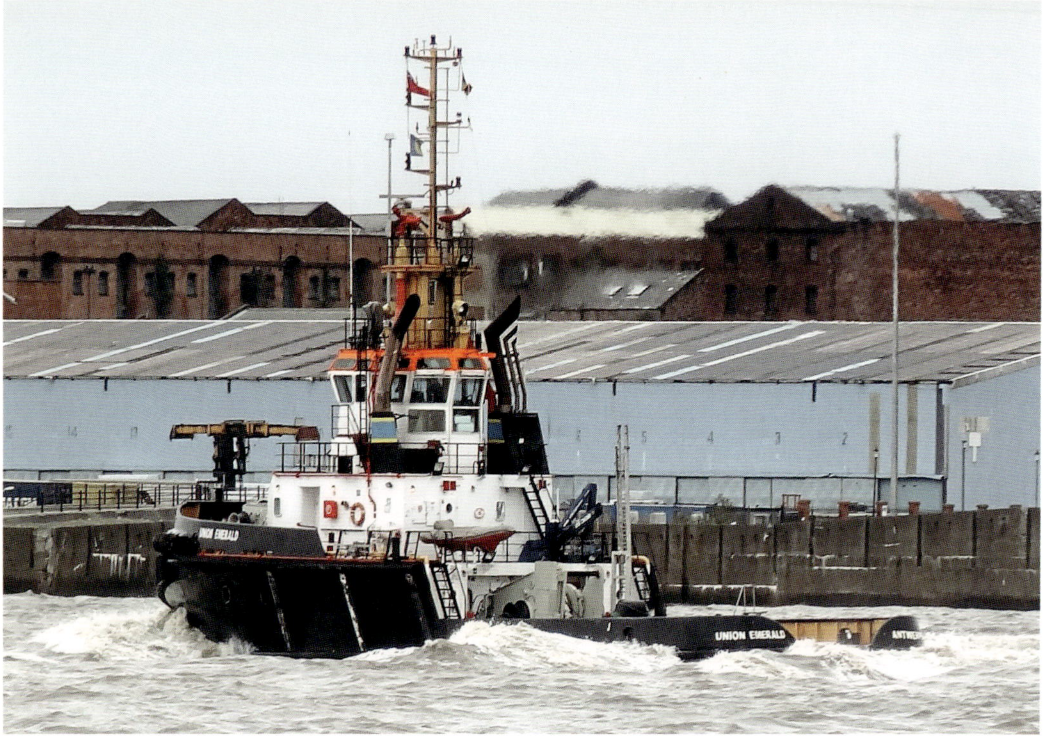
UNION EMERALD
UNION EMERALD

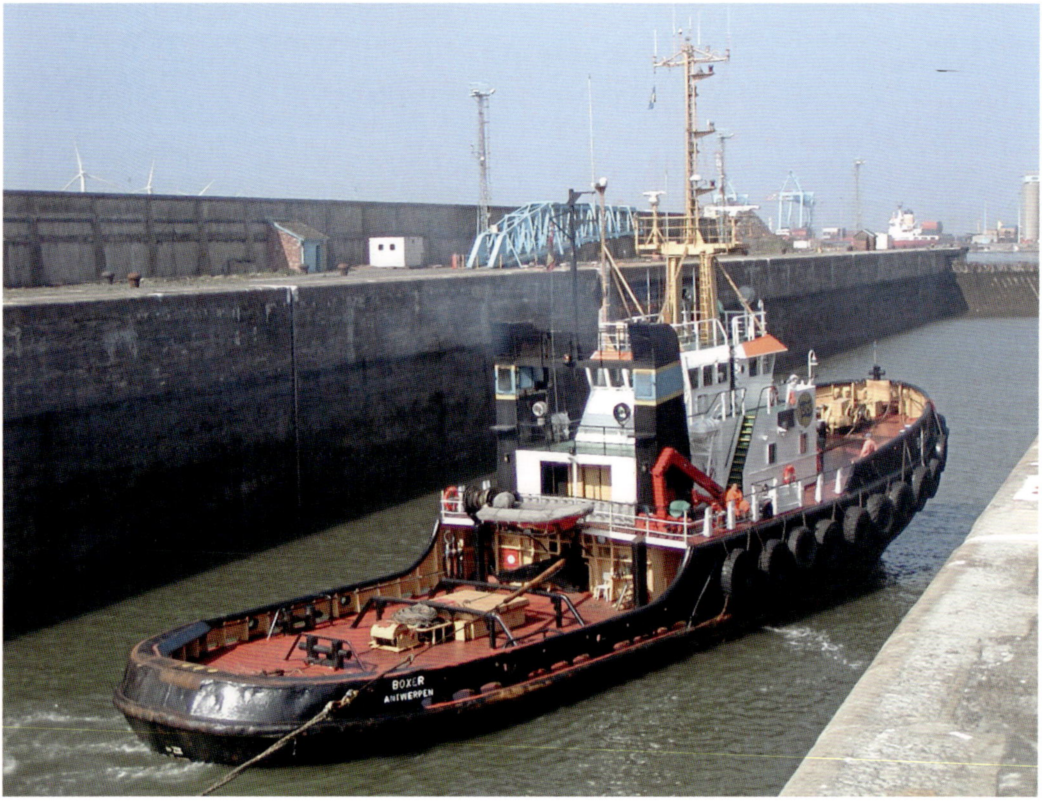
BOXER
ANTWERPEN

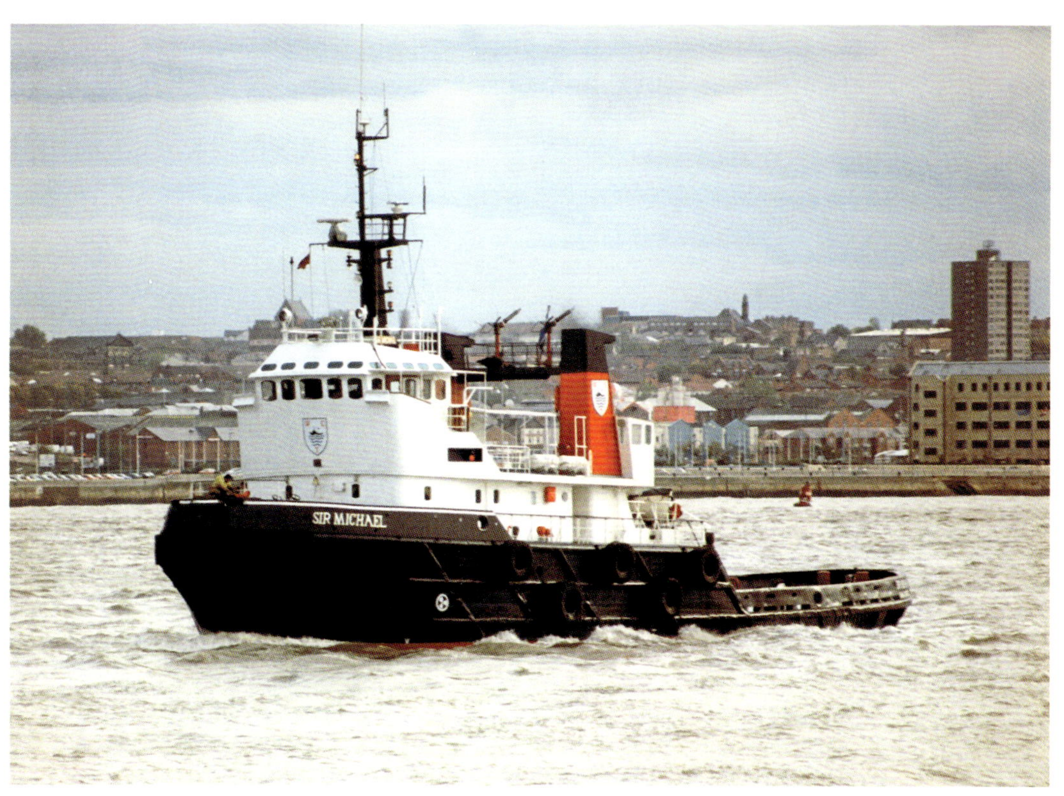

Sir Michael (1973/475 grt).

1973:	Delivered as *Bever*.
1981:	To 'Pacific Offshore' at Singapore (SGP), renamed *Cherdas*.
1985:	To 'BBT International Inc' at San Lorenzo, renamed *ABU SAMIR*.
1995:	To 'Yale Invest & Finance SA, West Coast Towing Offshore Ltd' at Swansea, renamed *Sir Michael*.
28 October 2003:	Entered Cabnave Yard at St Vincent (VCT) with engine failure.
13 April 2004:	Ready to leave, but was arrested.
11 January 2006:	Remaining under arrest at St Vincent.
2011:	In service (owner: Yale Invest & Finance S.A.)

Opposite above: Union Emerald (2005/493 grt) is owned by Urs Belgie, Antwerp, Belgium.

Opposite below: Boxer (1977/504 grt) arriving at Gladstone Dock. She was broken up at Ghent in 2007.

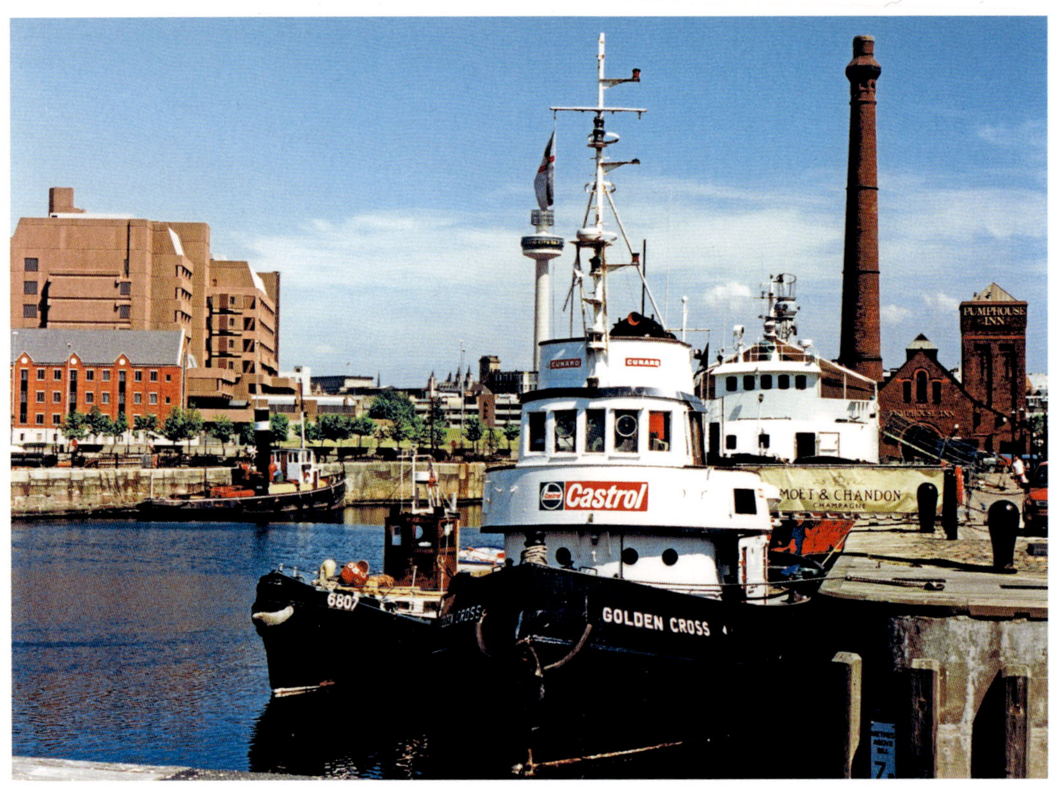

Golden Cross (1955/132 grt) in Albert Dock. She became *Dunheron* in 1968 and *Golden Cross* in 1997. In July 2012 she broke loose from her moorings and ran aground. The following April she ran aground again, and several weeks later it was discovered that she was taking on water and she was beached. In November that year she was raised and towed to Rosneath, where she was broken up by DRB Marine Services Limited.